OTHER TITLES OF INTERE

CODING AND REIMBURSEMENT

CPT Coders Choice®, Thumb Indexed
CPT TimeSaver®, Ring Binder, Tab Indexed
CPT & HCPCS Coding Made Easy!
HCPCS Coders Choice®, Color Coded, Thumb Indexed
Health Insurance Carrier Directory
ICD-9-CM, Coders Choice®, Color Coded, Thumb Indexed
ICD-9-CM, TimeSaver® Ring Binder, Tab Indexed
ICD-9-CM Coding For Physicians Offices
ICD-9-CM Coding Made Easy!
Medicare Rules and Regulations
Physicians Fees
Reimbursement Manual for the Medical Office
Working With Insurance and Managed Care Plans

FINANCIAL MANAGEMENT

A Physician's Guide to Financial Independence
Accounts Receivable Management for the Medical Practice
Financial Planning Workbook for Physicians
Financial Valuation of Your Practice
Pension Plan Strategies
Securing Your Assets
Selling or Buying a Medical Practice

RISK MANAGEMENT

Belli: For Your Malpractice Defense
Law, Liability and Ethics for Medical Office Personnel
Malpractice Depositions
Malpractice: Managing Your Defense
Medical Risk Management
Testifying in Court

DICTIONARIES AND OTHER REFERENCE

Drug Interactions Index
Isler's Patient Guide to Medical Terminology
Medical Acronyms, Eponyms and Abbreviations
Medical Phrase Index
Medical Word Building
Medico-Legal Glossary
Medico Mnemonica

**AVAILABLE FROM YOUR LOCAL MEDICAL
BOOK STORE OR CALL 1-800-MED-SHOP**

OTHER TITLES OF INTEREST

MEDICAL REFERENCE AND CLINICAL

Anesthesiology: Problems in Primary Care
Cardiology: Problems in Primary Care
Drugs of Abuse
Gastroenterology: Problems in Primary Care
Hematology: Diagnosis and Treatment of Blood Disorders
Medical Care of the Adolescent Athlete
Medical Procedures for Referral
Neurology: Problems in Primary Care
Orthopaedics: Problems in Primary Care
Patient Care Emergency Handbook
Patient Care Flowchart Manual
Patient Care Procedures for Your Practice
Pulmonary Medicine: Problems in Primary Care
Questions and Answers on AIDS
Sexually Transmitted Diseases
Urology: Problems in Primary Care

PRACTICE MANAGEMENT

365 Ways to Manage the Business Called Private Practice
Achieving Profitability with a Medical Office System
Choosing and Using a Medical Office Computer
Computerizing Your Medical Office
Doctor Business
Encyclopedia of Practice and Financial Management
Getting Paid for What You Do
Health Information Management
Managing Medical Office Personnel
Managing the Physician's Office Laboratory
Marketing Strategies for Physicians
Medical Marketing Handbook
Medical Practice Handbook
Medical Staff Privileges
Negotiating Managed Care Contracts
New Practice Handbook
Patient Satisfaction
Patients Build Your Practice
Physician's Office Laboratory
Professional and Practice Development
Promoting Your Medical Practice
Starting in Medical Practice
Spanish/English Handbook for Medical Professionals

**AVAILABLE FROM YOUR LOCAL MEDICAL
BOOK STORE OR CALL 1-800-MED-SHOP**

GETTING PAID FOR WHAT YOU DO

Coding For Optimal Reimbursement

Fourth Edition

Gary M. Knaus

Library of Congress Cataloging-in-Publication data

Knaus, Gary M.
       Getting paid for what you do : coding for optimal reimbursement /
Gary M. Knaus. -- [4th ed.]
             p. cm.
       Includes index.
       ISBN 1-57066-071-9
       1. Medicine--Practice--Economic aspects. 2. Medical claims
processing industry--Code numbers. I. Title.
       R728.5.K62 1997
       610'.68'1--dc21   97-30411
                                                                CIP

ISBN 1-57066-071-9

PMIC (Practice Management Information Corporation)
4727 Wilshire Blvd, Suite 300
Los Angeles, California 90010
1-800-MED-SHOP

http://www.medicalbookstore.com

Printed in the United States of America

FOREWORD

This book is dedicated to the tens of thousands of people I have had the privilege of teaching over the past ten years. Their thought provoking questions, insights, knowledge, and support give credence to the adage that teachers learn more from their students than they would like their students to know. Without them, this book would not have been possible. Thank you one and all.

Many individuals contributed their substantial talents to this fourth edition. Denise Knaus reorganized the text into more meaningful sections, edited away many of my grammatical errors, transformed unintelligible passages into the intelligible, and kindly brought me up-to-speed on key Medicare regulations. Her assistance, patience, and perseverance were invaluable. Leslie Garvey of Context Software Systems tirelessly input changes to this edition, as she has for the previous three editions. She's the best problem spotter I know in the business, and because of her, numerous errors that I had overlooked will not appear in this text. Finally, I owe much to my publisher, Jim Davis, and his editorial director, Kathy Swanson, for their patience and support awaiting this fourth edition.

All errors in this book are mine. If in the course of reading this text you find mistakes or feel strongly about a point of view that differs from mine, please let me know. Constructive criticism will be welcomed and appreciated. Send your comments to me in care of Context Software Systems, Inc. at the address provided below.

If you have ever attempted to write a how-to book, you well know the difficulty of selecting a form of gender when illustrating a point. Since the English language provides no gender neutral term to replace "he" or "she," I have attempted to mix the use of gender in this text. Selected use is for convenience, and not out of disrespect for females when I use "he," or for males when I use "she."

This book is intended to offer expert advice on the proper use of CPT, HCPCS, and ICD-9-CM coding in the context of helping physician practices obtain legitimate third party payment and reduce audit liability. However, you should take my advice (and the advice of others in the field) with a grain of salt. The interpretation of the proper use of coding systems may vary substantially from region to region and payer to payer.

Finally, the names and examples used in this text are purely fictitious and any resemblance to real people or events is coincidental.

Gary M. Knaus

July, 1997

Context Software Systems, Inc.
241 S. Frontage Road, Suite 41
Burr Ridge, Illinois 60521

DISCLAIMER

This publication is designed to offer basic information regarding coding and billing of medical services, supplies and procedures using the CPT, HCPCS and ICD-9-CM coding systems and additional information regarding forms, insurance claims processing and superbill design. The information presented is based on the experience and interpretations of the author. Though all of the information has been carefully researched and checked for accuracy and completeness, neither the author nor the publisher accept any responsibility or liability with regard to errors, omissions, misuse or misinterpretation.

THE AUTHOR

Gary M. Knaus

Gary Knaus is a leading expert in the areas of medical coding and the application of software technologies to improve the medical reimbursement process. As president and co-founder of Context Software Systems, Mr. Knaus has overseen the development and marketing of a wide range of reimbursement-related applications including the CodeLink family of programs, Claims Editor Professional, and Claims Analyzer. He has also been instrumental in developing Context's UCR fee databases and custom fee reports. In addition to these activities, Mr. Knaus has authored numerous texts and articles on the subject of coding and reimbursement, including *Getting Paid for What You Do*, which is now in its fourth edition, and given more than 400 presentations to professional groups on subjects ranging from physician reimbursement to technology. He is a Special Advisor to the Board of Directors of the International Billing Association and a member of the Association for Electronic Healthcare Transactions, on whose behalf he recently testified before the U.S. Department of Health and Human Services. Mr. Knaus received his MBA from the University of Chicago.

CONTENTS

CONTENTS

CHAPTER ONE:
ASPECTS OF
INSURANCE PROCESSING

OVERVIEW

A humorist is reputed to have said that there is not a human alive who fully understands how to complete a health insurance form. With forms ranging from the HCFA-1500 to managed care encounter forms to superbills—not to forget the 400 plus unique electronic claims submission formats—many physician office staff will likely argue that he knew not how true his amusing insight really was. There is very little about completing an insurance form which could be considered straightforward. And perhaps understandably so since more than $300,000,000,000 per year, which is about one twenty-fifth of the entire U.S. economy, rides on the proper completion of these forms.

In this chapter you will learn that the health insurance claim form and related support documentation is, in essence, a communication device. Via these forms and documents the physician practice communicates what services were performed and why, on whom and by whom, when they were performed and where, and asks the payer to reimburse for the services. In turn, the payer's claims processing staff uses this information to adjudicate the claim. Optimizing your practice's third party reimbursements is directly related to your ability to understand and effectively utilize the claims form and related documentation as communication tools.

This communication process can be viewed as comprising two components: a technical component, which includes proper completion and filing of the claim form, and appropriate use of coding systems; and a human component, which involves the people at both the provider's and the payer's offices. There is potential for errors that affect the outcome of a claim in both the technical and the human aspects. Codes can be wrong, fields can be left blank, and claims can be submitted too late. On the human side, information on a claim can be misinterpreted and an incorrect decision can be made. Or, the wrong information can be sent to the payer, leading to a claim delay or denial.

It is important to understand both aspects of the communication process to ensure prompt and accurate payment of claims. To this end, this chapter provides information to help you learn about the human aspect of insurance processing, including how third party payers operate and tips on interacting with the payer to ensure that your claims are paid promptly and appropriately. Also included is a discussion of the two types of claims as well as information related to the different types of information which can be obtained electronically.

The next chapter, Chapter Two, contains information related to the technical aspect of insurance processing, understanding and using the coding systems properly.

By studying the material in this chapter, you will:

- Understand how payers process claims.
- Learn tips for interacting with payers.
- Understand the advantages and disadvantages of different methods of submitting claims.
- Learn about other types of electronic interactions.

HOW THIRD PARTY PAYERS OPERATE

Although each third party payer has its own unique method of processing claims, most payers perform a similar set of functions from the time your claim arrives until it is either paid or denied. The claims processing cycle is referred to as claims adjudication, which literally means "to judge" the claim. The mechanics of adjudication will vary somewhat depending upon whether your claims are being submitted electronically or on paper. They will also vary as a function of the payer's sophistication and whether a third party claims administrator (TPA) is involved. About 50 percent of payers and TPAs utilize advanced claims editing programs which scan claims for a host of coding, billing, utilization, fragmentation and charge errors. Others may be so overloaded with claims volume that they simply pay most or all of the amounts you submit.

The following discussion takes a step-by-step look at a paper claims adjudication.

1. *Claim is received:* Claims are received by the payer's mail room and date-stamped. They are then microfilmed or microfiched. If your claim includes any additional support documentation, such as an operative report, it is removed and separated so that each element can be microfilmed. Immediately, your claim could have a problem if the "staple-remover" in the mail room cannot associate your operative report (consult report, etc.) with your claim. This is one way items can be misplaced. Be sure to include the following information on all attachments:

    * physician's name;
    * physician's identification number;
    * patient's name;
    * patient's policy number; and,
    * date of service.

    Including this data on your support documents will help enable the "staple-remover" to reattach the documents correctly.

2. *Claim is key punched or data entered:* After microfilming, claims are sent to data entry. The people in this department key the claims data into the payer's computer system, enabling the payer's computer to adjudicate claims. Due to the vast number of claims the payer must process on a given day, your claim will spend between two to three minutes with the data-entry person. If the information your practice has provided is incomplete or illegible, the claim may be delayed or denied.

    Some payers use scanning as a means of inputting claims data. A scanner machine "reads" the data on the claim and "places" it in the payer's computer system. In addition to reducing claims processing costs, scanning eliminates errors made by data entry personnel.

3. *Claim undergoes review*: At this point your claim is analyzed by either the data entry staff or review staff in conjunction with the payer's claims review software. The automated review verifies necessary elements, such as the eligibility of the patient for benefits, whether the deductible has been satisfied, and coverage of the billed services. Other types of "simple" checks include certification of the provider, timeliness of filing, and whether the policy is in force.

    The automated review also begins checking the appropriateness of the services provided using a set of edits. These edits can be simple, such as the validity of a code or whether the gender of the patient can have the procedure provided, to complicated, such as whether the diagnosis is justification for the service provided. Other typical edits include utilization of services, amount of charges, and total dollar amount billed on the claim.

    If at any point a claim "fails" the automated review, it is suspended for manual review. A claim can be suspended for manual review if it is missing necessary information, such as the patient's identification number, the date of service, procedure or diagnosis codes, or the patient's or physician's signature. (Claims that need additional information before they can be processed are said to require development.) Claims that exceed utilization screens or that don't meet coverage conditions, for example, are also suspended.

4. *Development:* Payers usually contact the patient or physician by phone or mail for missing information. It is advisable to produce the information as quickly as possible because these claims can be rejected if the payer can not obtain the necessary information within a certain time period.

5. *Manual Review:* Manual review of a claim is done by a claims examiner or reviewer. Usually, an examiner has received no formal training in medicine or medical terminology but has been trained to review claims for medical necessity using guidelines and parameters created by the payer's medical director and other medical personnel. The examiner looks at the claim and any support documents sent with it.

6. *Initial Determination:* After all the information is reviewed, the examiner makes one of three decisions regarding the claim:

    a. Pay it. If the claim is paid, a check is issued.

    b. Deny it. If all charges are denied, a denial notice is issued.

    c. Down code or partially pay it. When the service rendered exceeds that which was necessary for the treatment of the patient's problem, the examiner can "reduce" or down code the service and pay at the lower level. In other cases, some services may be denied in full and others paid. Both the patient and the physician are notified of this modification and a check for the approved services is issued.

    In addition to the above three decisions, claims can also be sent to other payer staff, such as nurses and/or physicians, who have more formal background in medicine and are able to make determinations that the examiner may not feel qualified to make.

While the claims adjudication process can be much more involved than this explanation provides, it does illustrate the basic process followed by payers when adjudicating a claim. Having an awareness of the communication process that takes place between the payer and the practice through the claim form will help the practice anticipate the needs of the people involved in processing claims and, therefore, submit claims that address those needs. In short, understanding how the system works helps you work with the system.

TIPS FOR INTERACTING WITH PAYERS

Now that you have an understanding of how payers process your claims, you are ready to learn some basic human interaction—and protection—skills. This chapter provides tips on dealing with payer staff in a manner that will help your practice.

Establish a Relationship

It is important to establish a rapport with a representative from each of the major payers in your area and with the benefits managers of major employers in your area. This initial investment in your time may well pay off handsomely later when dealing with problem claims and reimbursement. An easy way to make a first contact is to get the name of the person and either write an introductory letter or place a call to him or her to introduce yourself and "get acquainted." Another valuable contact to make are customer service representatives at each of the payers. By calling and asking these representatives questions, and getting the person's name, you can begin to get to know them and build a valuable contact.

Be Professional and Courteous

Anyone who has attempted to obtain information, including preauthorizations, from a payer has probably experienced frustration. They keep you on hold too long, they don't respond as promptly as you would like, they don't know the answer to your question, they give you an answer and then change their mind, etc., etc. It is very understandable that you could become frustrated and even angry. However, conveying these feelings will not "make friends and influence people" in a way that will be beneficial to your practice.

Remember when contacting a payer that you are talking to a *person* at the other end of the line. And that person, just like you, does not want to be yelled at or otherwise treated badly. It will not motivate them to help you nor will it build a relationship that could work in your favor later. When dealing with a payer, keep in mind that you are dealing with *people*—not just an institution. Be professional, courteous, and remember to say "thank you." This applies to any contact you make with a payer, either by phone or by letter.

Reduce Human Error

In 1970, the Pogo cartoonist Walt Kelly wrote, "We have met the enemy and he is us." Although not written with physician practices in mind, given that nearly one-third of claims submitted to third party payers contain errors, the saying has its application. Valid gripes and complaints about payer shortcomings aside, many of the problems physician offices confront are of their own making.

Improper, incomplete and inaccurate claims, which often result in unnecessary delays and denials, are referred to as "dirty" claims and can easily be avoided by your practice. The following types of problems are often the cause:

- Illegible handwriting
- Lack of physician name, identification number, or signature
- Lack of patient name or policy number
- Out-of-date patient information
- Outdated codes (CPT, HCPCS, and ICD-9-CM)
- Improper place of service code
- Lack of referring physician name or identification (when appropriate)
- Illogical relationships between services provided and patient diagnoses

Many practice management computer systems and electronic claims submission programs "force" you to submit cleaner claims by requiring basic claim information (see discussion of electronic claims later in this chapter). Whether keeping claims "clean" is ensured by your computer system or by the office manager double-checking all claims, it should be a policy in your practice to ensure that claims submitted are correct and that the information being used is current and accurate.

Document All Phone Contacts

Payers' staff who answer phone calls are not usually trained in medical terminology or coding nor are they experts on claims adjudication. As such, they may give you inaccurate information. For this reason, any time you receive an answer from a payer, document it. Keep the first and last name and department of the person you speak to and the date of the conversation in a file. Also, when you obtain information from a payer, it may be helpful to send a letter to the person you spoke with, confirming your understanding of the information you received and asking that they respond, in writing, if you have misunderstood. Doing so provides a backup for you should your actions be questioned. And, a letter is a way to also thank the person who helped you, thereby building a relationship that could be beneficial in the future.

If you have the misfortune to receive inaccurate information from a representative, do not hesitate to contact the supervisor or manager of the department. This allows the supervisor to educate the representative, thereby preventing the representative from giving out incorrect information in the future. It may also help to prevent any repercussions to your office.

Contact the Correct Department

Many practices have been frustrated when calling a payer and having to search for the department that can help them. This can be alleviated by thinking about the question you need answered, and then thinking about the appropriate department that could help you.

Alternatively, don't overlook your own resources, including your provider handbook. It may save you a phone call, some time, and frustration.

Keep Current

There are many changes occurring in third party reimbursement and coverage policies due to the many cost cutting efforts of government, business, labor, consumer groups, and the health insurance industry. These cost cutting efforts will affect the amount and availability of reimbursement for your practice. Keeping up-to-date with payer policies will help you deal more effectively with changes. Either you or someone in your office should be given the responsibility of keeping an eye on changes that might affect your practice. Contact the payers with whom you deal most frequently, such as Medicare, Blue Shield, and commercial payers, and get on their mailing list to obtain their newsletters and bulletins. Most payers publish information on changes to coverage and reimbursement which is found in these newsletters and bulletins.

Remember the Human Element and Anticipate the Payer's Needs

It cannot be stressed strongly enough that each payer is made up of people. People like to enjoy their jobs, but they have bad days and too much work to do. If you take the time to remember this, and then think about what you can do to make their job easier, you will be better off.

For example, if you have a claim that you believe may be difficult for the payer to understand (a new procedure or a lot of services in a short period of time), send a short letter in simple language explaining the service(s) provided and why they were provided. Add this to the claim in addition to your support documentation. In this way, the staff can quickly and easily see what was done and why and, as such, make a more favorable determination on your claim. You saved them time and made their job a little easier. In the long run, this saves you time in resubmitting claims and eliminates frustration. (For more information about this technique and other helpful techniques for optimizing reimbursement, refer to Chapter Four of this book.)

Also, try not to call around lunch time or right at the end of the day. During lunch, the payer is short-staffed and the people left to cover the shift may have a lot of phone calls to answer. If you call when they are already swamped, odds are the person won't be as helpful as he would if you had called earlier in the morning or after the "lunch rush." At the end of the day, staff are trying to finish up last-minute items or prepare to get out the door because they have to pick up their kids from daycare, etc. Again, staff may not be as helpful at this time of day, thus causing you frustration.

Although these tips may seem like basic common sense, many practices overlook them when dealing with insurance carriers. Remembering the Golden Rule: "Do unto others as you would have them do unto you" and using some common sense can go a long way in alleviating your frustration and providing benefits to your practice.

METHODS OF CLAIMS SUBMISSION

There are two options for submitting claims: paper and electronic media claims (EMC). In addition to submitting your own claims, some practices use a billing service or service bureau. Each option is discussed below.

Paper Claims

Paper claims are claims submitted in writing. About one-third of physician practices still submit paper claims to third party payers. Paper claims include the HCFA-1500 form (also called the Universal Claim Form), superbills and other types of itemized bills provided to patients by the provider, and proprietary forms issued by individual payers.

A sample HCFA-1500 form is shown in Figure 1.1. Note that the form provides areas for payer, patient, physician, and place-of-service information. Space is also allowed for diagnosis codes, procedure codes, fees, and other relevant information.

Contrast the HCFA-1500 to the example superbill shown in Figure 1.2. Each practice creates its own superbill and lists information and codes relevant to the practice's needs. These forms are often designed with the assistance of a consultant familiar with payer requirements and coding issues, or with the help of a trained printer representative.

Medicare will not accept superbills or charge tickets. *When submitting paper claims to Medicare you must use the HCFA-1500 form.* In addition to Medicare, virtually all third party payers accept the HCFA-1500. Commercial payers, many Blue Shield plans and other payers (as well as service bureaus), will typically accept superbills.

Proprietary forms are those created by individual insurers. While most all insurers now accept the HCFA-1500 form (if not require it), some Workers' Compensation programs and other programs still create and require use of their form.

Advantages

Paper claims have many advantages. First, they are easy to obtain; forms supply companies, the U.S. Government Printing Office, and other direct mail marketing firms sell Universal Claim Forms for a minimal cost. Second, because many paper forms come in two parts, it serves not only as the bill sent to the payer, but also as a back-up copy for the office. Third, the form is relatively easy to complete and provides room for all the necessary elements of a claim. The latter point is especially important since many payers may delay or deny a claim that does not contain all the necessary information. Sending additional documentation with a paper claim is also a simple procedure. The office staff can simply attach the operative report, consult report, etc., to the claim when it is mailed to the payer. Finally, the HCFA-1500 is usually accepted by all payers. This makes claim submission easier for the office staff because they do not have to remember which insurance company accepts which form—the same one can be purchased and used for all patients.

Disadvantages

Paper claims have four basic disadvantages: they can be lost, they require storage space, different forms can be required for different payers, and the industry is rapidly moving to electronic claims. Most insurers and the U.S. Postal Service have been known to lose a claim or two. For the practice, this means finding the office copy and resubmitting the claim, both of which take time and cause a delay in payment. Storage of completed and paid forms can be difficult for an office with limited space or one that sees a large number of patients. Finally, and probably most significantly, different payers may require use of different paper forms. This means keeping track of each form, completing each separately, and being sure the correct form is sent to the correct insurer. This is time consuming and can be frustrating for office staff.

Electronic Media Claims (EMC)

Electronic media claims (EMC) are those submitted via computer over telephone lines. Most major payers accept EMC and provide guidelines and information to practices regarding their require-

Figure 1.1: Sample HCFA-1500 Form (Universal Claim Form)

PLEASE
DO NOT
STAPLE
IN THIS
AREA

APPROVED OMB-0939-0008

PICA	**HEALTH INSURANCE CLAIM FORM**	PICA

1. MEDICARE MEDICAID CHAMPUS CHAMPVA GROUP HEALTH PLAN FECA BLK LUNG OTHER	1a. INSURED'S I.D. NUMBER (FOR PROGRAM IN ITEM 1)
[X] (Medicare #) (Medicaid #) (Sponsor's SSN) (VA File #) (SSN or ID) (SSN) (ID)	A987654321

2. PATIENT'S NAME (Last Name, First Name, Middle Initial)	3. PATIENT'S BIRTH DATE MM DD YY SEX	4. INSURED'S NAME (Last Name, First Name, Middle Initial)
Peter N. Aught	4 30 31 M [X] F	Same

5. PATIENT'S ADDRESS (No., Street)	6. PATIENT RELATIONSHIP TO INSURED	7. INSURED'S ADDRESS (No., Street)
321 Fading Lane	Self [X] Spouse Child Other	Same

CITY	STATE	8. PATIENT STATUS	CITY	STATE
Indolants	NY	Single Married [X] Other		

ZIP CODE	TELEPHONE (Include Area Code)	Employed Full-Time Student Part-Time Student	ZIP CODE	TELEPHONE (Include Area Code)
00009	(212)555-4444			

9. OTHER INSURED'S NAME (Last Name, First Name, Middle Initial)	10. IS PATIENT'S CONDITION RELATED TO:	11. INSURED'S POLICY GROUP OR FECA NUMBER
a. OTHER INSURED'S POLICY OR GROUP NUMBER	a. EMPLOYMENT? (CURRENT OR PREVIOUS) YES NO	a. INSURED'S DATE OF BIRTH MM DD YY SEX M F
b. OTHER INSURED'S DATE OF BIRTH MM DD YY SEX M F	b. AUTO ACCIDENT? PLACE (State) YES NO	b. EMPLOYER'S NAME OR SCHOOL NAME
C. EMPLOYER'S NAME OR SCHOOL NAME	c. OTHER ACCIDENT? YES NO	c. INSURANCE PLAN NAME OR PROGRAM NAME
d. INSURED PLAN NAME OR PROGRAM NAME	10d. RESERVED FOR LOCAL USE	d. IS THERE ANOTHER HEALTH BENEFIT PLAN? YES NO If yes, return to and complete item 9 a–d.

READ BACK OF FORM BEFORE COMPLETING & SIGNING THIS FORM.

12. PATIENT'S OR AUTHORIZED PERSON'S SIGNATURE I authorize the release of any medical or other information necessary to process this claim. I also request payment of government benefits either to myself or to the party who accepts assignment below.	13. INSURED'S OR AUTHORIZED PERSON'S SIGNATURE I authorize payment of medical benefits to the undersigned physician or supplier for services described below.
SIGNED On File DATE	SIGNED On File

14. DATE OF CURRENT: ILLNESS (First symptom) OR INJURY (Accident) OR PREGNANCY (LMP) MM DD YY	15. IF PATIENT HAS HAD SAME OR SIMILAR ILLNESS. GIVE FIRST DATE MM DD YY	16. DATES PATIENT UNABLE TO WORK IN CURRENT OCCUPATION MM DD YY MM DD YY FROM TO
2 9 97		

17. NAME OF REFERRING PHYSICIAN OR OTHER SOURCE	17a. I.D. NUMBER OF REFERRING PHYSICIAN	18. HOSPITALIZATION DATES RELATED TO CURRENT SERVICES MM DD YY MM DD YY FROM TO

19. RESERVED FOR LOCAL USE	20. OUTSIDE LAB? $ CHARGES [X] YES NO

21. DIAGNOSIS OR NATURE OF ILLNESS OR INJURY. (RELATE ITEMS 1,2,3 OR 4 TO ITEM 24E BY LINE)	22. MEDICAID RESUBMISSION CODE ORIGINAL REF. NO.
1. 719.07 3.	23. PRIOR AUTHORIZATION NUMBER
2. 4.	

24. DATE(S) OF SERVICE From To MM DD YY MM DD YY	B Place of Service	C Type of Service	D PROCEDURES, SERVICES OR SUPPLIES (Explain Unusual Circumstances) CPT/HCPCS MODIFIER	E DIAGNOSIS CODE	F $ CHARGES	G DAYS OR UNITS	H EPSDT Family Plan	I EMG	J COB	K RESERVED FOR LOCAL USE
03 17 97	11		20605	1	75 00	1				

25. FEDERAL TAX I.D. NUMBER SSN EIN	26. PATIENT'S ACCOUNT NO.	27. ACCEPT ASSIGNMENT? (For govt. claims, see back)	28. TOTAL CHARGE	29. AMOUNT PAID	30. BALANCE DUE
987-65-4321 [X]		[X] YES NO	$ 75 00	$ 0 00	$ 75 00

31. SIGNATURE OF PHYSICIAN OR SUPPLIER INCLUDING DEGREES OR CREDENTIALS (I certify that the statements on the reverse apply to this bill and are made a part thereof.) SIGNED 17/March/98 DATE	32. NAME AND ADDRESS OF FACILITY WHERE SERVICES WERE RENDERED (If other than home or office)	33. PHYSICIAN'S SUPPLIER'S BILLING NAME, ADDRESS, ZIP CODE & PHONE # Thomas Sticker, M.D. 1000 One Thousand Lane Thousand Lakes, NY 10000 PIN# 987-65-4321 GRP#

(APPROVED BY AMA COUNCIL ON MEDICAL SERVICE 8/88)   **PLEASE PRINT OR TYPE**   FORM HCFA-1500 (12-90) FORM OWCP-1500 FORM RRB-1500

CARRIER

PATIENT AND INSURED INFORMATION

PHYSICIAN OR SUPPLIER INFORMATION

Figure 1.2: Sample Superbill

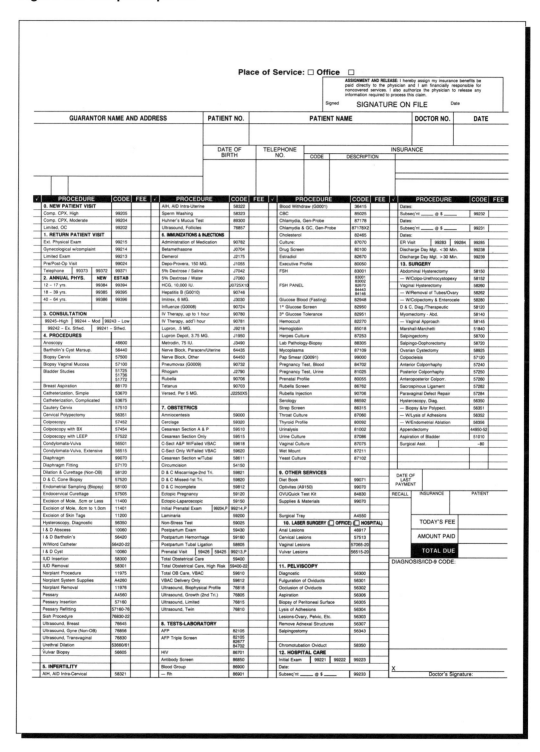

ments. To submit electronically, the practice must be computerized and have a modem or some other means of electronically transmitting the claims. Physician service bureaus or billing services can also submit claims electronically for physicians.

Advantages

Although there are numerous advantages to submitting claims electronically, they boil down into four key benefits. First, the nature of the electronic claims process requires that you submit cleaner claims. Claims with errors, such as missing information, invalid patient and provider numbers, etc., will be prescreened either by the claims clearinghouse you use or by the payer's pre-adjudication system. Problems that would cause delays and denials with paper claims are corrected *prior* to their acceptance by the payer. This results in improved cash flow and lower resubmission costs.

Second, electronic claims are generally paid more promptly than paper claims, which further enhances your cash flow. Third, a claim submitted electronically costs about a third less than had it been submitted on paper. (For payers, the savings are even more dramatic. Given sufficient volume, paper claims can reduce a payer's processing costs by more than 50 percent.) Finally, electronic claims submission reduces the possibility for human error. Because a computer sends the claims to the payer's computer, no one "loses" the claim or delays it during processing. And, many computer vendors and other software firms have created software that alerts the office staff when a mistake is made, such as missing information or a nonexistent code. This helps reduce errors on the part of the practice as well.

Disadvantages

Electronic media claims have a few drawbacks. First, while EMC is great for routine or simple claims, it is not the best vehicle for more complicated claims or claims that require additional documentation. The reason is simple; a computer processes the claim. Remember that a computer is not able to reason or interpret what you meant. If your claim is missing information or contains errors, or is for a large number of services, the computer may "kick it out" for manual processing. Think about this before sending a claim that should include additional documentation. Once payers begin receiving support documentation electronically, however, this drawback will disappear.

Second, decisions have to be made about how your claims will be submitted electronically. Will you utilize a clearinghouse, and if so, which one? Do you intend to submit some claims electronically and others via paper? If so, how will your system handle this? Do you want to submit some claims directly to a specific payer while other go via a clearinghouse? If so, how can you get your computer system to accomplish this? For most practices that are automated, the system vendor can help provide answers and/or solutions for these issues. But there are costs and time associated with implementing the EMC solution that best meets your practice's needs.

Other Electronic Information

There are many types of records that can be converted to an electronic format as well as many types of functions that can be automated. These include:

1. *Medical record.* Until recently, the only means of keeping and storing a patient's medical record was on paper. Maybe the computer was used to transcribe the physician's notes,

but the input, maintenance, and retrieval of this record was very manual. New technology and more involvement on the part of physicians is providing impetus for creation of an automated medical record. Many of these programs are prompt-driven, which means the user is prompted to choose from a list of standard clinical phrases and descriptions that are applicable to the particular patient. The advantages of these programs are the uniformity of records across patients and physicians, time savings, and a reduction in errors (which minimizes malpractice liability).

2.   *Accounts receivable.* Accounts receivable are much more manageable when automated. The computer provides a report of past due accounts which allows the person responsible for contacting the patient to make calls without looking up the phone number, account balance, etc.

3.   *Electronic remittance advice (ERA).* ERA is the electronic form of the remittance advice sent by insurance companies. It provides information related to the patient, date of service, services provided, charges made, charges approved, and amount paid. But, instead of mailing it to your office, you can receive it via your computer, similar to the way in which you transmit claims for EMC. While not all insurers provide ERA, many are beginning to because of the cost savings.

4.   *Electronic funds transfer (EFT).* Many people are familiar with EFT because it is used in their personal lives, for example, direct deposit of payroll checks and direct withdrawal of mortgage or other loan payments. Insurance companies use EFT to transfer payment on claims directly to the physician's bank account. The ERA or paper remittance advice then is used to notify the physician that payment has been made and at what amount. Again, use of EFT is growing because of the cost and time savings.

5.   *Electronic communication with third party payers.* With the increased use of computers in physician practices, insurance companies are automating common inquiries. For example, some insurance companies will allow your office computer to contact their computer to obtain policy coverage verification, pre-authorization for services, and claim status verification information. By automating these functions, both parties save time, reduce costs and hassles, and increase accuracy.

Billing Services

An alternative to complete automation is the use of a billing service. Also called a service bureau, these companies can perform all your billing and collection activities. Used traditionally by hospital-based physicians (anesthesiologists, radiologists, pathologists) and psychiatrists, billing services are now taking hold as an alternative to performing your own billing.

Advantages

Because the people who operate billing services are generally well-versed in billing, reimbursement, and regulatory issues, they can help you obtain the optimal reimbursement for your services. In addition, most billing services will also perform collection services on your behalf, which can also increase cash flow.

By removing the billing and insurance filing process from your office, the headaches and hassles associated with these functions are minimized. The level of expertise and knowledge required for this function is lessened, time spent following up unpaid and appealed claims is reduced or eliminated, and the process of sending claims, posting payments, etc., is simplified. And, removing the billing and insurance processing functions from the office will free staff time for other administrative work. Depending upon the size of the practice and the type of services offered, a billing service can often reduce administrative and other costs associated with billing and insurance processing. In many cases, the billing service is a more cost-effective method for performing these tasks. However, to determine whether this is true for your individual practice, you need to compare charges made by billing services to the costs of doing it yourself.

Also, the better job the billing service does, the happier your patient will be because their bills are being handled in a timely and professional manner. This makes them happier with their care and their physician as well.

Finally, most billing services provide financial and other important reports on a monthly basis for your review. Frequently, if there is a special report you would like to have, the service will create it for you. In this way, you still have access to all the information you need without having to utilize your staff to get the work done.

Disadvantages

Billing services do have some drawbacks. For many practices, the loss of control over the billing operation and its associated functions is too great a risk. Most practices want the control and daily hands-on operation because they feel they are at less risk should a mistake occur.

In addition to control, many practices also like the ability to review their daily billings, accounts receivable, etc., on a daily or weekly basis, information the billing service may only provide monthly.

A billing service does not perform other functions that an in-office computer can perform. If you intend to use your computer system for functions other than billing-related operations, the billing service may not be for you. Some practices feel it duplicates work to have a computer in the office for some functions and send the billing somewhere else. This is a determination only the physician and staff can make.

PROBLEM SET: CHAPTER ONE

Suggested solutions to the problems below can be found in Appendix A.

Mark the following statements true or false.

		True	False
1.	The vast majority of payers use sophisticated claims editing technology that scans your claim for coding, billing, clinical, utilization, and unbundling errors.	_____	_____
2.	Development of a claim refers to the process of obtaining additional information from the provider, such as a consultant's report or an operative report, so that the payer may properly adjudicate the claim.	_____	_____
3.	Establishing positive relationships with the payers and benefit administrators in your area is usually a worthwhile effort.	_____	_____
4.	About one out of every three claims submitted by physicians to payers contain errors.	_____	_____
5.	When reporting codes that are new to CPT or services that are rarely performed, it is helpful to provide support documentation which explains and/or justifies the service and your charges.	_____	_____
6.	Although less expensive to produce than paper claims, electronic claims generally have the same number of errors as paper claims.	_____	_____
7.	Virtually all payers accept the HCFA-1500 claim form.	_____	_____
8.	EFT is the abbreviation for "Error Free Transmission" of claims.	_____	_____
9.	Billing services can be a cost-effective alternative for practices that desire to out-source their billing, insurance filing and collection activities.	_____	_____
10.	Although counterintuitive, a "dirty" claim is NOT defined as one which is missing information, such as the patient name or policy number, that a payer needs to adjudicate a claim.	_____	_____

The following are multiple choice questions. Select the most correct answer(s).

11.   Advantages of submitting electronic claims generally include:

    a.   They are less expensive to submit than paper claims.
    b.   They reduce the likelihood that the payer will make an error with the claims.
    c.   They force providers to submit cleaner claims.
    d.   Payment turnaround is faster than with paper claims.
    e.   All of the above.

12.   Errors commonly found on "dirty" claims include:

    a.   Failure to list a referring provider when reporting consultation service.
    b.   Inconsistency between the patient's age and diagnosis or procedures.
    c.   Out-of-date insurance policy number.
    d.   Diagnosis does not support or adequately justify reported service.
    e.   All of the above.

CHAPTER TWO:
PROCEDURE AND
DIAGNOSIS CODING

Coding systems were created to allow health care providers the means of communicating to payers the services rendered to patients, as well as the reasons for those services. Considered the technical aspect of insurance processing, learning to properly code provides two immediate benefits to medical practices. First, your income and patient satisfaction is either directly or indirectly tied to coding. In the fee-for-service environment, appropriate use of codes helps ensure proper payment from both payers and patients. Payers may reject or delay payment on claims that are incorrectly coded. Under managed care plans where encounter forms are required, proper coding is essential for retrospective data analysis purposes (such as determining profitability of capitated arrangements or having clean data for provider report cards) and justifying the level of care provided. Accurate coding also has a positive impact on relations with those patients who are responsible for a portion of your charges. Poor coding on claims can lead to denials of covered services as well as co-payments that are higher than they should be, placing a needless financial burden on your patients.

Second, improper coding can adversely affect the practice's audit liability. The codes reported on a claim communicate to payers and others that specific services and procedures were performed. If the reported codes do not accurately describe the procedures and services rendered, the physician may be accused of fraudulent billing; that is, billing for services and procedures other than those that were provided. Thus, it is clearly in the practice's interest to learn how to code accurately and properly.

It is essential that you be familiar with and understand the use of coding systems to receive optimal reimbursement and minimize audit liability. By studying the material in this chapter you will:

- Learn when to use CPT codes.
- Learn when to use HCPCS National codes.
- Learn when to use HCPCS Local codes.
- Learn when to use ICD-9-CM codes.
- Learn the importance of keeping up with changes to these coding systems.

OVERVIEW OF CODING SYSTEMS

In years past, there was no one group of nationally accepted codes. Blue Cross & Blue Shield created and required use of its own coding system. Many private insurance companies accepted CPT codes, while others, especially in the western states, used California Relative Value Study codes. Several government programs required use of ICD-9 procedure codes. A Kansas Relative Value Study was even accepted by some payers in parts of the Midwest. Of course, the list could go on, but the point is well taken that until fairly recently the coding systems used to report services to insurance companies varied across the country.

An important event took place in 1983 which led to the standardization of coding systems nationwide: Medicare created a new coding system, HCPCS, and began requiring its use for the reporting of services and procedures provided to Medicare beneficiaries. The new HCPCS coding system consisted (and still does) of three levels of codes. The first level, and the largest portion of HCPCS, is CPT. National Codes comprise the second level of HCPCS while Local Codes comprise the third level. Each of these levels will be discussed in greater detail later on in this chapter.

Insurance companies that administer Medicare programs across the country began shifting from their then current coding systems to the HCPCS system. During the transition it became obvious to many of the Medicare carriers that if they were going to have to accept CPT codes for Medicare, they might as well accept them for all the policies they wrote. Other insurance companies started recognizing the fact that important health care statistics would be based on CPT codes due to Medicare's new requirement, and as such, felt it would be in their best interest to accept CPT codes. One event led to another, and within a three-year period virtually all insurance carriers in the U.S. began accepting, if not requiring, CPT codes. And, as of 1987 most Medicaid programs nationwide began accepting HCPCS codes.

The various coding systems discussed above have one element in common: they focus on the procedures, services, and supplies that physicians provide to patients. However, insurance companies do not base payment solely on *what* was done for the patient—they need to know *why* the services and procedures were provided. In the past, physicians simply wrote the patient's diagnosis on the claim form or superbill. Medicare now requires that you report ICD-9-CM codes on all claims for services rendered to Medicare patients. In fact, you risk a $2,000 per line item fine if you do not use ICD-9-CM codes when reporting to Medicare. Most other payers also require that you submit ICD-9-CM codes. If you fail to list them you run the risk of payment delays or denials. If you do not report a diagnosis code, a claims processor might choose one for you. This may result not only in delays, but the processor may pick a diagnosis code which does not justify or support the service you rendered, resulting in a denied claim.

Many beginning coders are so anxious to locate "correct" codes that they often overlook the context in which the codes exist. CPT, HCPCS, and ICD-9-CM codes do not exist in a vacuum by themselves. They are supported by a system of rules, symbols, notations, and formatting. To code properly requires both an awareness and an understanding of the support structure underlying the CPT coding system.

Now that you have a better understanding of why CPT, HCPCS, and ICD-9-CM are important to your reimbursement, let us turn our attention to the different coding systems and their application. The following chapters discuss each coding system in detail, including an overview of its use, organization, coding conventions and symbols used, and general coding rules.

CPT

Physicians' <u>C</u>urrent <u>P</u>rocedural <u>T</u>erminology, or CPT, is published annually by the American Medical Association (AMA). It lists codes for more than 7,000 procedures and services performed by physicians. CPT is the most widely used coding system for reporting services and procedures to health insurance companies. Virtually all payers, including Medicare and Medicaid, require CPT codes.

The first edition of CPT, published in 1966, was based on the California Relative Value Study. The 1966 edition contained four-digit codes with descriptions. In 1970, a second edition was published which contained five-digit codes and two-digit modifiers. A third edition was published in 1973 and a fourth edition in 1977. CPT is still in its fourth edition and the book is now updated on an annual basis. Each year's update is referred to as a volume. It is imperative that you obtain a new copy of CPT each year for several reasons:

- Hundreds of changes are made to the book each year.
- If you skip a year, you will have to spend endless hours determining the changes made during the previous year which apply to your specialty.
- Without the current codes your reimbursement will not be optimal.
- By not keeping up with changes to definitions you could expose yourself to audit liability.

CPT codes can be distinguished from other codes in that they consist of five numbers followed by a verbal description of the procedure or service associated with the code. Code numbers in CPT range from 00100 to 99199. The following is an example of a CPT code:

90701   Immunization, active; diphtheria and tetanus toxoids and pertussis vaccine (DTP)

CPT also contains modifiers that are to be listed after the codes which they modify. CPT modifiers are numeric, either two- or five-digit. The following is an example of a CPT modifier:

-59   Distinct Procedural Service

Organization

The CPT book is organized into six sections of codes which are divided based on the type of procedure or service performed. It also contains a table of contents, an introduction, guidelines, four appendices, and an index.

Evaluation and Management is the first section of CPT. Codes in this section range from 99201 through 99499. Open your CPT book to page 1 and you will not see codes; rather you will find information on how to use the codes in this section of the book. This information is entitled "Guidelines," and each of the six sections of the book contain guidelines. We will cover the important guidelines later.

The Evaluation and Management (E/M) section contains codes used by physicians to report services such as office visits, hospital visits, consultations, critical care, case management, and similar services. Eight pages of guidelines are provided to help you understand how to properly report these services.

Until recently, few physicians used codes from the second section of CPT, the *Anesthesia* section. Anesthesiologists usually reported their services to payers using CPT Surgery codes with time and patient condition notations. However, Medicare now requires that anesthesiologists use the CPT Anesthesia codes on their claims. At the time of this writing, most other payers still require the Surgery codes.

The CPT Anesthesia section is organized by general anatomic area, such as the head and the upper arm and elbow. Anesthesia services related to radiological and miscellaneous services are listed at the end of the section.

The *Surgery* section is both the longest and technically most difficult section of CPT. Code numbers in Surgery range from 10040 to 69979. It is important to note that the codes in this section are organized by body system. The first body system is the Integumentary System—the skin, subcutaneous, and areolar tissues (the outer portion of the human body). Next you will find the Musculoskeletal System which includes muscle and bone and is located anatomically beneath the Integumentary System. The last body system listed is the Auditory System (the ears).

In the *Radiology* section, codes are divided into four subsections:

1.   Diagnostic Radiology (Diagnostic Imaging)
2.   Diagnostic Ultrasound
3.   Radiation Oncology
4.   Nuclear Medicine

Within each subsection in Radiology the codes are arranged by anatomic areas from the top to bottom of the body as in Surgery. For example, Diagnostic Radiology codes begin with those for the Head and Neck and are followed by Chest, Spine and Pelvis, etc. Code numbers in the Radiology section range from 70010 to 79999.

The *Pathology and Laboratory* section contains codes for lab procedures performed both in the physician's office and independent labs. Code numbers range from 80002-89399. Additionally, codes used by pathologists appear toward the end of this section. Note that the individual clinical chemistry tests, listed under the heading "Chemistry and Toxicology," are arranged alphabetically.

Finally, the *Medicine* section contains codes used by a variety of medical specialists. Examples include ophthalmology services, dialysis, cardiovascular services and procedures, physical therapy, injections, and special services, such as codes for prolonged care. Procedures and services located in this section of CPT can be distinguished from those located in the Surgery section in that codes in the Medicine section primarily describe non-invasive (or minimally invasive) procedures and services. As an example, you would find codes for therapeutic injections in the Medicine section and codes for aspiration in the Surgery section. Codes in the Medicine section range from 90700 through 99199.

CPT's *Introduction* provides general information about the use and reporting of CPT codes. Format, modifiers, unlisted codes, and special reports are among the important issues discussed in the Introduction.

Appendix A contains a listing of all CPT modifiers. As you will learn, modifiers which apply to a particular section of CPT are listed in the Guidelines at the beginning of the section. Modifiers are covered in Chapter Three of this text.

A summary of the changes that have been made to CPT since the previous year's volume are listed numerically in *Appendix B*. Notations are made next to each code as to whether the code is new, changed, or has been deleted. In cases where a code has been deleted from CPT, a reference will be made to a code(s) that is to be used in place of the deleted code. An easier way to determine whether or not a code has been added or changed is discussed under "Symbols and Notations" later in this chapter.

The purpose of *Appendix C* is to provide the condensed verbal descriptions for new and revised codes. By using this appendix, purchasers of previous short procedure versions can update their computer database without having to spend a large sum for a new tape or diskette. (In addition to selling CPT in book form, the AMA also makes CPT available on computer diskettes and magnetic tape. The tape comes in two versions: long and short procedure descriptions. The long version contains both the five-digit codes and the complete verbal descriptions that appear with the codes. The short version contains the five-digit codes, but the verbal descriptions have been "condensed" to no more than thirty typewritten characters. This is the maximum number of characters that will fit in the procedure description area on the old version of the Universal Claim Form. The diskette version of CPT contains the condensed descriptions.)

In an attempt to help you more effectively utilize evaluation and management codes, clinical examples for various levels of different types of E/M services are provided in *Appendix D*. These examples supplement those provided with the E/M codes in the first section of CPT. Formerly termed "vignettes," the examples are designed to illustrate the types of services and patient problems for each level of service. Specialty specific examples are listed for relevance and realism. As you will learn later in this book, determining which level of E/M service should be reported is at best a difficult undertaking. The examples provided in *Appendix D* and those listed with E/M codes are an important reference tool.

The CPT *Index* is a great asset, and should be used as such. Over the past few years the AMA has made substantial improvements to the Index, including enhanced instructions for its use. To fully benefit from the Index you need to understand how procedures and services can be located. Codes may be listed one or more ways in the Index. If you cannot locate the code using one of the methods, try another. To locate a code, you can look under any of the following:

1. *The name of the procedure or service.* For example, if the physician performed a kidney biopsy, you could begin by looking under the term "Biopsy."

2. *The name of the organ or anatomic site.* For example, if the physician performed a procedure on a patient's kidney, you could look under "Kidney," "Renal," or "Urinary" until you locate a reference to the code(s) you are seeking.

3. *The name of the condition being treated or diagnosed.* For example, if the physician was treating an ulcer, you could look up the word "Ulcer" in the Index.

4. *A synonym of the term being used.* The Index may have reference to the procedure you are seeking, but under a term different from that which you are using. Rather than giving up, look under a synonym of the term. For example, if you searched unsuccessfully using the word "Shoulder," try again using synonyms such as "Clavicle" or "Scapula."

5. *An eponym.* An eponym is the naming of a procedure or service after the person or persons who developed it. For example, the second procedure listed in the CPT Index is an eponym: Abbe-Estlander Procedure. When a procedure is commonly referenced in the

medical community by eponym, the AMA will often list the procedure in the Index under the eponym.

6.   *An abbreviation of the procedure or service.* Several procedures, especially lab tests, are listed under their abbreviation. For example, you could find a Thyrotropin Releasing Factor test listed under TRH in the Index. On the other hand, some tests or procedures are not listed under abbreviations commonly used in the medical community. As an example, a "Transurethral resection of prostate" could not be located by looking under "TURP." In this case you need to look under the term "Transurethral procedure" or "Excision, Prostate, Transurethral."

Structure

The CPT coding system uses a hierarchical structure for organizing procedures and services. The six *sections* of the book—Evaluation and Management, Anesthesia, Surgery, Radiology, Pathology and Laboratory, and Medicine—form the top of the hierarchy. Within each of the six sections, codes are grouped into *subsections*. These are the titles that appear in the Table of Contents found in the Guidelines for each section. For example, in the Evaluation and Management section the first subsection listed is Office and Other Outpatient Services. The last section is Other Evaluation and Management Services. Each subsection is further divided into groups of codes called *headings*. If you open your book to Office and Other Patient Services, you will see that the codes for these visits are organized into New and Established patient groups. "New" and "Established" are heading titles. In the Surgery section in particular, codes are usually arranged into smaller groups under *subheadings*. Turn to the beginning of the Digestive System codes. The first anatomic site listed is the Lips, followed by the Mouth, Tongue, etc. Within the Lips anatomic site, the codes are grouped by type of procedure performed, e.g., Excision, Repair, Other Procedures. The anatomic sites would correspond to headings, and the groupings by type of procedure (e.g., Excision) would be called subheadings. Finally, the individual *procedures* are listed. The hierarchy, then, for code 40490 would be as follows:

    SECTION: Surgery
     SUBSECTION: Digestive System
      HEADING: Lips
       SUBHEADING: Excision
        PROCEDURE: 40490 Biopsy lip

You may have noticed that throughout most of CPT, the subsection, section and code number range are listed at the top of each page, and the page number is listed at the bottom of each page, along with the section name and definitions of special symbols used in the section.

Format

Many of the procedural descriptions in CPT are indented. Consider the example below excerpted from the Medicine section of CPT:

    95120   Professional services for allergen immunotherapy in prescribing physician's office or institution, including provision of allergenic extract; single injection

95125	two or more injections
95130	single stinging insect venom
95131	two stinging insect venoms
95132	three stinging insect venoms
95133	four stinging insect venoms
95134	five stinging insect venoms

Note that the description for codes 95125, 95130, 95131, 95132, 95133, and 95134 are indented. Why? Instead of repeating information in each code of a group of codes, the common element is printed once and followed by a semicolon. Codes below the one with the semicolon are indented and refer back to the common element.

Continuing with the above example, note that the semicolon occurs between the words "extract" and "single injection." The element common to codes 95120 - 95134 is that which precedes the semicolon, or "Professional services for allergen immunotherapy in prescribing physician's office or institution, including provision of allergenic extract." As such, code 95133 should be interpreted as meaning:

> 95133 Professional services for allergen immunotherapy in prescribing physician's office or institution, including provision of allergenic extract; four stinging insect venoms

Thus, for four stinging insect venoms you would use code 95133. For a single injection, you would use code 95130.

The reason the AMA chose to format CPT in this manner was to save space. The CPT book would be at least twice as long, and more expensive, if this format had not been selected.
When using CPT it is important that you pay close attention to the placement of the semicolon where indentations occur. Remember that the common element which carries down to the indented codes below includes *all* the information that comes before the semicolon in the unindented code.

Symbols

Three symbols appear in the CPT book: circles, triangles and stars (formerly called asterisks). Circles (●) are printed to the left of a new code in the book. This feature makes it easier to identify new procedures and services which appear in each year's volume. Circles may also appear next to codes that were in previous volumes but have been relocated to a different code range. Take a moment to thumb through your CPT book to note codes that have circles next to them.

The appearance of a triangle (▲), or delta, next to a code signifies that the description of the procedure has been changed since the previous year's CPT book. The revision may be major or minor. You will need to compare the new description to the previous year's description of the procedure to discover the change and its relevance to your billing.

An examples illustrates the importance of noting the deltas. In the 1996 volume of CPT, code 20962 read as follows:

> 20962 Bone graft with microvascular anastomosis; other bone graft (specify)

The code's definition was revised in the 1997 CPT to:

▲   20962   Bone graft with microvascular anastomosis; other <u>than fibula, iliac crest, or metatarsal</u>

The underlined words (emphasis added by author) were added to the 1997 code. The definition reflects the revision required due to the addition of codes for the iliac crest (20956) and metatarsal (20957).

You may have noticed that stars (*) appear to the right of several codes in the Surgery Section of CPT. Code 36415 is an example of a starred procedure. The appearance of the star means that the "surgical package" does not apply to the procedure. (Discussion of the surgical package and other billing rules is contained in Chapter Three.) Stars appear only with codes in the Surgery section of CPT.

Though not noted with symbols, when a code is deleted from the CPT system a parenthetical notation is invariably placed where the code had been located. The note will mention which code(s) has been deleted, and in many cases, refers the coder to another code to use in its place. An example will help illustrate. Locate code 82140 in your CPT book. Immediately below this code is a note which reads:

    (82141 has been deleted. To report, use 82140)

It is unfortunate that many coders forget to review new volumes of CPT for new, revised, and deleted codes until after they experience reimbursement problems. When obtaining a new volume of CPT your first job should be to check the changes and modify your billing process accordingly.

Notations

If you are familiar with the ICD-9-CM coding system you know how many rules it contains. You also know that the rules are applied fairly consistently. That is, there are not many exceptions to the rules in ICD-9-CM. Unfortunately, the same is not true for CPT. CPT has so many exceptions that it is often referred to as a system of exceptions with a few rules. It is imperative that you be aware of the exceptions and how to locate them.

You can locate exceptions by taking the time to read all the notes and parenthetical information appearing near the codes you are using. Notes that contain rules regarding the use of a group of codes are usually placed at the beginning of the group. Notes related to the use of one code or an indented group of codes appear after the code or at the end of the indented group.

Notes may be brief, such as the note associated with the pulmonary codes. Alternatively, they may be quite extensive. A review of the ophthalmology notes in the Medicine section exemplifies this latter point.

Two examples will help you understand the importance of reading all the notes in CPT. Open your book to the page in the Medicine section which contains codes for immunization injections. Between the title "Immunization Injections" and the first code in this group, 90700, you will find five notes, three of which are surrounded by parentheses. If you read the long note that starts with "When an immunization... " you will discover that in some circumstances you have the option of adding a charge for an evaluation and management service in addition to your charge for the immunization itself. You will also find that your charge for the injection should include a charge for the injected substance. Thus, you would not charge separately for the injection and for the substance you injected. Had you not read this note, you could have incorrectly billed for an immunization.

Another example can be found immediately below code 95827. The note reads:

> (For ambulatory 24 hour EEG monitoring, see 95950)

It appears that the note applies to several codes above it (95816 through 95827) and not just to either the one code or the indented group of codes immediately above the note.

Of all the things you will learn related to CPT coding, taking the time to read and think about notes will probably have the greatest positive impact on your reimbursement.

HCPCS

HCPCS is an acronym for the Health Care Financing Administration's Common Procedure Coding System and is pronounced "hick picks." As you may know, the Health Care Financing Administration (HCFA) is the government agency responsible for administering the Medicare and Medicaid programs nationwide. HCFA created the HCPCS system so that there would be codes to meet the following general objectives:

- To allow for the reporting of specific supplies, devices and equipment
- To allow for the reporting of non-physician services
- To provide a mechanism that allows regional variation in the way procedures, services and supplies are reported
- To provide a mechanism for reporting new procedure, service and supply codes

To meet these objectives, HCFA created a three-level coding system. Level I includes CPT, Level II contains the National codes, and Level III contains Local codes. HCPCS Level I (CPT), as you have just learned, contains codes that describe procedures and services physicians provide to their patients. It is important to note that CPT is not a supply book; it contains codes for physician procedures and services. In all cases, CPT codes are used to report what the physician did, or procedures and services rendered by someone under the physician's supervision as permitted by state and federal laws. For example, the physician could bill Medicare using CPT codes for hospital visits performed by a certified physician assistant who is an employee of the physician, as permitted by law, provided that certain licensing and claim filing requirements are met.

Figure 2.1 shows the three levels of HCPCS and provides easy comparison of the differences between them.

National Codes

Since CPT contains neither supply codes nor codes for non-physician procedures, HCFA needed to create codes for supplies, procedures and services not listed in CPT. This led to the creation of a second "level" of codes to supplement CPT. Often referred to as HCPCS Level II or alpha-numeric codes, they are technically National codes.

Figure 2.1: A Comparison of Differences Between The Three Levels of HCPCS

	LEVEL 1: CPT	LEVEL II: NATIONAL CODES	LEVEL III: LOCAL CODES
TYPE OF CODES	Five-Digit Numeric	Five-Digit Alpha-Numeric	Five-Digit Alpha-Numeric
RANGE OF CODES	00100-99199	A0021-V5364	W0000 thru Z9999 Varies by State Medicare carrier
EXAMPLE OF CODES	23020	A4550	W1234
TYPE OF MODIFIERS	Two- or Five-Digit Numeric	One or Two Letters, or Alphanumeric	Two Letter or Alpha-Numeric
RANGE OF MODIFIERS	"-20" thru "-99"	"-AA" thru "-VP"	"-W1" thru "-Z9" Varies by State Medicare carrier
EXAMPLE OF MODIFIERS	"-62" or "09962"	"-K4"	"-W2" and "-XA"
USAGE	Nationwide	Nationwide	Statewide—but being phased out

National codes, in contrast to the five-digit numeric codes found in CPT, begin with a letter, A, B, D, E, G, H, J, K, L, M, P, Q, R, and V, followed by four numeric digits. As you might suspect, National codes are used by all Medicare carriers. The following are examples of National codes:

A4207   Syringe with needle, sterile 2cc
A4550   Surgical trays
J2175   Injection, meperidine HCl, per 100 mg
J9070   Cyclophosphamide, [cytoxin], 100 mg
V2500   Contact lens, PMMA; spherical, per lens

There are approximately 2,500 codes in the National system, many of which are for supplies. A look at a portion of the Table of Contents for the National code system in Figure 2.2 should help you understand what types of items are listed. We will review the codes of most interest to the typical physician practice in the discussion below.

Before proceeding, a word of caution is in order. Many coders mistakenly believe that the existence of a code guarantees reimbursement when it is used, especially when first discovering the vast array of codes contained in the National system. Be aware that many factors affect the payer's decision to reimburse for a particular item or procedure. These range from the patient's diagnosis to whether or not the code describes a covered service. Whenever you are in doubt, contact the Medicare carrier and inquire about both coverage and coding. Of course, with most payers, this is easier said than done. Throughout this book suggestions are offered that will help you in this regard. For now, focus on understanding the content and usage of HCPCS National codes.

Figure 2.2: HCPCS National Codes Table of Contents

CONTENTS

v

Medicare and Medicaid payers will not accept the all-purpose CPT supply code, 99070. They require that you list an appropriate code from the National or Local systems. Therefore, it is important that you familiarize yourself with the types of supply codes listed in the National system. (Note: The following presentation is not organized alphabetically. Rather, those code ranges which you are most likely to need are listed first.)

Injection Codes J0120 – J9999

The National system lists hundreds of therapeutic and diagnostic drugs which can be administered intramuscularly, subcutaneously, or intravenously. There are also several codes for orally administered medications, such as immunosuppressive drugs. Practices often refer to these as "J" codes because they begin with the letter "J."

The "J" codes are used to report the *supply* of the injectable. To report the administration of the injection, use CPT codes 90782-90788. It is important to note that payment for the administration of an injection is included in the payment for an E/M service (or any other service(s)) provided on the same day, regardless of the type of drug used. If no E/M code is billed, the administration can be paid separately. If the sole purpose of the visit is for the administration of an injection, Medicare will make payment for the injection service (codes 90782-90788) and supply of the injectable only; an E/M service code is not paid separately. If an E/M service is billed on the same day as an administration *because services were performed in addition to the administration of the injection*, the E/M service may be allowed but the administration code will not be reimbursed separately. So, if you see a patient in the office and decide to inject an antibiotic to treat his illness, for example, you would bill only for the supply of the antibiotic using a "J" code; no additional charge would be made for the administration of the injection because the administration is considered to already be included in the payment for the E/M service.

Common Therapeutic and Diagnostic Injectables J0120 – J3570

Drugs listed in this range include antibiotics, analgesics, steroids, antihistamines, and others. Note that the drugs are usually listed by generic rather than brand name.

Miscellaneous Drugs and Solutions J7030 – J7310

Codes in this range are for drugs such as Ringers lactate infusions, human antihemophilic factors, and vitamin therapy. You should review these codes to determine which ones apply to your practice.

Immunosuppressive Drugs J7500 – J8999

Azathioprine, cyclosporine, epinephrine, and other immunosuppressive drugs are listed in this group.

Chemotherapy Drugs J9000 – J9999

Most major cancer treatment drugs are listed in this section. You should note that these codes are for the *supply of the chemotherapeutic drugs only*. You may make additional charges, as appropriate, for the administration of the drugs by use of CPT codes 96400 through 96549.

Medical and Surgical Supplies Codes A4206 – A7505

Although the majority of codes in this section would not be used by the typical physician practice, there are several codes of interest. These include codes for surgical trays (A4550), slings, splints and casts (A4565-A4590), and various materials such as sterile saline solutions, etc. (A4206-4270). For reference, the majority of codes are for vascular catheters, external urinary supplies, ostomy supplies, reterostomy supplies, supplies for durable medical equipment (DME), supplies for radiological procedures, supplies for End Stage Renal Disease (ESRD), and incontinency appliances and supplies.

Procedure/Professional Services Codes G0001 - G0094

In addition to supplies the National system contains codes required by Medicare and Medicaid for certain procedural and professional services. This section includes codes for billing routine venipunctures (G0001), administration of vaccines (G0008-G0010), PET myocardial perfusion imaging (G0030-G0047), destruction of benign and premalignant lesions (G0051-G0053), physician supervision services (G0064-G0066), and individual psychotherapy services (G0071-G0094).

Dental D0120 - D9999

This section consists of a reproduction of the American Dental Association's Current Dental Terminology (CDT) coding system. Although Medicare does not generally cover dental services, some Medicaid programs do, which is why the codes are included. Covered services of dentists specializing in oral and maxillofacial surgery, such as an oral or dental exam prior to a renal transplant or repair of a fractured jaw, are usually reported using CPT codes.

Temporary Codes Q0034 – Q9940

"Q" codes are assigned by HCFA for use on a temporary basis. The majority of codes in this section are for injections of EPO, with miscellaneous codes for infusion therapy, screening Pap smears, occupational therapy evaluations, physical therapy evaluations, and other services. You should review codes in this section to see if they may be relevant to your billing.

Other

The HCPCS National system also provides an extensive listing of codes for supplies and related services for enteral/parenteral therapy ("B" codes), DME ("E" codes), orthotics and prosthetics ("L" codes), and vision and hearing ("V" codes). Refer to a HCPCS National code manual for a complete listing of these codes.

National Modifiers

The HCPCS National coding system contains a total of 120 modifiers. In addition there are modifiers for use with the ambulance service codes to describe ambulance place of origin and destination. Several of the National modifiers are for use by anesthesiologists and non-physicians. Examples of National modifiers are:

-AB Medical direction of own employee(s) by anesthesiologist (not more than four employees)

Figure 2.3: Utah Local Codes and Modifiers

```
1997 HCPCS LEVEL III CODES
CODE        DESCRIPTION
Z0112       Injection, Vitamin B Complex 1,000 mcg
Z0117       Injection, Vitamin B6 100 mgm (Pyridoxine Hydrochloride)
Z0123       Injection, Mandol 500 mgm (Cefamondole Nafate)
Z0137       Injection, Stadol 4mg (Butorphanol Tartrate)
Z0174       Injection, Sodium Bicarbonate 50 meg/50 ml
Z0193       Injection, Bumex 0.25 mgm/ml (bumetanide)

1997 HCPCS LEVEL III MODIFIERS
MODIFIER    DEFINITION
WU          Purchased Diagnostic Test
YP          Diagnostic Test(s) Not Purchased From Outside Suppliers
```

-AP Determination of refractive state was not performed in the course of diagnostic ophthalmological examination

-LT Left side (used to identify procedures performed on the left side of the body)

-RC Right coronary artery

The National modifiers range from "-AA" to "-VP." (Additional information about National modifiers can be found in Section Three, Modifiers.)

Local Codes

Each Medicare carrier is given the freedom to create Local codes and modifiers for use in the area it administers. Local codes begin with the letters "W," "X", "Y", or Z." Local modifiers also begin with these letters, but may include a letter followed by a number, such as "-W2. " Some Medicare carriers create Local modifiers, others do not.

Local codes have been used by Medicare carriers for the purposes of allowing health care providers to report relatively new procedures, services, and supplies which are being accepted on a local but not a national basis, to allow for regional variations in the way providers customarily report services and supplies, and to allow Medicare carriers the freedom to collect various types of information from providers so as to better manage their Medicare contract.

For your reference, Figure 2.3 provides a listing of the 1997 Local codes and modifiers used by the Utah Medicare carrier, Blue Cross and Blue Shield of Utah.

To help you better understand the use of Local codes, consider the following example based on the Local codes provided in Figure 2.3. Remember that the Local codes used in this example would only apply to physician practices in Utah.)

Consider the situation of a physician who is treating a Medicare patient with Vitamin B6 injections. Unfortunately, there are no codes for the supply of Vitamin B6 in either CPT or the HCPCS

National system. Thus, the physician would have to use the unlisted supply code (J3490) for unclassified drugs, and submit a report explaining what was injected, costs, medical necessity, etc. If the physician practices in Utah, he or she would be in luck as the Utah Medicare carrier has created a special code to cover the supply of the B6, code Z0117. The supply would be billed using this code in addition to either the appropriate E/M service or administration code. By reporting the local code rather than the unclassified National drug code, the provider has reduced the likelihood of denial and can expect faster claims payment. Clearly, you should obtain and carefully review the local codes and modifiers provided by your Medicare carrier to determine if any are relevant to your practice.

(Note: With the advent of the Medicare Fee Schedule and its attendant rules, Local codes are in the process of being phased-out. All Medicare carriers must now adhere to stricter payment and coverage guidelines. As a result, the conditions which lead to the need for Local codes are being removed. Until Local codes have been completely phased-out, you should use them as appropriate. Your Medicare carrier's bulletins should list Local codes and modifiers. Alternatively, your Medicare carrier can provide you with a list of Local codes and modifiers upon request.)

Which HCPCS Code To Use

Take a moment to review Figure 2.4, which provides a conceptual representation of the overlaps between CPT, HCPCS National, and HCPCS Local codes. One circle represents CPT codes, the others HCPCS National and Local codes, respectively. Note the overlap where circles intersect. This overlap symbolizes instances where, depending upon payer requirements, you might use a CPT code, a HCPCS code, or both to report a service. Examples will help clarify the issue.

CPT contains an all purpose supply code, 99070. Many private and managed care plans will accept this code when you bill for a supply. Invariably the payer will require that you describe the specific supply, in some cases providing documentation which shows what you paid for the supply. However, Medicare will not accept CPT code 99070. Instead, you need to list the appropriate supply code from the National or Local HCPCS system.

As another example, you would bill for an intramuscular injection of antibiotic by use of code 90788. For private and managed care plans your charge for this service may include both the injection and the supply of the antibiotic. For Medicare, the injection code does not include supply of the antibiotic; the antibiotic is to be listed using one of the J-codes from the National series, or a Local code if appropriate. Note that Medicare may not allow billing of the injection itself if provided in conjunction with an evaluation and management service, as it is assumed to be included with the service. However, in such situations, billing of the supply is still allowed.

With more than 1,500 payers, no guidelines related to which codes to use (CPT, HCPCS National or Local) will apply universally. However, you may want to consider the following when attempting to determine which codes to use.

- For Medicare, report the code (whether CPT, National or Local) which most accurately describes the service or procedure rendered, or the supply provided.

- Do not report code 99070 to Medicare. Use the appropriate National or Local code.

- For injections, bill Medicare separately for the supply of the injectable.

Figure 2.4: Potential Overlaps Between The Three Levels of HCPCS

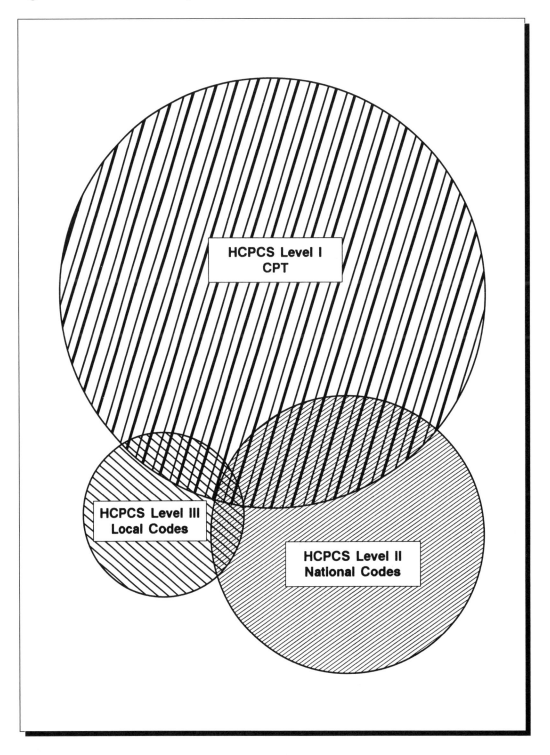

- For other payers with whom you deal frequently, determine if they accept HCPCS National or Local codes. If this is the case, inquire about their reporting requirements for injections and other services where there is overlap between the coding systems.

An increasing number of payers either have or are in the process of adopting the Medicare RBRVS payment system. Along with this system come reporting rules similar to those used by Medicare. You can anticipate that within a few years, virtually all payers will be requiring reporting of National (and Local, if still in use) codes as a supplement to CPT.

ICD-9-CM

ICD-9, or International Classification of Diseases, 9th Revision, was initially developed by the World Health Organization as a classification system for the reporting of mortality and morbidity statistics by physicians throughout the world. A United States version (the Clinical Modification variation, thus ICD-9-CM) is maintained and updated under the supervision of the National Center for Health Statistics. Changes to ICD-9-CM are released annually on October 1st. A comprehensive revision to this diagnosis coding system (ICD-10) is not scheduled for use in the U.S. until after the year 2000.

Within the past few years almost every payer has required physicians to use ICD-9-CM codes on claim forms and superbills when reporting patient conditions. There are three reasons for this. First, if you fail to report ICD-9-CM codes a payer may deny or delay payment on your claim. Most payers evaluate medical necessity as a function of reported diagnosis. If you do not list diagnosis codes, the payer may either send the claim back to your practice or attempt to locate a code for you. In either case, the impact on your reimbursement is adverse.

Second, if you do not report a diagnosis code and the payer attempts to assign one for you based on the written description of the patient's illness, an inappropriate code might be selected. The person who locates the diagnosis code may know little or nothing about your medical specialty and may well assign a code that does not support or justify your services. This can lead to denial of the claim or down-coding of your services.

And third, most major third party payers have either purchased or developed sophisticated software programs that compare reported CPT or HCPCS codes to the associated ICD-9-CM codes. These programs edit (or screen) your claims for logical relationships between procedure and diagnosis codes. For example, if you were to report the removal of a cyst with a primary diagnosis of hypertension, the claim is likely to be denied for lack of medical necessity.

In addition, Medicare began formally requiring ICD-9-CM codes as of April 1, 1989. Physicians can now be fined by Medicare up to $2,000 for each instance in which the physician does not report an ICD-9-CM code. As a practical matter, you should be listing ICD-9-CM codes on all your claims.

The material in this section is not intended to be exhaustive. It is included to provide an overview of the key concepts related to proper use of this complex and increasingly important coding system. Readers who want additional information about ICD-9-CM coding are encouraged to review texts devoted exclusively to the subject.

Three Volumes of ICD-9-CM

The complete ICD-9-CM coding system consists of three volumes, although many publishers now put two or three of these volumes in one book. Volume One is titled "Diseases: Tabular List" and contains a complete listing of codes and diseases. It is analogous to the front portion of the CPT book as it lists codes and their associated descriptions. The second volume of ICD-9-CM is an index to the first volume and is appropriately titled "Diseases: Alphabetic Index." Finally, some publishers offer the ICD-9-CM Volume Three which contains a listing of procedure codes and an index to the procedures. Since payers require that you submit CPT codes and not ICD-9-CM procedure codes, this third volume has limited use in the United States. For those who are curious, Volume Three is used by hospital billing staff when reporting the services of hospital-based physicians to the Medicare Part A program.

Like CPT and HCPCS, ICD-9-CM is updated annually. Although there are typically fewer changes to ICD-9-CM each year than there are changes to CPT, it is imperative that you keep up-to-date with each year's new, revised, and deleted codes. Revisions to ICD-9-CM are made public on October 1st of each year, and most publishers offer new or updated texts in November or December. Medicare and other payers do not usually begin accepting the revised codes until the first of each year. For example, the 1998 ICD-9-CM will be released in October 1997, become available from publishers in November or December 1997 and become effective January 1998.

Organization

The ICD-9-CM Volume One codes and descriptions are divided into 17 primary chapters. There are two additional supplemental chapters, one for "V" codes, the other for "E" codes. A listing of these primary and supplemental Volume One chapters and Volume Two sections is provided in the Table of Contents of ICD-9-CM books.

Within each chapter, codes are organized into three-digit *categories*, as in the following example:

810 Fracture of clavicle

For specificity of reporting purposes, categories often contain fourth-digit codes. These fourth-digit codes are called *subcategory* codes. For example:

810.0 Fracture of clavicle, Closed

Finally, fifth-digit or *subclassification* codes are sometimes provided for additional specificity and clarification. Continuing the above example, the following fifth-digit subclassifications are provided for the "closed" subcategory:

> **810.00 Fracture of clavicle, Closed, unspecified part**
> **810.01 Fracture of clavicle, Closed, sternal end of clavicle**
> **810.02 Fracture of clavicle, Closed, shaft of clavicle**
> **810.03 Fracture of clavicle, Closed, acromial end of clavicle**

As you will learn later, reimbursement often depends upon your level of coding specificity. That is, if fourth- or fifth-digit codes apply to the diagnosis code, you need to report them.

Symbols

Two symbols are used throughout ICD-9-CM to assist with your use of the codes. The first symbol is the section mark (§). A section mark to the left of a three-digit code signifies that fifth-digit codes apply to the category. For example, you would find the section mark listed as follows in - ICD-9-CM:

§ 644   Early or threatened labor

The appearance of the mark alerts you to the need for using fifth-digit codes when reporting a "644" series code.

The lozenge symbol (□) signifies that the code has been altered in some way from the original World Health Organization (WHO) version of ICD-9. Physicians need not be concerned with this symbol.

(Note: Many publishers of ICD-9-CM, including PMIC, provide special color-coding or other symbols for the purpose of alerting you to the need for additional fourth or fifth digits. If you are utilizing one of these annotated ICD-9-CM code manuals, be sure to review the publisher's notes related to the meaning of their symbols or colors.)

Punctuation

Four types of punctuation have special meaning in ICD-9-CM:

1.   Brackets [ ]. Brackets are used to enclose synonyms, alternative wordings or explanatory phrases. These terms and phrases can be especially helpful to coders who are working from the physician's diagnostic statement. For example, suppose the physician reports that the patient is being treated for PKU. Note how PKU is listed within brackets as part of the appropriate diagnosis code shown below:

270.1   Phenylketonuria [PKU]

2.   Parentheses ( ). The parentheses symbol is used to enclose supplementary words which may or may not be present in the disease statement, and which do not affect code selection per se, but can be of help to the coder. For example, consider the following Includes note which appears with category code 806 for fracture of vertebral column with spinal cord injury:

complete or incomplete transverse lesion (of cord)

If the physician's diagnostic statement included the terms "of cord," the coder would be more assured that this was the proper code group. However, absence of the term does not mean that the code group is inappropriate.

3.   Colon :. Colons have a special meaning in the Tabular List of ICD-9-CM. They are placed after an incomplete term which requires one or more of the modifying terms that follow it in order to make the code assignable to a given category. Consider the following example from ICD-9-CM:

493.0 Extrinsic asthma
Asthma:
allergic with stated cause
atopic
childhood
hay
platinum

If the patient were suffering from hay asthma, for example, the condition would be assignable to the 493.0 subcategory.

4.   Braces { }. Braces are used to enclose a series of terms, each of which is modified by the statement appearing to the right of the brace. For example, the subcategory code 667.0 for retained placenta without hemorrhage includes the following brace notation:

667.0 Retained placenta without hemorrhage
[0,2,4]
Placenta accreta
Retained placenta:
    NOS   without hemorrhage
    total

The terms "without hemorrhage" that appear to the right of the brace are used to modify the terms "Placenta accreta," "Retained placenta NOS," and "Retained placenta total."

To better understand how the above symbols apply to the codes you report most frequently, take a few moments to locate instances where they appear in your code manual and note how they affect code assignment.

Conventions

Two important conventions are used in ICD-9-CM. They are:

1.   **Bold** Type Face. Bold type face is used for all codes and titles in ICD-9-CM Volume One. For example:

462 Acute pharyngitis

2.   *Italicized* Type Face. Codes printed in the italicized type face are for manifestations and are *not* to be listed as the patient's primary diagnosis. However, you may use them as a secondary diagnosis. For example, never report the following diagnosis as the primary reason for treating a patient:

484.1 Pneumonia in cytomegalic inclusion disease

In addition to italicized type, some publishers use color coding or other methods of noting that codes should not be listed as primary diagnoses.

Abbreviations

Users of ICD-9-CM will be familiar with the two abbreviations, NEC and NOS. Each has a specific meaning and importance to coding and reimbursement.

1. NEC (Not Elsewhere Classifiable). The NEC abbreviation has two distinct uses in ICD-9-CM. First, it may be used by coders who do not have enough information available to determine which specific diagnosis code should be used in situations where ICD-9-CM provides very specific diagnoses. For example, suppose the physician is treating a patient for viral encephalitis which was transmitted by an arthropod (insect), but the specific insect that communicated the disease is not known. A review of the ICD-9-CM Index shows that codes for viral encephalitis are based upon whether the disease was transmitted by a mosquito or tick. There is a code for situations where the specific insect (vector) is unknown, and is listed in the Index as follows:

> Encephalitis...
> > viral, virus 049.9
> > <u>arthropod-borne NEC 064</u>
> > > mosquito-borne 062.9
> > > Australian X Disease 062.4
> > > California virus 062.5
> > > ...
> > > specified type NEC 062.8

The code of choice in this case will be for arthropod-borne NEC, 064 (as shown by underline). A review of the code in the Tabular List shows that 064 should be used in cases of reporting viral encephalitis transmitted by an insect, when the specific insect (vector) is not known.

> **064   Viral encephalitis transmitted by other and unspecified arthropods**
> > Arthropod-borne viral encephalitis, vector unknown
> > Negishi virus encephalitis
> > *Excludes: viral encephalitis NOS (049.9)*

The second use of NEC applies when the coder has more specific information available than is specified in ICD-9-CM. Continuing the above example, suppose the physician knew that the viral encephalitis was transmitted by a mosquito, and that it was a new strain not specified in ICD-9-CM. That is, the virus was not Japanese, Western equine, Eastern equine, or one of the other specified encephalitis viruses listed. Use of the Index refers you to:

> Encephalitis ...
> > viral, virus 049.9
> > arthropod-borne NEC 064
> > > mosquito-borne 062.9
> > > Australian X Disease 062.4
> > > California virus 062.5
> > > ...
> > > <u>specified type NEC 062.8</u>

Thus, the code of choice in this situation will be 062.8 (as shown by underline.) If you use an NEC code as in the example above, it may be helpful to inform the payer of the specific disease. Why? Some claims processors may refer claims to review which use codes such as "other specified ... " when the specific virus, in this case, is not shown on the claim. You should also note the NECs may be shown in the ICD-9-CM Index, but not in the Tabular List. In some situations, the NECs are provided both in the Index and Tabular List.

2.   NOS (Not Otherwise Specified). This abbreviation appears throughout the Tabular List. It is used to denote "unspecified" codes. In fact, not otherwise specified means the same as "unspecified." Codes with NOS as part of their definition may be used when the coder does not have enough information to select a more definitive diagnosis. Using the example above for NEC, suppose the physician has determined that the patient has viral encephalitis which was not transmitted by an arthropod, and furthermore, no other information which would help categorize the disease is currently available. In such a situation, you would look first in the Index as discussed above:

> Encephalitis ...
> > viral, virus 049.9
> > arthropod-borne NEC 064
> > > mosquito-borne 062.9
> > > Australian X Disease 062.4
> > > California virus 062.5
> > > ...
> > > specified type NEC 062.8

Note the subheading "viral, virus 049.9" which precedes the indented specific diagnoses below (underline provided to show correct code choice). Such Index subheadings often refer you to the NOS codes. By reviewing code 049.9 in the Tabular List you find the following:

> **049.9 Unspecified non-arthropod-borne viral diseases of central nervous system**
> > Viral encephalitis, NOS

When submitting NOS or "Unspecified" ICD-9-CM codes it is helpful to explain the disease more fully such that the payer can make a determination in your or your patient's favor.

Notations

As a user of ICD-9-CM, you have probably noticed the Includes and Excludes notes that appear with groups of codes as well as specific codes. These terms have specific meanings in ICD-9-CM. The Includes notes further define or give an example of the contents of a group of codes. Consider the following code:

> **055 Measles**
> > Includes: morbilli rubeola

Patients suffering from either type of measles could be coded using listings from the 055 series.

Excludes mean just the opposite of Includes. In ICD-9-CM the term "Excludes:" is always surrounded by a box so that it will be more easily noted. You need to be aware of conditions that are excluded from groups of codes, and therefore should take notice of the Excludes notes. An example of an Excludes note follows:

533 Peptic ulcer, site unspecified
Excludes: peptic ulcer: duodenal (532.0-532.9)
gastric (531.0-531.0)

Thus, if a patient is suffering from a gastric or duodenal ulcer, codes from the 533 group should not be reported.

Coding Underlying Diseases

In some situations, physicians use two ICD-9-CM codes to report a specific patient condition. Both the manifestation of the condition and its underlying cause need to be listed. The Tabular List provides help by giving references to underlying conditions. These are noted by the words "Code also underlying disease." Codes which list this note are also in italics. Please note that italicized codes are *never* to be reported without an additional code and they are *never* to be reported as the patient's primary diagnosis. An example will help clarify.

595.4 Cystitis in diseases classified elsewhere
Code also underlying disease, as:
    actinomycosis (039.8)
    amebiasis (006.8)
    bilharziasis (120.0-120.9)
    Echinococcus infestation (122.3, 122.6)

To report services related to a patient suffering from cystitis due to amebiasis, you would need two diagnosis codes: 006.8 for amebiasis and 595.4 for cystitis.

Basic ICD-9-CM Coding Rules

Coding with ICD-9-CM can be made easier by following the steps listed below.

1.   Locating Codes. Locating codes in ICD-9-CM does not have to be as difficult a task as it may appear to be. Simply by adhering to the following guidelines, your coding task will be much easier.

    A.   Identify the main terms in the physician's diagnostic statement. For example, if the physician has written the patient's diagnosis as, "The patient has an open fracture of the upper end of his left fibula," you would take note of the terms "fibula," "open," "fracture" and "upper end." With the terms noted, look first in the ICD-9-CM Index.

    B.   Locate the main term in the Volume Two Index. In the ICD-9-CM Index terms are listed by condition or problem, not by anatomic area or site. Using the above example, you would look under the term "fracture."

Figure 2.5: Sample of ICD-9-CM Index

Fracture—*continued*
    open 807.3
    Stieda's—*see* Fracture, femur, lower end
    stress—*see* Fracture, pathologic
    styloid process
       metacarpal (closed) 815.02
         open 815.12
       radius—*see* Fracture, radius, lower end
       temporal bone—*see* Fracture, skull, base
       ulna—*see* Fracture, ulna, lower end
    supracondylar, elbow 812.41
       open 812.51
    symphysis pubis (with visceral injury) (closed) 808.2
       open 808.3
    talus (ankle bone) (closed) 825.21
       open 825.31
    tarsus, tarsal bone(s) (with metatarsus) of one foot (closed) NEC 825.29
       open 825.39
    temporal bone (styloid)—*see* Fracture, skull, base
    tendon—*see* Sprain, by site
    thigh—*see* Fracture, femur, shaft
    thumb (and finger(s)) of one hand (closed) (*see also* Fracture, phalanx, hand) 816.00
       with metacarpal bone(s) of same hand 817.0
         open 817.1
       metacarpal(s)—*see* Fracture, metacarpus
       open 816.10
    thyroid cartilage (closed) 807.5
       open 807.6
    tibia (closed) 823.80
       with fibula 823.82
         open 823.92
       condyles—*see* Fracture, tibia, upper end
       distal end 824.8
         open 824.9
       epiphysis
         lower 824.8
           open 824.9
         upper—*see* Fracture, tibia, upper end
       head (involving knee joint)—*see* Fracture, tibia, upper end
       intercondyloid eminence—*see* Fracture, tibia, upper end
       involving ankle 824.0
         open 824.1
       lower end or extremity (anterior lip) (posterior lip) 824.8
         open 824.9
       malleolus (internal) (medial) 824.0
         open 824.1
       open NEC 823.90
       pathologic 733.16
       proximal end—*see* Fracture, tibia, upper end
       shaft 823.20
         with fibula 823.22
           open 823.32
         open 823.30
       spine—*see* Fracture, tibia, upper end
       tuberosity—*see* Fracture, tibia, upper end
       upper end or extremity (condyle) (epiphysis) (head) (spine) (proximal end) (tuberosity) 823.00
         with fibula 823.02
           open 823.12
         open 823.10
    toe(s), of one foot (closed) 826.0
       with bone(s) of same lower limb 827.0
         open 827.1

Fracture—*continued*
    open 826.1
    tooth (root) 873.63
       complicated 873.73
    trachea (closed) 807.5
       open 807.6
    transverse process—*see* Fracture, vertebra, by site
    trapezium (closed) 814.05
       open 814.15
    trapezoid bone (closed) 814.06
       open 814.16
    trimalleolar (closed) 824.6
       open 824.7
    triquetral (bone) (closed) 814.03
       open 814.13
    trochanter (greater) (lesser) (closed) (*see also* Fracture, femur, neck, by site) 820.20
       open 820.30
    trunk (bones) (closed) 809.0
       open 809.1
    tuberosity (external)—*see* Fracture, by site
    ulna (alone) (closed) 813.82
       with radius NEC 813.83
         open 813.93
       coronoid process (closed) 813.02
         open 813.12
       distal end—*see* Fracture, ulna, lower end
       epiphysis
         lower—*see* Fracture, ulna, lower end
         upper—*see* Fracture, ulna, upper, end
       head—*see* Fracture, ulna, lower end
       lower end (distal end) (head) (lower epiphysis) (styloid process) 813.43
         with radius (lower end) 813.44
           open 813.54
         open 813.53
       olecranon process (closed) 813.01
         open 813.11
       open NEC 813.92
       pathologic 733.12
       proximal end—*see* Fracture, ulna, upper end
       shaft 813.22
         with radius (shaft) 813.23
           open 813.33
         open 813.32
       styloid process—*see* Fracture, ulna, lower end
       transverse—*see* Fracture, ulna, by site
       upper end (epiphysis) 813.04
         with radius (upper end) 813.08
           open 813.18
         multiple sites 813.04
           open 813.14
         open 813.14
         specified site NEC 813.04
           open 813.14
    unciform (closed) 814.08
       open 814.18
    vertebra, vertebral (back) (body) (column) (neural arch) (pedicle) (spine) (spinous process) (transverse process) (closed) 805.8
       with
         hematomyelia—*see* Fracture, vertebra, by site, with spinal cord injury
         injury to
           cauda equina—*see* Fracture, vertebra, sacrum, with spinal cord injury
           nerve—*see* Fracture, vertebra, by site, with spinal cord injury
         paralysis—*see* Fracture, vertebra, by site, with spinal cord injury

867

38

C.   Check any notes appearing after the main term. If you look up "fracture" in the ICD-9-CM Index, you will see the following:

Fracture (abduction) (adduction) (avulsion) (compression) (crush) (dislocation) (oblique) (separation) (closed)

In addition, there are several notes that describe open and closed fractures which are helpful, in this instance, when attempting to determine whether the fracture should be reported as open or closed.

D.   If necessary, look for indented subterms under the main term. There are many pages of fracture references in the Index. To locate a fibula fracture you will need to find fibula within the fracture section of the Index (Figure 2.5). Once located you will see many different references to fibula fractures ranging from those with the tibia to the upper end. You should select the reference which best fits the patient's condition (in this example, upper end, open, 823.11) and review the code in Volume One.

E.   Verify and check the code in the Volume One Tabular List. Never code directly from the ICD-9-CM Index as there are many notes, Includes, Excludes, fourth digits, fifth digits, etc., which may affect your selection of a code for reporting as shown in Figure 2.6. After locating a code using the Index, always look it up in the Tabular List and review the rules which apply to the code.

Using the above example, in Figure 2.6 you will see an Excludes note which appears with the category code 823. This note tells you about specific types of fractures that are excluded from this classification. And, you will also see the fifth-digit codes that are required with the 823 category.

2.   Code to the highest level of certainty. Coding would be much easier if the typical patient who walked into your practice said something like, "Doctor, could you please treat my reticuloendothelial cytomycosis?" Unfortunately, for some patients it may take several visits and many tests to determine the exact cause of a problem. And since you may need to submit claims prior to having a final diagnosis, it is important that you use the most specific diagnosis available at the time of billing. That is, always report using the most accurate information you have at the time you submit the claim.

For example, suppose a patient is seen on Monday with mild chest pain. Various tests are ordered, and when the patient returns the following Thursday it is determined that he has arteriosclerotic cardiovascular disease (ASCVD). The first visit on Monday would be coded using the most certain diagnosis at the time of the visit, chest pain (a code from the 786.5 series). The following Thursday visit would be coded using the diagnosis most certain at the time of the visit, 429.2 for the ASCVD.

3.   Only code the reason for the visit or encounter. Do not list old or irrelevant diagnoses on patient claims. For example, if you are currently treating a patient for diabetes but saw the patient last year for a foot infection, do not list the foot infection on the current claim. Although you may believe that by listing every reason the patient has ever sought your help, with the idea that the more diagnoses reported the more likely the claim will be paid, by doing so you are making yourself liable for a lawsuit. Why? By reporting an old diagnosis

Figure 2.6: Sample of ICD-9-CM Tabular Text

INJURY AND POISONING

821.29 **Other**
    Multiple fractures of lower end

821.3 **Lower end, open**

821.30 **Lower end, unspecified part**

821.31 **Condyle, femoral**

821.32 **Epiphysis, lower (separation)**

821.33 **Supracondylar fracture of femur**

821.39 **Other**

822 **Fracture of patella**

822.0 **Closed**

822.1 **Open**

⑤ 823 **Fracture of tibia and fibula**

    Excludes: *Dupuytren's fracture (824.4-824.5)*
       ankle (824.4-824.5)
       radius (813.42, 813.52)
       Pott's fracture (824.4-824.5)
       that involving ankle (824.0-824.9)

The following fifth-digit subclassification is for use with category 823:

    0 tibia alone

    1 fibula alone

    2 fibula with tibia

☐ 823.0 **Upper end, closed**
    Head   Tibia:
    Proximal end   condyles
                              tuberosity

☐ 823.1 **Upper end, open**

823.2 **Shaft, closed**

823.3 **Shaft, open**

☐ 823.8 **Unspecified part, closed**
    Lower leg NOS

☐ 823.9 **Unspecified part, open**

824 **Fracture of ankle**

824.0 **Medial malleolus, closed**
    Tibia involving:
       ankle
       malleolus

824.1 **Medial malleolus, open**

824.2 **Lateral malleolus, closed**
    Fibula involving:
       ankle
       malleolus

824.3 **Lateral malleolus, open**

824.4 **Bimalleolar, closed**
    Dupuytren's fracture, fibula
    Pott's fracture

824.5 **Bimalleolar, open**

824.6 **Trimalleolar, closed**
    Lateral and medial malleolus with anterior or posterior lip of tibia

824.7 **Trimalleolar, open**

824.8 **Unspecified, closed**
    Ankle NOS

824.9 **Unspecified, open**

825 **Fracture of one or more tarsal and metatarsal bones**

825.0 **Fracture of calcaneus, closed**
    Heel bone   Os calcis

825.1 **Fracture of calcaneus, open**

● Code new to this edition	▲ Revision of existing code	④ ⑤ Fourth or fifth digit required

377

you are telling the payer that the problem is currently active. If the patient were to attempt to obtain new health insurance, the illness would be excluded from coverage in the patient's new health insurance plan as a pre-existing condition.

4. Use the most specific code available. Many practices rely too heavily on the "unspecified" and "other" codes listed in ICD-9-CM when more specific codes are available. Never use "unspecified" codes unless there are no codes that accurately describe the patient's illness. Similarly, do not use the "other" codes in situations where there are specific codes that describe the illness. Your claims may be delayed or denied when the "unspecified" and "other" codes are used improperly.

5. If there are fifth digits, *use them.* ICD-9-CM is replete with coding situations that require use of fifth digits to identify special circumstances. Always refer to the Tabular List (Volume One) to see if fifth digits apply to the code you are reporting. If there are fifth digits, select the proper one and use it. For example, to code the open upper end fibula fracture discussed above, you would use a fifth-digit code, 823.11.

6. If there are no fifth digits, use fourth digits. In most diagnosis coding situations, if there are no fifth-digit codes, there will be fourth-digit codes for your use. For example, to report a closed fracture of the alveolus you would use code 802.8 "Other facial bones, closed," a fourth-digit code.

7. If there are no fifth- or fourth-digits, use the third-digit code. In some areas of ICD-9-CM there are no fourth- or fifth-digit codes, so a third-digit code will need to be reported.

8. List next to the service the diagnosis which is the reason for the service. To ensure proper reimbursement you must properly associate diagnoses with services. In the claim shown on the following page reporting the treatment of respiratory failure (Figure 2.7), note that two patient illnesses are identified: the respiratory failure and the malignant neoplasm of the upper lobe of the lung. Although the physician is only treating the respiratory failure, the malignancy does affect the delivery of care and is thus reported. Additionally, you should note that the respiratory failure diagnosis is the primary diagnosis associated with the treatment.

9. *Never* use "rule out," "probable," "suspected," or "questionable" diagnoses as if they exist. Code using signs, symptoms and ill-defined conditions instead. There are two reasons you should not use the above "maybe" illnesses. First, third party payers will generally not pay on claims listing such diagnoses. If they did, some of your less scrupulous colleagues could get rich making a career of "ruling out" patient illnesses. Second, if you report a diagnosis code, for example for congestive heart failure, and the words "rule out," "probable," etc., are written next to the code, the claims processor may not see your notation and enter the patient illness into the payer computer system. If it turns out that the patient does not have the illness, the patient's insurance records nonetheless report the illness. This could make it difficult for the patient to obtain different health insurance in the future, and even more difficult for your practice should the patient learn you were the reason for their inability to obtain insurance.

    ICD-9-CM provides codes for use until a more definitive diagnosis is reached. These codes are found in Chapter 16 of ICD-9-CM under "Symptoms, Signs and Ill-Defined Conditions." In this section you will find codes for conditions ranging from coma and stupor to cachexia.

Figure 2.7: Associating Diagnoses with Procedures

APPROVED OMB-0939-0008

PLEASE DO NOT STAPLE IN THIS AREA

CARRIER

| | PICA | | | | | | HEALTH INSURANCE CLAIM FORM | PICA | |

HEALTH INSURANCE CLAIM FORM

1. MEDICARE / MEDICAID / CHAMPUS / CHAMPVA / GROUP HEALTH PLAN / FECA BLK LUNG / OTHER — **X** (Medicare #) ☐ (Medicaid #) ☐ (Sponsor's SSN) ☐ (VA File #) ☐ (SSN or ID) ☐ (SSN) ☐ (ID)

1a. INSURED'S I.D. NUMBER (FOR PROGRAM IN ITEM 1): **B12345678**

2. PATIENT'S NAME (Last Name, First Name, Middle Initial): **Tunes, Mary**

3. PATIENT'S BIRTH DATE MM | DD | YY: **2 | 14 | 21** — SEX: M ☐ F **X**

4. INSURED'S NAME (Last Name, First Name, Middle Initial): **Tunes, Mary**

5. PATIENT'S ADDRESS (No., Street): **010 Melody Lane**

6. PATIENT RELATIONSHIP TO INSURED: Self **X** Spouse ☐ Child ☐ Other ☐

7. INSURED'S ADDRESS (No., Street): **Same**

CITY: **Hollywood** — STATE: **CA**

8. PATIENT STATUS: Single ☐ Married **X** Other ☐

CITY: — STATE:

ZIP CODE: **90012** — TELEPHONE (Include Area Code): **(213) 555-1234**

Employed ☐ Full-Time Student ☐ Part-Time Student ☐

ZIP CODE: — TELEPHONE (Include Area Code):

9. OTHER INSURED'S NAME (Last Name, First Name, Middle Initial):

10. IS PATIENT'S CONDITION RELATED TO:

11. INSURED'S POLICY GROUP OR FECA NUMBER:

a. OTHER INSURED'S POLICY OR GROUP NUMBER:

a. EMPLOYMENT? (CURRENT OR PREVIOUS): YES ☐ NO ☐

a. INSURED'S DATE OF BIRTH MM | DD | YY — SEX: M ☐ F ☐

b. OTHER INSURED'S DATE OF BIRTH MM | DD | YY — SEX M ☐ F ☐

b. AUTO ACCIDENT? PLACE (State): YES ☐ NO ☐

b. EMPLOYER'S NAME OR SCHOOL NAME:

C. EMPLOYER'S NAME OR SCHOOL NAME:

c. OTHER ACCIDENT? YES ☐ NO ☐

c. INSURANCE PLAN NAME OR PROGRAM NAME:

d. INSURED PLAN NAME OR PROGRAM NAME:

10d. RESERVED FOR LOCAL USE:

d. IS THERE ANOTHER HEALTH BENEFIT PLAN? YES ☐ **X** NO — If yes, return to and complete item 9 a–d.

READ BACK OF FORM BEFORE COMPLETING & SIGNING THIS FORM.

12. PATIENT'S OR AUTHORIZED PERSON'S SIGNATURE I authorize the release of any medical or other information necessary to process this claim. I also request payment of government benefits either to myself or to the party who accepts assignment below. SIGNED **Signature on File** DATE **12/10/97**

13. INSURED'S OR AUTHORIZED PERSON'S SIGNATURE I authorize payment of medical benefits to the undersigned physician or supplier for services described below. SIGNED **Signature on File**

14. DATE OF CURRENT: ILLNESS (First symptom) OR INJURY (Accident) OR PREGNANCY (LMP) MM | DD | YY

15. IF PATIENT HAS HAD SAME OR SIMILAR ILLNESS, GIVE FIRST DATE MM | DD | YY

16. DATES PATIENT UNABLE TO WORK IN CURRENT OCCUPATION MM | DD | YY FROM TO

17. NAME OF REFERRING PHYSICIAN OR OTHER SOURCE

17a. I.D. NUMBER OF REFERRING PHYSICIAN

18. HOSPITALIZATION DATES RELATED TO CURRENT SERVICES MM | DD | YY FROM TO

19. RESERVED FOR LOCAL USE

20. OUTSIDE LAB? YES ☐ NO ☐ — $ CHARGES

21. DIAGNOSIS OR NATURE OF ILLNESS OR INJURY. (RELATE ITEMS 1,2,3 OR 4 TO ITEM 24E BY LINE)
1. **518 81** Resp. Failure
2. **162 3** M-Neop. Lung
3.
4.

22. MEDICAID RESUBMISSION CODE — ORIGINAL REF. NO.

23. PRIOR AUTHORIZATION NUMBER

24. A DATE(S) OF SERVICE		B Place of Service	C Type of Service	D PROCEDURES, SERVICES OR SUPPLIES (Explain Unusual Circumstances) CPT/HCPCS	MODIFIER	E DIAGNOSIS CODE	F $ CHARGES	G DAYS OR UNITS	H EPSDT Family Plan	I EMG	J COB	K RESERVED FOR LOCAL USE
From MM DD YY	To MM DD YY											
12 10 97	12 10 97	7		99285		12	75 00	1				

25. FEDERAL TAX I.D. NUMBER / SSN EIN: **38-1234567** ☐ **X**

26. PATIENT'S ACCOUNT NO.

27. ACCEPT ASSIGNMENT? (For govt. claims, see back) **X** YES ☐ NO

28. TOTAL CHARGE: $ **75 00**

29. AMOUNT PAID: $ **0 00**

30. BALANCE DUE: $ **75 00**

31. SIGNATURE OF PHYSICIAN OR SUPPLIER INCLUDING DEGREES OR CREDENTIALS (I certify that the statements on the reverse apply to this bill and are made a part thereof.) SIGNED *Peter Kramer* DATE **12/10/97**

32. NAME AND ADDRESS OF FACILITY WHERE SERVICES WERE RENDERED (If other than home or office)

33. PHYSICIAN'S SUPPLIER'S BILLING NAME, ADDRESS, ZIP CODE & PHONE #
Peter Kramer, M.D.
101 1st St.
Los Angeles, CA 90010
PIN# **M1234** GRP#

(APPROVED BY AMA COUNCIL ON MEDICAL SERVICE 8/88)

PLEASE PRINT OR TYPE

FORM HCFA-1500 (12-90)
FORM OWCP-1500 FORM RRB-1500

PATIENT AND INSURED INFORMATION

PHYSICIAN OR SUPPLIER INFORMATION

10. Never code directly from the ICD-9-CM Index! ICD-9-CM is replete with Includes, Excludes and other notes which affect the codes you will report. Just as you should never code directly from the CPT Index for this reason, you should make it a habit to always review diagnosis codes in the Volume One Tabular List before listing them on claims.

11. For diagnostic services, consider using "V" codes. Radiology and pathology/laboratory services are usually listed with a "V" code as the primary diagnosis and patient complaints, symptoms, signs, or other diagnoses secondarily. For example, if a patient with fever and cough is given a chest X-ray for suspected pneumonia, the radiologist would report V72.5 (radiological exam not elsewhere classifiable) as the primary diagnosis for the X-ray service, and the fever (780.6) and cough (786.2) as secondary diagnoses. As another example, if lab work is being performed for this patient, the lab would report code V72.6 (laboratory examination) as the primary diagnosis and the fever and cough as secondary diagnoses.

Use of "V" and "E" Codes

"V" codes can be located toward the end of ICD-9-CM's Tabular List under the title "Supplementary Classification of Factors Influencing Health Status and Contact with Health Services." They are most commonly used for reporting diagnostic services (as discussed above), for routine treatments (such as physical therapy and chemotherapy), for situations where the patient is being followed postsurgically (such as to have a cast removed after a fracture has healed), or for instances when the patient being seen does not have a current illness (such as a routine annual physical).

In circumstances where the use of "V" codes is appropriate, it is often the case that additional diagnoses will be reported secondarily to the "V" codes. For example, suppose a patient is receiving physical therapy for treatment of paralysis due to a stroke. The physical therapy "V" code (V57.1 for other physical therapy) would be listed as the primary diagnosis and the paralysis and/or late effect of cerebral vascular disease code(s) would be listed as secondary diagnoses.

"E" codes are supplementary and used to describe a variety of <u>external</u> causes of injuries and poisonings. You may find it interesting to review the "E" codes as there are many unusual causes of injuries and poisonings. For example, there are codes for reporting injuries due to laundry machinery on a boat and due to accidents from air drops of emergency supplies.

You should not list "E" codes as primary diagnoses; they are supplementary. As a practical matter, most physician practices do not use these codes and most payers do not require them. However, the codes can be of help if you need to explain to a payer the unusual cause of an injury or poisoning.

PROBLEM SET: SECTION TWO

Suggested solutions to the problems below can be found in Appendix A.

Mark the following statements true or false.

		True	False
1.	In Kansas, you must use Kansas Relative Value Study codes to ensure proper reimbursement.	_____	_____
2.	CPT is published by the Health Care Financing Administration once every year.	_____	_____
3.	CPT is organized into six sections of codes.	_____	_____
4.	You would find the CPT nuclear medicine codes in the Medicine section of CPT.	_____	_____
5.	The abbreviation "TURP" is an example of an eponym.	_____	_____
6.	CPT's indentation format was created to save space.	_____	_____
7.	HCPCS is pronounced "hick-pucks."	_____	_____
8.	ICD-9-CM stands for International Classification of Diagnoses - Ninth Revision — Clinical Modifications	_____	_____
9.	In ICD-9-CM braces —{ }— are used to enclose a series of terms which are modified.	_____	_____
10.	Reporting "rule-out" diagnoses is inappropriate coding.	_____	_____
11.	HCPCS National codes are being phased-in for the purpose of eventually replacing CPT.	_____	_____
12.	Assuming medical necessity has been established, Medicare will accept any code you submit from the HCPCS National code system.	_____	_____
13.	HCPCS National codes may contain either one letter followed by four numbers or two letters followed by three numbers.	_____	_____
14.	Unless you are billing for anesthesia, ambulance or nurse anesthetist services, it is unlikely that you will have occasion to use the HCPCS National or Local modifiers.	_____	_____
15.	Q2331 could be a HCPCS National code.	_____	_____

	True	False
16. The diagnosis code(s) you report support and justify your services.	_____	_____
17. ICD-9-CM manifestation codes should never be used as a primary diagnosis.	_____	_____
18. NOS abbreviations are printed only in ICD-9-CM Volume One; they are never listed in the Volume Two index.	_____	_____
19. ICD-9-CM is updated once every three years.	_____	_____
20. HCPCS Local codes and modifiers can be obtained free from your local Medicare carrier.	_____	_____

The following are multiple choice questions. Select the most correct answer(s).

21. Correct ICD-9-CM coding involves the following steps:

   a. Locate the code in the Tabular list, then verify it by use of the Index.

   b. Locate the code in the Index by use of the provider's diagnostic statement, then check the notes associated with the code in the Index before reporting it.

   c. Locate the code in the Tabular by use of the provider's diagnostic statement, then check notes associated with the code before reporting it.

   d. Using the provider's diagnostic statement, find the code in Volume #3 and then crosswalk it to the appropriate Volume #1 code.

   e. None of the above.

22. When billing Medicare for individual psychotherapy services you would:

   a. Use HCPCS National "P" codes.

   b. Use CPT codes for psychotherapy services.

   c. Use CPT Evaluation and Management service codes.

   d. Use ICD-9-CM Volume 3 codes.

   e. None of the above.

23. In CPT:

    a. The circle to the left of a code number signifies that the code cannot be reported by itself, but must be reported in conjunction with another service.

    b. A triangle or delta to the left of a code number signifies that the code's description has been revised.

    c. The star to the right of a code number signifies that special surgical package billing rules apply.

    d. A triangle or delta to the left of a code number signifies that the code is new.

    e. A triangle or delta to the left of a code number signifies that the code has been deleted.

24. In general:

    a. Under special circumstances, you can report the all purpose CPT supply code to Medicare.

    b. Only Medicare and Medicaid accept HCPCS National and/or Local codes.

    c. When billing Medicare in Utah you would use code Z1094 for injecting Bumiterol 150 meg/50ml.

    d. CPT code 95120 would be found in the Medicine section.

    e. None of the above.

Problems 25 through 27 refer to the following excerpt from the 1997 CPT book.

Destruction, Benign or Premalignant Lesions

17000* Destruction by any method, including laser, with or without surgical curettement, all benign facial lesions or premalignant lesions in any location, or benign lesions other than cutaneous vascular proliferative lesions, including local anesthesia; one lesion

17001   second and third lesions, each

17002   over three lesions, each additional lesion

17010   complication lesion(s)

25. To bill for destruction of five non-complicated benign facial lesions you would list which of the following on your claim?

    a. Code 17000 with five units of service

    b. Code 17000 with one unit of service and code 17002 with four units of service

    c. Code 17002 with two units of service

    d. Code 17000 with one unit of service, code 17001 with two units of service, and code 17002 with two units of service.

    e. None of the above.

26. The physician destroys one benign facial lesion with a laser, two premalignant lesions on the patient's back via cryosurgery, and one benign lesion on the patient's arm with an electrodesiccation treatment. These services would be coded as:

    a. Code 17000 with one unit of service, code 17001 with two units of service, and code 17002 with one unit of service.

    b. Code 17001 with three units of service and a code from another range for the arm lesion destruction.

    c. Code 17002 with four units of service.

    d. Code 17000 with one unit of service for the laser on the face, code 17001 with two units of service for the cryosurgery on the back, and code 17000 again with one unit of service for the electrodesiccation treatment on the arm.

    e. None of the above.

27. Two 0.5 cm malignant facial lesions are destroyed by laser. This service would be coded as:

    a. Code 17001 with two units of service.

    b. Code 17000 with one unit of service and code 17001 with one unit of service.

    c. Code 17281 with one unit of service.

    d. Code 99203 and code 17001 with two units of service.

    e. None of the above.

28. Mr. Lopez develops pneumonia as a result of his non-congenital cytomegalic inclusion disease. Dr. Klein admits Mr. Lopez to the hospital to treat the pneumonia. Assuming Dr. Klein performs a Level III initial hospital care service, which of the following should appear on the claim.

Procedure	Diagnoses	
a. 99223	484.1	Pneumonia in cytomegalic inclusion disease
	078.5	Cytomegaloviral disease
b. 99223	484.1	Pneumonia in cytomegalic inclusion disease
	771.1	Cytomegalovirus infection
c. 99223	771.1	Cytomegalovirus infection
	484.1	Pneumonia in cytomegalic inclusion disease
d. 99223	078.5	Cytomegaloviral disease
	484.1	Pneumonia in cytomegalic inclusion disease

e. None of the above.

29. A cameraman sitting on the sidelines of a basketball game was struck on his knee by an errant basketball causing a tear of the lateral cartilage of this left knee. To report the services of the emergency room physician who treats the cameraman, assuming a Level III service was performed, you would list which of the following combinations of procedure and diagnosis(es) on the claim:

a. Procedure:	99283	Emergency care
Diagnoses:	717.0	Old bucket handle tear of medial meniscus
	E917.0	Struck by thrown ball
b. Procedure:	99283	Emergency care
Diagnosis:	836.1	Knee dislocation, tear of lateral cartilage
c. Procedure:	99283	Emergency care
Diagnoses:	836.1	Knee dislocation, tear of lateral cartilage
	E917.0	Struck by thrown ball
d. Procedure:	99283	Emergency care
Diagnoses:	717.0	Old bucket handle tear of medial meniscus
	E894.4	Place of occurrence, Basketball court

e. None of the above.

Coding Questions

Locate the appropriate diagnosis codes for the following conditions.

30. Arnold-Chiari syndrome, type II, lumbar region   _____

31. Blue Diaper syndrome   _____

32. Amaurotic family idiocy   _____

33. Resistance to chloramphenicol   _____

34. Rat-bite fever   _____

35. Eyelid Yaws   _____

CHAPTER THREE:
KEY CODING AND
BILLING RULES

INTRODUCTION

Now that you have an understanding of the coding fundamentals discussed in Chapter Two, you are ready to begin getting down to specifics. That is, learning the key coding and billing rules associated with the various sections of CPT. Integral to this learning process is proper use of the numerous CPT and HCPCS modifiers, a topic which is also covered in the following pages.

Like medicine itself, coding is a mixture of art and science. Deciding which code to report is not always straightforward. One payer may require that you list a specific service one way while another payer requires that you use an entirely different code if you are to expect reimbursement. Some code definitions are subject to varying interpretations as to what they do and do not include, leading to confusion as to which code or codes should be reported to accurately describe the actual service(s) rendered. In other situations, notably with evaluation and management services, deciding which code to report is a function of determining the appropriate level of subcomponents performed, which in turn is a function of documentation which if handled poorly, may not correctly reflect what was actually done. And, for newer services, there may not be codes that define the procedure or service, forcing you to either select a very close code and add a modifier or select one of the unlisted service codes. Despite these factors, it is the provider's responsibility to be as accurate as possible when reporting his/her services.

This Chapter is not meant to provide you with an "end all" understanding of CPT coding. If you take the time to carefully read the material and work through the problem sets you will have more than a basic understanding of CPT coding; you will also have the framework in place that is often required when reviewing other texts and articles which deal in depth with specific areas of coding.

In this Chapter you will learn about the following topics:

- Selection of E/M codes based upon levels of key components and time.
- Determining whether a patient is new or established.
- Selecting appropriate types of services.
- Distinguishing between consultations and other visits.
- How to report modifiers.
- How and when to use CPT and HCPCS modifiers.
- What information payers may need to justify payment of modified services.
- How to properly code the most frequently reported CPT medicine services.
- Surgical package concepts.
- Separate procedure concept.
- Reporting starred procedures.

- Basics of anesthesia coding and billing.
- Reporting radiology services, including professional and technical components.
- Radiological services involving injections.
- Coding laboratory tests and pathology services.

EVALUATION AND MANAGEMENT SERVICES

If you are ever unfortunate enough to have your office audited by an insurance company, chances are you will discover that the "jugular vein" which the auditors go for, so to speak, is your evaluation and management (E/M) services coding. Evaluation and management services make up about 35 percent of all claims submitted by physicians. Also, E/M services are the easiest to miscode, making them a prime target for auditors. Visit charges, whether office, outpatient, hospital, home, emergency department, consultation and the like, are based on the content of the service you provide to the patient. It is imperative that you learn how to code E/M services, because if you report and bill for levels of care greater than those that were actually provided, you run the risk of being charged with fraudulent billing.

Overview of E/M Codes

Before learning the specific rules related to the E/M codes, it will be helpful for you to review the sample E/M code below (taken from page 10 of the 1997 CPT book). Code 99203 describes a new patient visit (office or outpatient). Note the key features associated with this E/M code.

> **99203**   **Office or other outpatient visit** for the evaluation and management of a new patient, which requires these three key components:
>
> > ■ **a detailed history;**
> >
> > ■ **a detailed examination; and**
> >
> > ■ **medical decision making of low complexity.**
>
> Counseling and/or coordination of care with other providers or agencies are provided consistent with the nature of the problem(s) and the patient's and/or family's needs.
>
> Usually, the presenting problems are of moderate severity. Physicians typically spend 30 minutes face-to-face with the patient and/or family.

A.   **Bolded Components**. The bolded bullet points are key to the selection of this code. At a minimum, you should have performed a detailed history, detailed exam and the patient's condition(s) should have required medical decision making of low complexity if this code is selected. Each of these components will be defined in detail later in this Chapter.

B.   **Three Key Components Required.** This tells you that all three components—history, exam, and medical decision making—are required. Some codes, such as for established patient office/outpatient visits, require only two of the three components.

C. **Counseling and/or Coordination of Care.** Counseling and/or coordination of care is not used as a basis for selecting a code <u>unless</u> more than 50 percent of your service involved providing these components. In such cases, time will be used to determine code selection.

D. **Presenting Problems.** This information is provided primarily for reference. In general, you will not use this component when selecting a code.

E. **Time.** When counseling or coordination of care comprise more than 50 percent of the service, time becomes the factor which determines the code you report. This is discussed in more detail below. Time is not listed with all E/M codes.

OFFICIAL DOCUMENTATION GUIDELINES FOR EVALUATION & MANAGEMENT SERVICES

A few years ago, the American Medical Association and Health Care Financing Administration jointly prepared guidelines for documenting E/M services. For your reference, relevant portions of these guidelines are included in Appendix A at the back of this text. The *General Principles of Medical Record Documentation* for E/M services are as follows:

1. The medical record should be complete and legible.

2. The documentation of each patient encounter should include:

    •   reason for the encounter and relevant history, physical examination findings, and prior diagnostic test results;

    •   assessment, clinical impression or diagnosis;

    •   plan for care; and

    •   date and legible identity of the observer

3. If not documented, the rationale for ordering diagnostic and other ancillary services should be easily inferred.

4. Past and present diagnosis should be accessible to the treating and/or consulting physician.

5. Appropriate health risk factors should be identified.

6. The patient's progress, response to, and changes in treatment, and revision of diagnosis should be documented.

7. The CPT and ICD-9-CM codes reported on the health insurance claim form or billing statement should be supported by the documentation in the medical record.

The above documentation guidelines should be kept in mind when creating, updating, and maintaining patient charts and records.

General E/M Coding Rules

Your selection of evaluation and management codes will depend upon several factors. Is the patient new or established? Where was the service performed? What type of service was provided? Did face-to-face counseling dominate the service? Which specific levels of history, examination, and medical decision making apply to the patient encounter? By adhering to the following steps, each of which is explained in detail later in this chapter, you are much more likely to report appropriate E/M codes. Each of the three key components is defined below:

1. *Determine Whether the Patient Is New or Established.* In several cases, CPT provides different codes depending upon whether the patient is new to the physician or established. For each patient you will need to determine whether they are considered new or established.

2. *Determine the Type and Place of Service.* E/M codes are organized into categories by place and type of service. For example, hospital visits are distinguished from office and outpatient visits, and consultative services are differentiated from all other types of services. For each E/M service, you will need to determine both the type of service and the place of service.

3. *Determine if Counseling Was the Primary Service.* If face-to-face counseling comprises more than one-half of the service provided to the patient, time will be utilized to determine the level of E/M service that should be reported. However, be aware that not all E/M codes may be selected on the basis of time.

4. *Identify the Levels of Key Components That Were Provided.* Each of the three key components—history, examination, and medical decision making—have varying levels. Proper code selection will depend upon your identifying which levels of each were provided during the encounter with the patient.

5. *Match Key Components to Code Definitions.* Finally, unless counseling has dominated the service, you will select a specific code based upon matching the levels of the key components with the code definitions in CPT.

New and Established Patients

New patients are those for whom the physician has not provided professional services within the past three years. Obviously, patients provided professional services within the past three years are considered to be established. There are two key exceptions to this rule.

1. If you are on call or covering for another physician (including "locum tenens" physicians, according to Medicare) and bill your services, you would report using the same code the regular physician would have used.

2. If you have never before provided professional services to a patient but are a member of a group practice that bills under a single group identification number, and the patient has received services within the last three years from another physician in your specialty billing under the group ID, then Medicare and most other payers consider the patient to be established. If the patient received services from a member of the group who is in another specialty, you may consider the patient new.

Key Components and Code Selection

In most cases, selection of codes is dependent upon the factors (or components) which comprise the *content* of the service provided. CPT defines seven components, three of which are key, four of which are contributory. The components are listed below. Note that the three key components are printed in bold. Time is italicized.

1. History
2. Examination
3. Medical Decision Making
4. Counseling
5. Coordination of Care
6. Nature of Presenting Problems
7. *Time*

For the majority of E/M codes your selection will depend upon the extent of history taken, the extent of the examination provided, and the level of decision making involved. These three components are said to be the *key components*. In addition to the key components, three of the contributory factors may influence your code selection: counseling, coordination of care, and the nature of the patient's presenting problem(s).

Time is used *only* in selecting E/M codes when counseling or coordination of care comprises more than 50 percent of the service. In such cases you will use time to select the appropriate code and time becomes the controlling factor in code selection.

Key Component #1: History

CPT defines four levels of history, ranging from problem focused to comprehensive. The four levels are as follows:

1. Problem Focused
   Includes:
   - Chief complaint
   - Brief history of present illness or problem

2. Expanded Problem Focused
   Includes:
   - Chief complaint
   - Brief history of present illness
   - Problem pertinent system review

3. Detailed
   Includes:
   - Chief complaint
   - Extended history of present illness
   - Extended system review
   - *Pertinent* past, family and/or social history

4.   Comprehensive
      Includes:
          • Chief complaint
          • Extended history of present illness
          • Complete system review
          • *Complete* past, family and social history

The patient's medical record should note the level of history that was taken. For example, if a detailed history was performed, in addition to the complaint, history of the illness, and extended system review, the medical record should document information about the patient's past, family, and/or social history relevant to the complaint for which he is being seen. Documentation guidelines related to the history component of E/M services can be found in Appendix A.

Key Component #2: Examination

Four levels of examination are provided and each involve an increasingly extensive level of service. Like history, examinations range from problem focused to comprehensive as follows:

1. Problem Focused
     • An exam limited to the affected body area or organ system.

2. Expanded Problem Focused
     • An exam of the affected body area or organ system
     • An exam of other symptomatic or related organ systems.

3. Detailed
     • An extended exam of the affected body area(s).
     • An extended exam of other symptomatic or related organ systems.

4. Comprehensive
     • A complete single system specialty exam *or,*
     • A complete multisystem exam.

Your examination of the patient, including any findings or other observations, should also be documented in the patient's medical record. Documentation guidelines related to the examination component of E/M services can be found in Appendix A.

Key Component #3: Medical Decision Making

Of the key components, medical decision making is the most complex because three variables are involved. Selection of one of the appropriate four levels of decision making is a function of the following factors:

1.   The number of possible diagnoses and/or the number of management options that must be considered.

2.   The amount and/or complexity of medical records, diagnostic tests, and/or other information that must be obtained, reviewed, and analyzed.

3.   The risk of significant complications, morbidity and/or mortality, as well as co-morbidities, associated with the patient's presenting problem(s), the diagnostic procedure(s), and/or the possible management options.

To determine the appropriate level of decision making, the following chart (or that appearing in your CPT book) can be utilized:

Type of Decision Making	Number of Diagnoses or Management Options	Amount and/or Complexity of Data to Be Reviewed	Risk of Complications and/or Morbidity or Mortality
Straightforward	minimal	minimal or none	minimal
Low Complexity	limited	limited	low
Moderate Complexity	multiple	moderate	moderate
High Complexity	extensive	extensive	high

To select the appropriate level, *two of the three table elements must be met or exceeded.* To assist with your understanding of this concept, two examples are provided below.

1. The following applies to a patient:
   - limited number of diagnoses;
   - limited amount of data to be reviewed;
   - risk of complication is moderate.

In this case, the low complexity level would be selected as the elements met the three criteria established for low complexity.

2. The following applies to a patient:
   - extensive management options;
   - limited data review;
   - moderate risk of complications.

The moderate complexity level would apply in this example because two of the three elements met or exceeded the criteria. Documentation guidelines related to the medical decision making component of E/M services can be found in Appendix A.

Time

Time is used to determine selection of an E/M code *only* when more than 50 percent of the service rendered consists of counseling or coordination of care. Two types of time are defined in CPT based on the location of where the counseling or coordination of care services was provided.

When counseling or coordination of care services are performed in the office or other outpatient location, time is measured as the minutes the doctor spends *face-to-face* with the patient or family. This applies to office and outpatient visits and office consultations. The time spent performing tasks related to the visit, such as writing reports, reviewing medical records, calling other health care professionals, assessing lab results, etc., but that are not performed face-to-face, are not included in the time measurement.

For inpatient hospital care, initial and follow-up consultations, and nursing facility services, time related to counseling or coordination of care services is measured in *unit or floor time*. This includes time the doctor is actually in the patient's unit and at the bedside rendering services. Communicating with other professionals and/or family, updating or reviewing the patient's chart, writing notes or orders, and examining the patient would also be included. Time spent away from the patient's unit or floor in another part of the hospital or facility performing services such as reviewing X-rays or lab work are not considered part of unit or floor time.

For example, if an established patient received 30 minutes of face-to-face counseling in your office about the risks and benefits of treatment options under consideration, and this was the primary service provided, code 99214 for a Level IV established patient office visit would be selected.

When using time as the basis for selecting E/M codes, state the amount of time spent performing these services in the patient's medical record. Also include specifics related to the counseling or coordination of care services provided, as appropriate, and documentation of the history, examination, and medical decision making. (Refer also to "E/M Documentation Guidelines.")

Contributing Components

In addition to history, examination, and medical decision making, three other components may contribute to the selection of E/M codes. These include counseling, coordination of care, and the nature of the presenting problem(s).

Counseling and coordination of care affect selection of codes only if more than 50 percent of the service involves one or both of these components. Specifics related to the definitions of counseling can be found in your CPT book. The nature of the patient's presenting problem(s) is included as part of some E/M descriptions to assist the physician in determining the appropriate level of coding and is described fully in your CPT book.

Matching Key Components to Definitions

When reviewing the definitions of E/M services you will note that some require performance of all three key components (such as new patient office services) while others require only two of the components (such as established patient office services). In all cases, appropriate selection of an E/M code depends upon meeting or exceeding the stated requirements. Two rules for selection are:

1. When all three components are required, you must meet or exceed those described in the code. For example, to code for a new patient whose office visit included a detailed history, expanded problem focused examination, and medical decision making of low complexity, you would select code 99202. Note that although the detailed history and low complexity medical decision making are included as part of code 99203, the expanded problem focused exam is of lower intensity than required for code 99203, thus the lower level code is reported.

2. When only two components are required, two of the three components must meet or exceed those described in the code's definition. For example, you would code a subsequent hospital

visit for a patient who receives a detailed history, detailed exam, and with a problem requiring medical decision making of moderate complexity with code 99233 because two of the three components meet the code's requirements.

Examples

To help guide your selection of E/M codes, the American Medical Association provides examples (or vignettes) which illustrate encounters typically associated with each level of care. Examples are specialty specific and may be found in two locations in your CPT book. The first set of examples may be found immediately below the E/M codes to which they apply. Two examples provided for follow-up inpatient consultation code 99263 are as follows:

> Follow-up inpatient consultation with 58-year-old diabetic female, with bacterial endocarditis, continued fever after 2 weeks of intravenous antibiotic therapy, and new onset of ventricular ectopia. (Cardiology)

> Follow-up inpatient consultation for a 62-year-old male, status post-op acute small bowel obstruction; now with acute renal failure. (Family Medicine)

A second set of examples are provided for E/M codes in the CPT book's Appendix D titled "Clinical Examples Supplement."

Using a Crib Sheet

Due to the complexity of the E/M coding rules and the vast number of codes involved, it may be helpful to use a crib sheet similar to that shown in Figure 3.1. For each code the crib sheet lists the type of history, examination, medical decision making, number of key components required, and the amount of time spent with the patient when counseling or coordination of care are the determining factors. Practices may also choose to list their fees in the crib sheet cells. An example showing how to interpret the components of a crib sheet cell is provided below.

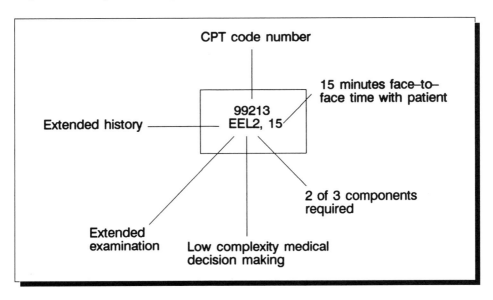

59

Figure 3.1: CPT E/M code Crib Sheet

	9920 OV NEW	9921 OV EST	9924 CON OP	9925 CON IP	9927 2-3 OP	9928 E/R
L1	99201 PPS3, 10	99211 PPSOn, 5	99241 PPS3, 15	99251 PPS3, 20	99271 EES3	99281 PPS3
L2	99202 EES3, 20	99212 PPS2, 10	99242 EES3, 30	99252 EES3, 40	99272 EES3	99282 EEL3
L3	99203 DDL3, 30	99213 EEL2, 15	99243 DDL3, 40	99253 DDL3, 55	99273 DDL3	99283 EEM3
L4	99204 CCM3, 45	99214 DDM2, 25	99244 CCM3, 60	99254 CCM3, 80	99274 CCM3	99284 DDM3
L5	99205 CCH3, 60	99215 CCH2, 40	99245 CCH3, 80	99255 CCH3, 110	99275 CCH3	99285 CCH3

	9921 IOC	9922 HOSP H&P	9923 HOSP V	9926 CON IP V	9932 RH H&P	9933 RH V	9934 HOME NEW	9935 HOME EST
L1	99218 D/C, D/C, S/L3	99221 D/C, D/C, S/L3, 30	99231 PiPS/L2, 15	99261 PiPS/L2, 10	99321 PPS/L3	99331 PiPS/L2	99341 PPS/L3	99351 PiPS/L2
L2	99219 CCM3	99222 CCM3, 50	99232 EiEM2, 25	99262 EiEM2, 20	99322 EEM3	99332 EiEM2	99342 EEM3	99352 EiEM2
L3	99220 CCH3	99223 CCH3, 70	99233 DiDH2, 35	99263 DiDH2, 30	99323 DDH3	99333 DiDH2	99343 DDH3	99353 DiDH2

OV NEW = office or outpatient visit, new patient
OV EST = office or outpatient visit, established patient

E/R = emergency department
RH = rest home

HOSP H&P = initial inpatient hospital visit
HOSP V = subsequent hospital visit

IOC = initial observation care

CON IP = consultation, inpatient, initial
CON IP V = consultation, inpatient, follow-up
CON OP = consultation, outpatient
2-3 OP = confirmatory consultation

P = problem focused
E = extended problem focused
D = detailed
C = comprehensive
S = straightforward

L = low complexity
M = moderate complexity
H = high complexity

D/C = detailed or comprehensive
S/L = straightforward or low complexity

On = nurse may perform task
i = interval

2 = 2 of 3 required
3 = 3 of 3 required

Although a crib sheet can be quite helpful when selecting E/M codes, it should only be used by those who fully understand the E/M coding rules and the requirement that services be properly documented in the patient's medical record.

Types of E/M Services

There are 16 types of E/M services listed in the CPT book in addition to one code for unlisted E/M service. Each type of service and its application are discussed below.

Office and Other Outpatient Services (99201–99215)

The codes in this group are used to report E/M services provided by the physician in the office or other outpatient setting. Separate codes are listed for new and established patients. Note that the new patient codes require *all* three key components; the established patient visits require *at least* two of the three key components.

In situations where services provided to a patient in the office (or outpatient facility) are related to a hospital or nursing facility admission made on the same day, you should generally bill for the admission only and not for the office visit; it will be considered by payers as part of the admission. However, there may be instances where you can bill both office and admission services on the same day. As an example, if you see a patient in the morning for a diabetes check and the patient develops severe chest pain in the afternoon which requires that you admit her to the hospital later in the day, you can bill for both the office and hospital admission services. Be sure that you list the diabetes diagnosis for the office visit and chest pain for the admission so that it is clear to the patient's insurance company why both services were warranted for the patient on that day.

Hospital Observation Services (99217–99220)

These codes allow you to bill for patients who are being seen in the hospital for observation, but have not been admitted (or are not) admitted as a hospital inpatient. As with the office and outpatient codes, any E/M services you provide to the patient on the same day as the admission to the hospital observation area and which are related to the admission (whether they were performed in the office, outpatient facility, emergency department, nursing home, etc.) are to be included in your observation care charge. Separate payment will not be made for both.

In situations where the physician provides observation care services to the patient and later that same day, admits the patient to the hospital, the physician would only bill for the hospital admission service. Finally, the observation discharge service code (99217) should only be used when the observation discharge services are performed on a different day than the initial observation service. For example, if the patient is placed into observation care at 4:00 pm on a Thursday and discharged at 2:00 pm the next day, the physician would bill the appropriate initial observation care code for Thursday's services and the observation care discharge code, 99217, for Friday's service.

Hospital Inpatient Services (99221–99238)

Hospital visits, including those provided in a "partial hospital" setting are billed by using codes from this group. Initial hospital, subsequent hospital, and hospital discharge service codes are all listed.

Initial hospital care codes apply to the first hospital inpatient encounter with the patient by the *admitting physician*. If you are seeing the patient for the first time in the hospital but did not admit the patient, use the subsequent hospital care codes (99231-99233) or, if you are performing a consultation, use the appropriate consultation code (99251-99255).

The initial hospital care codes include non-hospital services provided to the patient on the day of admission that are related to the admission, even if such E/M services were provided in the office, emergency department, observation area, or other location. For example, if an examination was performed in the physician's office and the patient is admitted to the hospital later that day, an initial hospital care E/M code would be listed.

Subsequent hospital care codes are to be reported for follow-up (subsequent) hospital services. Evaluation and Management services provided to an inpatient by the admitting physician, beginning the day after admission, and E/M inpatient services provided by physicians who did not admit the patient, would be listed via these codes.

CPT provides two codes (99238 and 99239) for reporting all services provided to a patient on the day of discharge. The total amount of time spent by the physician related to the discharge of a patient, which would include the final examination of the patient, discussion of continuing care and the hospital stay with the patient, and preparation of discharge records, is used to select the appropriate discharge code. Note that if the patient is discharged on the same day that he or she is admitted, the pertinent initial hospital admission code would be used rather than the hospital discharge management service code.

Consultations (99241–99275)

Four types of E/M consultation services are listed in CPT: office or other outpatient, initial inpatient, follow-up inpatient, and confirmatory. With the exception of follow-up inpatient consultations which can be provided only to established patients, no distinction is made between new and established patients.

The coding of consultation services has always been a challenge to physicians and staff alike. Because consult services pay at a rate which is nearly double that for equivalent office and hospital services, it is tempting to list consults when non-consult services were more likely provided. To help you understand how and when consults can legitimately be billed, consider the following guidelines:

1. The consultation *must be requested* by another physician or appropriate source. (Confirmatory consultations, discussed below, are an exception to this rule.) Medicare requires that you list the requesting physician's name and UPIN (Unique Physician Identification Number) on your claim for consult services. Other payers may also require that you list the requesting physician's name on the claim.

2. The purpose of the service is to provide an *opinion or advice* related to the evaluation or management of a specific patient problem.

3. The consulting physician may *initiate* diagnostic or therapeutic services during the course of the consultation.

4. The request and need for the consultation must be *documented* in the patient's medical record. The medical record should also state the name of the physician or other source requesting the opinion or advice.

5. The opinion, advice, and services ordered or performed by the consulting physician must be *documented* in the patient's record **and** *communicated* to the requesting physician or appropriate source.

Guideline 5 deserves special mention. Although the CPT book does not specify the form of communication, it is highly recommended that you have a formal, typed consult report sent to the physician or source who requested the consultative services. For hospital consults performed at the request of the patient's attending physician, it is generally permissible to write a consult report and make it a part of the patient's hospital record where it can be accessed by the attending physician and other health care providers. If you are ever audited by a payer and your consult charges are reviewed, the auditor will request copies of consult reports. Should the reports not exist, the auditor is likely to claim that you did not perform consultative services.

You may report only one initial inpatient consultation per patient admission. Additional consultations provided during the patient's same stay in the hospital should be listed using the follow-up inpatient consult codes. For example, an internist is asked by a surgeon to evaluate a patient for a fever following abdominal surgery. The internist evaluates the patient, initiates antibiotic therapy, and writes the results of her findings, treatment plan, and therapy in the patient's hospital chart. She would bill an initial inpatient consultation. However, the patient fails to improve during the course of the hospital stay and the surgeon asks the internist to reevaluate the patient and recommend an alternative therapy. This second consult service would be billed using the follow-up inpatient consultation codes.

Be careful, however, to avoid billing follow-up consultations when subsequent hospital services should be reported. In the above example of the follow-up inpatient consult, the internist would have had to write another consult report related to the second consult. If the internist had taken over management of the fever problem, she would bill subsequent hospital visits instead of consultation. To be billable, consultations, whether initial or follow-up, must meet the five criteria defined above.

Confirmatory, or additional opinion consultations, are reported only when the physician is aware that he or she is confirming or denying the opinion of another physician. For example, suppose a patient visits the doctor because another physician has told her that she needs a hysterectomy due to the presence of ovarian cysts. The patient would prefer not to have the surgery and is inquiring about the accuracy of the other physician's diagnosis and recommended treatment. This visit could be billed as a confirmatory consultation because the physician is being asked by the patient to confirm or deny another doctor's opinion. If the patient had simply come in and stated "Doctor, I've been having irregular periods and discomfort in my abdomen, and want your opinion because I am afraid I have cancer," the E/M services would be billed as an office visit, not confirmatory consultation because there is no reference to another physician or health care provider's opinion.

When you can legitimately bill for confirmatory consultations, it is highly recommended that the patient's medical record note the patient's request, name of the physician(s) (or provider source) whom the patient previously saw, results of the evaluation and discussion of management options.

Emergency Department Services (99281-99288)

Emergency department E/M codes are used most frequently by physicians who specialize in emergency medicine. However, any physician can use these codes as appropriate. Difficulties tend to arise when both a physician who normally works in the emergency department and another physician bill the same patient for emergency department services provided on the same day.

Physicians who do not normally work in the ER but nonetheless provide E/M or invasive services there have several billing options. First, if the ER physician requests an opinion or advice regarding the ER patient's problem(s) from a specialist, the specialist may be able to bill for a consultation. Second, if the non-assigned physician admits the patient to the hospital, he could charge for a hospital admission. Third, if the physician performs specific procedures or services, such as a fracture reduction in the ER, the procedure or service can be billed.

Also note that the CPT emergency department code notes refer specifically to an "organized hospital-based facility for the provision of unscheduled episodic services to patients who present for immediate medical attention. The facility must be available 24-hours a day." Thus, physicians who see patients in a free-standing emergency care facility would not bill emergency department service codes. In such a case you should report office/outpatient visit codes.

Unlike most other E/M codes, time is not considered a factor when billing emergency department services because the physician may be concurrently caring for several patients and it is therefore virtually impossible to determine how much time is spent with each patient. Also, no distinction is made between new and established patients.

Other Emergency Services (99288)

CPT provides a code (99288) for billing the services of a physician who is remotely directing emergency care or advanced life support. To use this code, the physician must be in two-way voice communication with rescue or ambulance personnel who are outside the hospital. And the physician must be located in the hospital emergency department or critical care unit when directing this service.

Critical Care (99291–99292)

Critical care services include constant physician attendance, procedures normally provided as part of critical care, and are usually provided in a critical care area such as a coronary care unit, intensive care unit, respiratory care unit, or similar area. Procedures and services defined as being included in critical care are as follows:

- Interpretation of cardiac output measurements (CPT codes 93561, 93562)
- Interpretation of chest X-rays (CPT codes 71010, 71020)
- Interpretation of blood gases and information data stored in computers (e.g., ECG, blood pressure, hematologic data) (CPT code 99090)
- Gastric intubation (CPT code 91105)
- Temporary transcutaneous pacing (CPT code 92953)
- Ventilator management (CPT codes 94656, 94657, 94660, 94662)
- Vascular access procedures (CPT codes 36000, 36410, 36415, 36600)

According to CPT, if services other than those listed above are provided, such services can be billed separately. For example, if during the critical care period the physician is monitoring blood gases and also performs cardioversion, in addition to the critical time charge, the physician can bill separately for the cardioversion service.

Critical care services are reported on a time basis. The first hour of critical care provided to a patient on a given day is listed using code 99291, even if care was not continuous. Additional half-hour segments are reported by use of code 99292. For example, if the physician provided 45 minutes of critical care in the morning and an additional 75 minutes of critical care in the afternoon for a total of two hours of critical care, the claim would list code 99291 once (for the first hour) and code 99292 twice (for the two additional half-hour segments). If critical care is provided to the patient the next day, the first hour would be listed using code 99291, etc.

Specific time guidelines for the billing of critical care services are provided in CPT. If the time spent is one-half hour or less, then a subsequent hospital care codes is to be listed (99232 or 99233). Codes that should be reported along with their associated units are shown below for various time durations:

1-30 Minutes	99232 (one unit) or 99233 (one unit)
31-74 Minutes	99291 (one unit)
75-104 Minutes	99291 (one unit) and 99292 (one unit)
105-134 Minutes	99291 (one unit) and 99292 (two units)
135-164 Minutes	99291 (one unit) and 99292 (three units)
165-194 Minutes	99291 (one unit) and 99292 (four units)

Neonatal Intensive Care (99295–99287)

These codes are used by physicians providing care to neonates and infants in a neonatal intensive care unit (NICU). Services are billed on a per-day basis per patient. The specific procedures and services included with neonatal intensive care, of which there are many, are outlined in CPT under the neonatal intensive care notes and, additionally, with each code. Physicians are allowed to bill separately for services not specifically listed as included with neonatal intensive care, or specifically associated with one of the codes. If you use these codes, you should become familiar with the full range of services that are and are not included with neonatal intensive care.

Nursing Facility Services (99301–99313)

Nursing facility services are defined to include those E/M services provided in skilled nursing facilities, intermediate care facilities, long term care facilities, and psychiatric residential treatment centers. Two types of nursing facility services are defined: comprehensive nursing facility assessments and subsequent nursing facility care.

Comprehensive nursing facility assessments are typically billed when the physician admits the patient to the nursing facility, when performing an annual assessment of the patient, or when a patient's condition or status changes so significantly as to require a comprehensive reassessment. With the exception of hospital discharge services which may be reported separately, the comprehensive assessment codes include all E/M services provided by the physician in facilities other than the nursing facility which are related to a nursing facility admission. The subsequent care codes are used to report routine nursing facility services.

Domiciliary, Rest Home (eg, Boarding Home), or Custodial Care (99321–99333)

Codes from this group are separated into new and established patients and are generally used to report E/M services provided to patients who are being seen in a facility which provides basic patient care (such as room, board, and personal assistance services) on a long term basis. These services are billed on the basis of the three key E/M components, as time is not identified separately as a factor.

Home Services (99341–99353)

These codes are used to bill for services provided to patients in their residence, or in the case of someone who is traveling, in their hotel room. Two categories of codes are provided, one for new patients, a second for established patients. Times have not been established for these services, so you they are to be billed using the three E/M key components. Pay special attention to the presenting problem definitions associated with these codes. For example, you will note that for established patients, presenting problems range from a stable, recovering or improving patient to a patient who is unstable or has developed complications or a significant new problem.

Prolonged Services (99354-99360)

CPT identifies three types of prolonged physician services: those involving direct face-to-face contact with the patient, those without direct face-to-face contact, and standby services. With the exception of standby services, when warranted, these services are to be reported in addition to other physician services, including other E/M services. Only one prolonged service code may be reported per day for a patient, even if the prolonged services were not continuous. These codes are not to be used if the prolonged service was for less than 30 minutes.

Two types of direct face-to-face prolonged services are defined. The first is for patients seen in the office or other outpatient setting (99354 and 99355). A second set is for patients being cared for in an inpatient setting (99356 and 99357). As with critical care services, the selection of codes is based upon the duration of the prolonged service. Codes 99354 and 99356 are for the first hour of prolonged care and codes 99355 and 99357 are for each additional 30 minutes. Your CPT book provides examples of which codes and units to report for various durations of prolonged services.

Two codes (99358 and 99359) are available for reporting prolonged services not involving direct face-to-face contact with the patient. An example of these types of services would be prolonged discussions with a family member who is caring for the patient related to treatment options and home care. These non-face-to-face services are also reported using the time duration table in CPT.

In instances where a physician has been requested by another physician to standby in case his or her services are required, such as being available to perform an emergency cesarean section and newborn resuscitation for a patient in early labor, code 99360 should be reported. There are several restrictions on the use of this code. First, the physician may not be providing care to other patients while on standby. Second, the physician may not be teaching other physicians, such as residents, while on standby. Finally, if the physician performs a surgical procedure on the patient for whom he was standing by, and the procedure has an associated surgical package, the standby service will be assumed to be included in the charge for the surgery and may not be billed separately. Standby services are reported in 30 minute increments. A minimum of 30 minutes of standby is required to list code 99360. Each additional full 30 minute increment is also reported via use of code 99360.

Case Management Services (99361–99373)

Case management service codes are provided in CPT as a means of reporting services performed by a physician who is responsible for directing the care of a patient. Two types of codes are listed. The first is for medical conferences between the physician and a team of other health care providers or community agencies involved in coordinating patient care. These services are reported based upon the amount of time spent performing case management activities for a patient. The second set of codes is for telephone calls related to consulting, medical management, or coordinating care with other healthcare providers. Three levels of telephone call services are listed.

It is worth noting that Medicare and many other payers generally do not allow payment for services provided when the patient is not physically present, as would be the situation with case management-related telephone calls. Exceptions to this rule include reading X-rays, ECGs, pathology, and other services which allow the physician to "visualize" or directly examine an aspect of the patient. Since some third party payers to not cover case management services, it may be necessary to inform the patient that he or she will be responsible for payment.

Care Plan Oversight Services (99375-99376)

CPT provides two codes for use in reporting the services of a physician related to overseeing and planing for the care of a patient. These care planing oversight codes are to be used on a monthly basis and are listed in addition to any other E/M services provided to the patient during the month. Typical care plan oversight services include those related to developing and revising care plans, tests, review of reports, adjusting treatment plans, telephone discussions with other healthcare professionals who are caring for the patient, and the like. These services are usually billed for patients under the care of a home health agency, hospice, or nursing facility. Refer to the notes for these codes in CPT for additional requirements related to their use.

Preventive Medicine Services (99381–99429)

Codes from this section are to be utilized when providing E/M services to healthy individuals. These would include pediatric care and routine examinations of healthy adolescents and adults. Note that if a patient presents with complaints or a problem, or if a problem is discovered during the course of a preventive E/M service, an office visit (or other appropriate) E/M code should be used instead of these codes.

A group of counseling and risk factor reduction intervention service codes are also provided in this section. Such services would include counseling to obese patients about diet and weight reduction, helping individuals stop smoking, counseling about substance abuse or high-risk sexual practices, and the like. These services are to be reported for healthy individuals only and should not be listed for patients with symptoms or patients who are being seen for an established illness. In such cases you would report the appropriate office, outpatient or other service code.

Newborn Care (99431–99440)

Use of the E/M codes in this section is fairly straightforward: physicians who provide services to normal or high-risk newborns will report their services using these codes. Note that a special code for newborn resuscitation (99440) should be used when reporting services (such as inhalation therapy, aspiration, and administration of medication) related to stabilizing a high-risk newborn.

Special Evaluation and Management Services (99450-99456)

This group of codes is provided to allow for the reporting of life and disability insurance examinations as well as work related and medical disability examinations. Any other E/M services or other procedures performed on the same patient on the same day as these special services can be separately reported.

It is worth noting that Medicare and many other payers generally do not allow payment for services provided when the patient is not physically present, as would be the situation with case management-related telephone calls. Exceptions to this rule include reading X-rays, ECGs, pathology and other services which allow the physician to "visualize" or directly examine an aspect of the patient. Since some third party payers to not cover case management services, it may be necessary to inform the patient that he or she will be responsible for payment.

MODIFIERS

Before jumping headlong into the remaining sections of CPT codes, you will require an understanding of modifiers and how they are used. New coders are often confused about modifiers and their application. As you will learn, their primary purpose is to denote circumstances which affect the performance of a procedure or service. They are also used to provide supportive information to payers that can directly aid your practice's reimbursement.

After reviewing the information on modifiers in this chapter, you will know how to add modifiers to codes, know how and when to use CPT modifiers, know how and when to use the HCPCS modifiers, and obtain an understanding of what information payers may need to justify payment of modified procedure and service codes.

An Overview of Modifiers

On some occasions it is necessary to note circumstances which affect the way services and procedures are performed. For example, a physician performs a procedure bilaterally, and the procedure as listed in CPT is unilateral. Or a normally simple procedure becomes unusually complicated because the patient suffers from diabetes. When these and other circumstances arise, it will be helpful if you add modifiers to the procedures and services you report. The following discussion provides information to help you learn how to report modifiers and learn how and when to use CPT and HCPCS National modifiers. Each modifier and its usage is discussed in detail.

In addition to understanding how to use a modifier, you need to be aware of the effect the addition of a modifier can have on your claims. A key concept with modifiers is not the addition of the modifier itself, but rather that you often need to support the modified code with additional information which justifies the service, procedure or supply being reported. In many cases the addition of the modifier itself will not guarantee appropriate payment. You should always remember that you are adding a modifier because something different happened, and that something different may have to be explained to the insurance carrier. This means sending some type of support documentation, whether it is a special report or letter, with the claim. Where support documentation should be sent with a claim containing a specific modifier, it is noted.

Reporting Modifiers

There are five distinct types of modifiers you may find need for when billing services. CPT provides two types—two digit modifiers and five digit modifiers. The HCPCS National and Local systems have three types of modifiers—a letter followed by a number, two letters, or one letter. Between CPT and the HCPCS National system there are 180 different modifiers. Examples of modifiers are provided below.

    CPT Modifiers - Two Digit Form   "-51"

    CPT Modifiers - Five Digit Form   09951

    HCPCS Modifier - Letter/Number Form   "-F1"

    HCPCS Modifier - Two Letter Form   "-QY"

    HCPCS Modifier - One Letter Form   "-H"

Because both the HCFA-1500 claim form and most electronic claim formats provide two spaces for representing each modifier (that is, for each modifier you can report up to two letters, two numbers, or a letter and a number), it is unlikely that you will use the five digit CPT modifier. The five digit modifier was created for use on what are now legacy computer systems. These older systems could not handle a two digit modifier, so rather than being placed next to the CPT code to which it applied, the five digit modifier was placed on the service line below the code.

In Figure 3.2 you will find an example of how modifiers are reported on the HCFA-1500 claim form. In this example the physician is treating a neuroma on the left inferior alveolar ridge. The procedure consists of microdissection of the nerve (code 64830), excision of the neuroma (code 64784), and mobilization of the proximal nerve with primary reanastomosis (code 64874). An operating microscope (noted by modifier "-20" placed next to code 64784) was used when performing the procedures. The multiple procedure modifier, "-51", is listed next to the secondary procedures. The decision for the surgery was made the day before during a consultation at the surgeon's office (code 99244). Note that the decision for surgery modifier "-57" is listed next to the consultation code.

Problems with modifiers may arise for offices using superbills or charge tickets. Too often these forms either omit needed modifiers or have designs which will not accommodate the addition of modifiers. In either case, patient or physician reimbursement may suffer from improper reporting.

You should be aware that you can use CPT modifiers on HCPCS National and Local codes. Conversely, you can use HCPCS National and Local modifiers on CPT codes. You can even use National Modifiers on Local codes, and Local Modifiers on National codes. In other words, when billing a payer that accepts the full HCPCS system, you can use any modifier on any code, as long as the use is appropriate.

Figure 3.2: Modifiers Listed Next to Code

21. DIAGNOSIS OR NATURE OF ILLNESS OR INJURY. (RELATE ITEMS 1,2,3 OR 4 TO ITEM 24E BY LINE)	22. MEDICAID RESUBMISSION CODE / ORIGINAL REF. NO.
1. 225.1 3.	23. PRIOR AUTHORIZATION NUMBER
2. 4.	

24.	A DATE(S) OF SERVICE						B Place of Service	C Type of Service	D PROCEDURES, SERVICES OR SUPPLIES (Explain Unusual Circumstances) CPT/HCPCS MODIFIER	E DIAGNOSIS CODE	F $ CHARGES	G DAYS OR UNITS	H EPSDT Family Plan	I EMG	J COB	K RESERVED FOR LOCAL USE
	From MM	DD	YY	To MM	DD	YY										
1									64784 20	1						
2									64876 51	1						
3									64830	1						
4																
5																
6																

25. FEDERAL TAX I.D. NUMBER SSN EIN	26. PATIENT'S ACCOUNT NO.	27. ACCEPT ASSIGNMENT? (For govt. claims, see back) YES NO	28. TOTAL CHARGE $	29. AMOUNT PAID. $	30. BALANCE DUE $
31. SIGNATURE OF PHYSICIAN OR SUPPLIER INCLUDING DEGREES OR CREDENTIALS (I certify that the statements on the reverse apply to this bill and are made a part thereof.) SIGNED DATE	32. NAME AND ADDRESS OF FACILITY WHERE SERVICES WERE RENDERED (If other than home or office)		33. PHYSICIAN'S SUPPLIER'S BILLING NAME, ADDRESS, ZIP CODE & PHONE # PIN# GRP#		

(APPROVED BY AMA COUNCIL ON MEDICAL SERVICE 8/88)   **PLEASE PRINT OR TYPE**   FORM HCFA-1500 (12-90) / FORM OWCP-1500   FORM RRB-1500

PHYSICIAN OR SUPPLIER INFORMATION

CPT Modifiers

The 1997 CPT system contains 30 modifiers. You will find modifiers listed in two areas of the CPT book. First, all modifiers are listed in Appendix A of CPT. Second, the modifiers that apply to a specific section of CPT (e.g., Medicine, Surgery, etc.) are listed in the Guidelines for that section. Modifiers and their use are also mentioned in the Introduction to CPT.

"–20" Microsurgery

In situations where the physician uses an operating microscope to aid with the performance of a surgical procedure, the microsurgery modifier "-20" is to be listed with the procedure code. It is also common for physicians to increase charges for procedures which require use of the operating microscope due to their inherently greater difficulty.

Not all microsurgical procedures warrant use of the "-20" modifier. There are three circumstances under which you would not report this modifier. First, if the procedure is *always* performed microsurgically by the physician and he includes use of the microscope in the procedure's standard charge, reporting the microsurgery modifier may be considered inappropriate. Second, some procedures are described as involving microsurgical techniques. In such cases, the modifier would be redundant. As an example of this, refer to CPT code 15842 for the grafting of muscle for facial nerve paralysis by microsurgical technique. When billing code 15842, you do not need to also list the "-20" modifier as microsurgery is an element of the procedure. Finally, when reporting nerve repair by suture procedures (CPT codes 64831-64876), instead of the "-20" modifier you add an additional code, 64830, to report the use of microsurgical techniques. For example, if the physician repaired the posterior tibial nerve by microsurgical means, two codes, each with a separate charge, would be listed on the claim: 64840 for the repair and 64830 for the microsurgery.

Note that microsurgery implies the use of an operating microscope, and, as stated in CPT, "... is not to be used when a magnifying surgical loupe is used, whether attached to the eyeglasses or on a headband." Note also—when you use an operating microscope to assist with a procedure for which use of the microscope is rare, submission of a special report with the claim that explains why the microscope was required will improve the likelihood of prompt and proper payment.

"–21" Prolonged Evaluation and Management Services

This modifier is to be used exclusively with E/M codes. It is reported in situations where the E/M services provided to a patient are greater than those defined in the highest E/M level. For example, suppose that the physician is performing a consultation for a patient who is suffering from severe pancreatitis complicated by respiratory and renal problems. The patient is moderately retarded and does not speak English, thus requiring the need for an interpreter. Due to the severity of the patient's problems, the language barrier, and retardation, the consultation requires over two and one-half hours to perform. In this case it may be appropriate to add the "-21" modifier for prolonged evaluation and management services to the consultation code as follows:

99255—21

As with the unusual services modifier below, it may be necessary to supply a special report with the claim which explains the unusual nature of the consultation service. Without such a report, additional charges for the prolonged service are likely to be denied.

Situations where a prolonged evaluation and management services modifier is applicable should not be confused with those instances where the prolonged service codes (99354-99360), discussed earlier in this chapter, would apply. An example will help clarify this issue. A physician is treating an asthmatic patient in his office. In addition to the office visit services, the physician spends a total of 45 minutes over the course of the patient's stay personally monitoring response to the asthma treatment. The physician can bill both the appropriate office visit as well as code 99354 for the prolonged care he provided. As a general rule, if the "prolonged" component of care is separate and apart from the standard history, examination, and medical decision making components of an E/M service and is at least 30 minutes in duration, then it may be billed in addition to the E/M service.

"–22" Unusual Services

The unusual services modifier has conceptually distinct uses in CPT. Its primary purpose is to denote circumstances for which a procedure or service required an "unusual" amount of time or effort to perform. As such a higher fee is usually charged. A word of caution regarding the use of the unusual service modifier: its use implies that the procedure or service was distinctly more time-consuming or difficult to perform than usual. When using the modifier you <u>must</u> also send a special report to the insurance carrier that describes the unusual nature of the service and justifies the additional charge. Even when justified, it may be difficult at best to obtain higher than normal reimbursement from the majority of payers.

Consider a surgical procedure which typically requires one to two hours to perform. Reimbursement from payers will be the same whether the procedure takes one or two hours. Why? Reimbursement averages out across patients over time. The use of the unusual services modifier would be inappropriate if the procedure took two hours, just as use of the reduced service modifier would not be appropriate if the procedure took one hour. However, use of the unusual services modifier would be more appropriate with the above hypothetical surgery if the operation was very difficult and required three hours to perform because the patient was obese.

The "-22" modifier has other specific uses in CPT. For example, the CPT Psychiatry notes explain that the unusual services modifier is used to communicate that the patient was seen for a period greater than is customary.

"–23"   Unusual Anesthesia

Under some circumstances general anesthesia is given when normally either a local or no anesthesia is provided. For example, performing a cystoscopy on a three-year-old child would likely require a general anesthesia, whereas the same procedure on an adult would not. Thus, use of a general anesthetic when performing a cystoscopy is an example of unusual anesthesia.

In these cases insurance companies will want to know why the unusual anesthesia was required. Therefore, when submitting the unusual anesthesia modifier be sure to include a report that focuses on the circumstances which required that the patient receive a general anesthetic. The use of this modifier is generally restricted to anesthesiologists.

"–24"   Unrelated Evaluation and Management Service by the Same Physician During a Postoperative Period

Under Medicare's (and several other payers') surgical package definition, the follow-up services related to most surgical procedures may not be billed separately; they are included as part of the surgery charge. This modifier is provided to communicate to Medicare and other payers that an E/M service provided to a patient during a follow-up period is unrelated to the recent surgery and therefore is not covered under the surgical package. For example, consider a patient who undergoes abdominal surgery. Three days after the operation, the patient falls. The surgeon evaluates the injury and when billing for E/M services related to the injury, uses the "-24" modifier, as follows:

99232-24

As another example, suppose a dermatologist excised lesions from a patient's back. Five days later the patient returns to the physician for evaluation of a contact dermatitis. Billing for the E/M service related to the contact dermatitis would include use of the "-24" modifier. Note that when the unrelated E/M service during a postoperative period modifier is reported, it is invariably for a diagnosis that is different from that for which the surgery was performed. Payers will anticipate a diagnosis different from that reported for the surgery, and if a different one is not used, even if the "-24" modifier is listed, the claim is likely to be denied.

"–25"   Significant, Separately Identifiable Evaluation and Management Service by the Same Physician on the Day of a Procedure or Other Service.

This modifier communicates essentially the same information as the "-24" modifier, with one exception, it is for unrelated E/M services provided by the physician on the day of a procedure or other service. Continuing the examples provided above for the "-24" modifier, suppose the surgeon evaluated a fall that took place on the day of the surgery, or the dermatologist examined a contact dermatitis on the same <u>day</u> as excising a lesion. In these and analogous circumstances, the physician would list the E/M services using the "-25" modifier. Again, note that the diagnosis code(s) reported with the E/M service will be different from the diagnosis code(s) listed for the surgical service(s).

"–26" Professional Component

Many listed procedures consist of both technical and professional components. Technical components include such things as equipment, technician time, and supplies that are used in the performance of a procedure. The professional component refers to the physician's time, skill, and judgment in interpreting the results of tests and procedures.

To illustrate, consider the two view chest X-ray described by code 71020. The X-ray is typically taken in a hospital radiology department and then "read" by a radiologist who has a contract with the hospital for professional services. The hospital will bill for the technical components of the service (usually by adding technical component modifier "-TC" to code 71020) and the radiologist will report code 71020 with the professional component modifier, "-26" as shown below.

Hospital's charge: 71020-TC

Radiologist's charge: 71020-26

In some situations the physician practice may have its own radiological equipment and the bill submitted by the physician is inclusive of both the technical and professional components. If this is the case, no professional or technical component modifiers will be added to code 71020. However, you should note that some payers are now requiring that the technical and professional components of these services be reported separately, even if provided by the same billing entity.

The professional component modifier is generally not appropriate when the procedure as described is only for interpretation. Refer to the first code in the Radiology section of CPT, code 70010. Note that the description is for the supervision and interpretation of a myelogram, posterior fossa. If a radiologist supervises the taking of the myelogram and then interprets the radiographs, he would simply use code 70010. The radiologist would not need to add the "-26" modifier as the code is for the professional component already. This and other issues related to billing radiology are discussed in later in this book.

"–32" Mandated Services

Mandated services are those requested by an insurance carrier, peer review organization, utilization review panel, HMO, PPO, or other entity. Typically, the request is for a second or third opinion regarding a patient's illness or treatment. When mandated services are requested, the physician performing the service is usually required to accept assignment from the payer, and in turn, the payer reimburses the doctor 100 percent of the payer's allowable for the service. An example of a mandated service would be a Level III confirmatory consultation. This would be reported as:

99273-32

The "-32" modifier is used to alert the payer's claim processors that the service was mandated and should receive special handling.

"–47" Anesthesia by Surgeon

When the surgeon renders regional anesthesia services in conjunction with a procedure, or furnishes general anesthesia services normally provided by an anesthesiologist, the circumstance can be noted by adding the "-47" modifier to surgical procedure(s). This modifier might be used, for example, by a surgeon working in an underserved area, where an anesthesiologist or nurse anesthetist is not available, and an emergency procedure must be performed on a patient that requires the surgeon to concurrently administer general anesthesia. More commonly it is used to report regional anesthesia services, such as the block of an extremity by an orthopedic surgeon in conjunction with an in-office service.

The anesthesia by surgeon modifier is reported by listing the CPT code to which it applies on a separate line and adding the "-47" modifier. For example, an emergency appendectomy and associated general anesthesia rendered by a rural surgeon would be coded as in the following example:

44960	Appendectomy for ruptured appendix with abscess or generalized peritonitis
44960-47	Anesthesia for the appendectomy

Listing separate charges for the surgery and anesthesia services would be appropriate.

"–50" Bilateral Procedures

Procedures listed in CPT are assumed to be unilateral unless they are either always performed bilaterally or otherwise noted. The most commonly accepted method of reporting bilateral procedures is to list the procedure twice and add the "-50" modifier to the second procedure as shown below for otoplasties of a patient's left and right ears:

69300 Otoplasty, protruding ear RIGHT
69300-50 Otoplasty, protruding ear LEFT

Note that the words "right" and "left" have been added to clarify that the procedures were indeed performed bilaterally. The HCPCS National modifiers "-RT" and "-LT" for right and left, respectively, can also be added for clarification. For example, continuing the above example, the physician might report his services as follows:

69300-RT
69300-50 LT

Also, it is common for physicians to report their full charge for each procedure and let the payer reduce the amount on the second, or bilateral, procedure. (Billing of multiple procedures is discussed in more detail below.)

Some payers accept an alternative method of billing bilateral procedures. This method involves listing the procedure once and adding the "-50" modifier as shown below:

69300-50 Otoplasty, protruding ear, bilateral

If this method is used, place a "2" in the UNITS column of the HCFA-1500 claim form so that the payer is aware that two procedures were performed, and place both the "-RT" and "-LT" modifiers next to the code. The charge reported on the claim for the procedures is typically twice that of what the physician charges for performing one of the procedures.

Physicians and staff may become confused by the definition of bilateral. Bilateral procedures are identical procedures (i.e., you use the same CPT code) performed on the same anatomic site but on opposite sides of the body. Furthermore, each procedure should be performed through its own separate incision to qualify for bilateral.

"–51" Multiple Procedures

This modifier has traditionally been used to identify multiple surgical procedures performed on a patient during the same operative session. For example, the repair of a simple neck wound and the closed treatment of a clavicle fracture would be coded as:

23500 Closed treatment of clavicle fracture., without manipulation
12005-51 Simple closure 18cm neck wound

Note that the higher charge procedure (fracture treatment) is listed first and the multiple procedure modifier is added to the lesser or secondary service. If three procedures had been performed, the services would be ranked from highest to lowest charge on the claim form and the "-51" modifier added to all but the first (highest charge) procedure.

The definition of multiple procedures includes not only multiple procedures performed during the same operative session, but also to multiple medical and/or surgical services performed on a patient on the same day. For example, if a primary care physician saw a patient for chronic obstructive pulmonary disease, congestive heart failure and a skin tag, the services could be reported as shown in Figure 3.3. Note that the modifier is listed next to all but the highest charge service.

Although it is acceptable to use the "-51" modifier when reporting multiple services and procedures as illustrated in Figure 3.3, the author is not aware of many practices who do this or of payers who require the "-51" modifier under these circumstances. Use of the "-51" modifier is usually limited to reporting multiple surgeries performed in the same operative session. However, payer policies can change overnight and you should keep abreast of the requirements of your major payers with regard to use of this modifier.

Physician practices that regularly bill multiple procedures have usually established policies for handling fees in these situations. Some practices have a policy of leaving their full normal charge for each procedure and then let the payer in question apply reductions for the secondary (multiple) procedures. Other practices reduce fees on the secondary procedures. Finally, some practices may make multiple procedure fee reductions for select payers, such as Medicare, but not for other payers. If your practice's policy is to reduce fees on the secondary services, make sure some payers are not reducing your reductions. For example, a payer's claims adjudication software system may automatically apply a 50 percent reduction to secondary procedures and be incapable of taking into consideration the fact that you already reduced your fees for these procedures. Since payers are increasingly employing new technologies in their claims administration process, this is likely to be a greater problem for your practice in the future.

Fig. 3.3: Multiple Procedures Modifier

PLEASE DO NOT STAPLE IN THIS AREA	APPROVED OMB-0939-0008

HEALTH INSURANCE CLAIM FORM

			PICA
PICA			

1. MEDICARE (Medicare #) ☐ MEDICAID (Medicaid #) ☐ CHAMPUS (Sponsor's SSN) ☐ CHAMPVA (VA File #) ☐ GROUP HEALTH PLAN (SSN or ID) ☐ FECA BLK LUNG (SSN) ☐ OTHER (ID) ☒

1a. INSURED I.D. NUMBER (FOR PROGRAM IN ITEM 1): XI 153-62-1175

2. PATIENT'S NAME (Last Name, First Name, Middle Initial): **Henry, Robert James**

3. PATIENT'S BIRTH DATE: 5 17 48 SEX: M ☒ F ☐

4. INSURED'S NAME (Last Name, First Name, Middle Initial): **Same**

5. PATIENT'S ADDRESS (No., Street): **371 Sixth Street**

6. PATIENT RELATIONSHIP TO INSURED: Self ☒ Spouse ☐ Child ☐ Other ☐

7. INSURED'S ADDRESS (No., Street): **Same**

CITY: **Newberry** STATE: **NC**

8. PATIENT STATUS: Single ☐ Married ☒ Other ☐

CITY: STATE:

ZIP CODE: **48888** TELEPHONE (Include Area Code): **(630) 654-8800**

Employed ☒ Full-Time Student ☐ Part-Time Student ☐

ZIP CODE: TELEPHONE (Include Area Code):

9. OTHER INSURED'S NAME (Last Name, First Name, Middle Initial):

10. IS PATIENT'S CONDITION RELATED TO:

11. INSURED'S POLICY GROUP OR FECA NUMBER: **RR6-71**

a. OTHER INSURED'S POLICY OR GROUP NUMBER:

a. EMPLOYMENT? (CURRENT OR PREVIOUS): YES ☐ NO ☒

a. INSURED'S DATE OF BIRTH: 5 17 48 SEX: M ☒ F ☐

b. OTHER INSURED'S DATE OF BIRTH: SEX: M ☐ F ☐

b. AUTO ACCIDENT? YES ☐ NO ☒ PLACE (State):

b. EMPLOYER'S NAME OR SCHOOL NAME: **Joe's Factory & Warehouse**

c. EMPLOYER'S NAME OR SCHOOL NAME:

c. OTHER ACCIDENT? YES ☐ NO ☒

c. INSURANCE PLAN NAME OR PROGRAM NAME: **Prudential**

d. INSURED PLAN NAME OR PROGRAM NAME:

10d. RESERVED FOR LOCAL USE:

d. IS THERE ANOTHER HEALTH BENEFIT PLAN? YES ☐ NO ☐ If yes, return to and complete item 9 a–d.

READ BACK OF FORM BEFORE COMPLETING & SIGNING THIS FORM.

12. PATIENT'S OR AUTHORIZED PERSON'S SIGNATURE I authorize the release of any medical or other information necessary to process this claim. I also request payment of government benefits either to myself or to the party who accepts assignment below.

SIGNED **On File** DATE **12/3/97**

13. INSURED'S OR AUTHORIZED PERSON'S SIGNATURE I authorize payment of medical benefits to the undersigned physician or supplier for services described below.

SIGNED

14. DATE OF CURRENT: ILLNESS (First symptom) OR INJURY (Accident) OR PREGNANCY (LMP): 6 9 98

15. IF PATIENT HAS HAD SAME OR SIMILAR ILLNESS. GIVE FIRST DATE MM DD YY

16. DATES PATIENT UNABLE TO WORK IN CURRENT OCCUPATION: FROM — TO —

17. NAME OF REFERRING PHYSICIAN OR OTHER SOURCE:

17a. I.D. NUMBER OF REFERRING PHYSICIAN:

18. HOSPITALIZATION DATES RELATED TO CURRENT SERVICES: FROM — TO —

19. RESERVED FOR LOCAL USE:

20. OUTSIDE LAB? YES ☐ NO ☐ $ CHARGES

21. DIAGNOSIS OR NATURE OF ILLNESS OR INJURY. (RELATE ITEMS 1,2,3 OR 4 TO ITEM 24E BY LINE)

1. **810 02**
2. **910 8**
3. ____
4. ____

22. MEDICAID RESUBMISSION CODE: ORIGINAL REF. NO.

23. PRIOR AUTHORIZATION NUMBER:

24. A DATE(S) OF SERVICE						B Place of Service	C Type of Service	D PROCEDURES, SERVICES OR SUPPLIES (Explain Unusual Circumstances)		E DIAGNOSIS CODE	F $ CHARGES		G DAYS OR UNITS	H EPSDT Family Plan	I EMG	J COB	K RESERVED FOR LOCAL USE
	From MM	DD	YY	To MM	DD	YY			CPT/HCPCS	MODIFIER								
1	12	3	97				11		23500		1	275	00	1				
2	12	3	97				11		12995	51	2	250	00	1				
3																		
4																		
5																		
6																		

25. FEDERAL TAX I.D. NUMBER: **678-90-1234** SSN ☐ EIN ☒

26. PATIENT'S ACCOUNT NO.:

27. ACCEPT ASSIGNMENT? (For govt. claims, see back) YES ☐ NO ☒

28. TOTAL CHARGE: $ **525 00**

29. AMOUNT PAID: $ **0 00**

30. BALANCE DUE: $ **525 00**

31. SIGNATURE OF PHYSICIAN OR SUPPLIER INCLUDING DEGREES OR CREDENTIALS (I certify that the statements on the reverse apply to this bill and are made a part thereof.)

SIGNED [signature] DATE 12/3/98

32. NAME AND ADDRESS OF FACILITY WHERE SERVICES WERE RENDERED (If other than home or office):

33. PHYSICIAN'S SUPPLIER'S BILLING NAME, ADDRESS, ZIP CODE & PHONE #: **Dr. Albert E. Stein 93 Sixth Street Newberry, NC 48888**

PIN# GRP#

(APPROVED BY AMA COUNCIL ON MEDICAL SERVICE 8/88) **PLEASE PRINT OR TYPE** FORM HCFA-1500 (12-90) FORM OWCP-1500 FORM RRB-1500

"–52"   Reduced Services

Just as the unusual services modifier ("-22") is used to denote abnormally difficult or time-consuming procedures, the reduced service modifier "-52" signifies the opposite: that a procedure was reduced or eliminated in part.

Consider the physician who removes a coccygeal pressure ulcer and performs a coccygectomy but does not use a primary suture or skin flap closure. (The physician wants to continue cleansing the wound for a period of time before closing.) The proper way to report the procedure would be:

15920-52

Since the procedure as described was not performed in its entirety, the "-52" modifier is used to indicate that the procedure is "reduced," or less than what is described. At a later date the physician would code for the appropriate wound closure procedure.

Many coders mistakenly use the "-52" modifier to reduce a charge for a patient who is indigent. The physician performs the procedure or service as described, but does not want to charge the patient the full amount. The "-52" modifier should not be used for this purpose. If the reduced fee results in a charge that is less than that which you would charge a Medicare or Medicaid patient for the same service or procedure, a legal argument could be made that you are violating Medicare and Medicaid regulations. Remember, for any service, procedure or supply, you cannot charge other patients an amount less than you charge your Medicare or Medicaid patients.

There are ways around this difficulty. You could treat the patient for no charge. Alternatively, you can charge your normal amount and bill them as you would other patients. You can explain to indigent patients that regulations require you to charge them an amount equal to what you charge your Medicare and Medicaid patients. You can also explain that you understand their financial situation and that you will be satisfied with whatever amount they are able to pay. After submitting three or so statements to the patient, it may be possible to write any remaining amount due off your books.

However, be sure to note in the patient's record that you have written off, or not pursued collection of unpaid balances, as a result of his or her financial situation. Failure to do so could create problems if your practice is audited.

Many physicians are not aware that approximately 40 percent of the indigent population who are eligible for Medicaid benefits are not Medicaid beneficiaries. Often this is due to ignorance (or pride) on the part of the patient. You may find that many of the hospitals in your area are willing to help indigent patients become Medicaid enrollees. The physician should check with the hospital(s) where he has staff privileges to see if he can help eligible patients obtain Medicaid benefits.

Finally, a physician may wish to reduce fees for a "professional courtesy" given to a colleague, colleague's family member or for a friend. It is not uncommon for the physician to accept assignment from the payer in such cases, and consider the amount paid by the third party payer to be payment in full. This custom can cause problems if the practice is audited by the payer, as it is considered insurance fraud. In such situations, inform the payer that as a professional courtesy you accept their payment as payment in full. The payer is likely to reimburse you 64 percent of the allowable for the service(s) (80 percent of their normal 80 percent payment, or 64 percent of the allowed charge). Use of the reduced service modifier would not be appropriate for billing professional courtesies.

"-53"   Discontinued Procedure

There are occasions when a physician needs to terminate a surgical procedure or diagnostic service prior to completion. Situations necessitating termination might include a patient's inability to tolerate the procedure, or the development of complications arising during a surgery which do not allow the surgical procedure to be completed. In such cases the "-53" modifier is listed with the code for the procedure that was terminated. It is to your benefit to provide a special report with the claim that explains the unusual circumstances that lead to termination and describes what portions of the procedure were rendered so that the payer is able to a make a payment determination.

This modifier is not to be confused with the reduced service modifier "-52", which applies when the physician's services were completed, but consisted of something less than described by the code. Also, as cautioned in CPT, "This modifier ("-53") is not used to report the elective cancellation of a procedure prior to the patient's anesthesia induction and/or surgical preparation in the operating suite."   In such cases, the physician may bill for any preoperative services provided, such as E/M visits, that would normally be included with in the surgical package for the procedure that was canceled.

"–54"   Surgical Care Only
"–55"   Postoperative Management Only
"–56"   Preoperative Management Only

The surgical package applies to codes in the Surgery section (except those procedures with stars) and includes the operation, postoperative care, and in some cases, the preoperative care. However, there may be occasions when it is necessary for one physician to perform only a portion of the package with a different physician performing the remainder. Consider the physician who handles the preop and operation on a patient and then must leave town to attend a medical conference. Another physician manages the operative follow-up. Modifiers can be used by each physician to charge for that portion of the package which he performed. The surgical package modifiers are defined as follows:

"–54"   This modifier is used when charging for the operation itself and includes any digital blocks, local anesthetics or topical anesthetics given by the surgeon.

"–55"   This modifier is for billing the postoperative management portion.

"–56"   Bill the preoperative management portion using this modifier.

Continuing the above example, assume that the surgeon performed the preoperative work and a bone cyst excision and then left for a medical conference. He codes:

28100-56/54

The physician who managed the postoperative care could code:

28100-55

Note that the second physician could have chosen to bill hospital visits and/or office visits as appropriate instead of listing the surgical procedure with the "-55" postoperative care modifier. In such cases, the second surgeon may wish to add the "-55" postop modifier to the hospital and/or office visit charges.

Should the surgeon who performed the preoperative care and operation fail to limit the charge to that portion of the package which he performed, the second physician who provides the postop will not be paid by the insurer. From the insurance company's point of view, the postop was paid when the first surgeon was paid. Furthermore, if the first surgeon bills for the complete service, but does not provide follow-up, the surgeon is billing for services he did not render. In legal terms this is called *fraud*. Some exceptions to this situation exist, for example, when the physician bills for the complete surgery but makes arrangements with another physician to cover while he is out of town. If the other physician does not bill the patient and does not accept a fee from the surgeon for following the patient, then there is probably nothing inappropriate about the arrangement. Many physicians have a relationship with other physicians, as in group practices and clinics, where they cover for each other under such circumstances, and the only form of compensation is reciprocation.

"–57" Decision for Surgery

In response to cost containment concerns in healthcare, many third party payers are embracing increasingly stringent surgical package guidelines. This is especially true of those adopting the Medicare fee schedule and its attendant billing rules. Modifier "-57" was originally placed in CPT by the AMA (as were several other modifiers) so that Medicare could better administer its RBRVS-related surgical package payment guidelines, despite the fact that Medicare had a special HCPCS National modifier ("-QI") for this purpose. These Medicare guidelines include denial of payments for presurgical E/M services performed the day of or the day before surgery—unless the decision for the surgery was made during one of those E/M services. In such cases the "-57" modifier is added to the E/M service during which the decision for surgery was made, so as to alert payers utilizing preoperative payment guidelines, that the service is compensable.

To illustrate appropriate use of the modifier, consider the situation where a neurosurgeon consults on a trauma patient in the ER. The patient is admitted by a general surgeon and it is agreed that the neurosurgeon will wait until the patient stabilizes and make further evaluations of the patient's neurological problems before determining if a neurosurgical procedure is warranted. The neurosurgeon sees the patient in the hospital on the day after admission and decides that neurosurgery is necessary. On the next day the neurosurgery is performed. Assuming the payer utilizes the same preoperative service guidelines established by Medicare, the neurosurgeon's E/M services might be billed as follows:

99244   Consultation in ER

99254-57 Consultation on admitted patient during which decision for surgery was made

"-58"   *Staged or Related Procedure or Service by the Same Physician During the Postoperative Period*

This modifier was created to minimize confusion that can arise when a provider performs services during a postoperative period that are either related to or part of a planned series of services. Without this modifier, a payer might assume that the second and subsequent procedures in a series are repeat procedures and deny on the basis of duplicate billing. Or, in the case of a related procedure performed during a surgical package, deny the service believing it to be included in the surgical package. This modifier is designed for use in three distinct billing situations.

1. If at the time of the original procedure it was known that an additional procedure(s) would be performed, the "-58" modifier is to be added to the additional procedure(s) when it is performed. For example, an ophthalmologist performs trabeculoplasty by laser service on a patient over three treatment sessions. Billing would be as follows:

65855	Reported on claim listing the first session
65855-58	Reported on the claim identifying the second session
65855-58	Reported on the claim which lists the final session

2. If a surgery performed during the postoperative period is more extensive or difficult than the initial procedure, the "-58" modifier is added to the postoperative surgical procedure code. As an example, a dermatologist removes lesions from a patient's back during the first visit. The laboratory report identifies several of the lesions as malignant, requiring additional surgery to ensure that the lesion margins are clear. Assuming that the second series of procedures is more difficult that the initial procedure, the "-58" modifier would be used on the second series procedures.

3. When therapeutic services are provided following diagnostic surgical procedures, the "-58" modifier should be added to the therapy service codes. Using the dermatological example above, suppose the dermatologist biopsied a lesion (the diagnostic surgical procedure). Three days later the lab identified the lesion as malignant, and the dermatologist excised the lesion. The "-58" modifier would be listed with the code for the excision.

The "-58" modifier is not to be used when reporting <u>unrelated</u> procedures performed during the postoperative period. These situations are to be handled by use of modifer "-79." Modifier "-58" should also not be listed when reporting a <u>related surgery performed in the operating room</u> during the postoperative period. Use modifier "-78" in these circumstances.

"-59" *Distinct Procedural Service*

This modifier has been added to assist Medicare and other payers in distinguishing procedures that were performed separate from other procedures performed by the physician on the patient on the same day. CPT identifies the following types of situations where this modifier would be relevant:

- Different sessions
- Different patient encounters
- Different procedures or surgeries
- Treating different sites or different organ systems
- Separate incisions or excisions

- Separate lesions
- Separate injuries

There are two caveats related to use of modifier "-59". First, if the procedures or services are normally reported together, then use of the "-59" modifier is not considered appropriate. Second, if another modifier, such as for multiple procedures or bilateral procedure, better explains the circumstances of the services, do not use the "-59" modifier.

"–62" Two Surgeons

The two surgeons modifier is utilized in situations where two physicians, usually in different specialties, perform different aspects of the same procedure. Both physicians would generally list the same CPT code along with the "-62" modifier. For example, if a neurosurgeon and an orthopedic surgeon performed different aspects of a laminectomy, each would report the following:

63045-62

If two surgeons are treating the patient during the same operative session but are performing different procedures (i.e., they report different CPT codes) then the two surgeon modifier is not required. Each surgeon will report his or her services as he would normally.

Due to increasing third party payer restrictions, it may be helpful to send a special report (KISS letter) with the claims which explains and justifies the need for two primary surgeons. Some payers will assume the procedure can be successfully performed by a primary surgeon and an assistant surgeon, and thus delay payment until support documentation justifying the need for a second primary surgeon is supplied. If the surgery is elective or nonemergency and requires precertification by the patient's health insurer, it is advisable to seek approval for the second primary surgeon at the time of precertification. This will help minimize payment delays and denials.

"–66" Surgical Team

Certain complex surgical procedures require the skills of more than two surgeons. A good example is the surgical team which transplants a liver. As with the "-62" modifier, the physicians performing the surgery usually have different skills or specialties. Each member of the team would add the "-66" modifier to the procedures he performed as part of the surgical team.

As with the two surgeons situation, it may be necessary to communicate the need for the team of surgeons to the insurance company. This is especially true in cases where the need for the team may not be immediately obvious to the claims processor.

"–76" Repeat Procedure By Same Physician
"–77" Repeat Procedure By Another Physician

These two modifiers are to be used when the procedure has been "... repeated subsequent to the original service." You will need to submit these modifiers when applicable as, without them, the insurance company may think you accidentally double-billed for the service. Consider a patient who is brought to the hospital with internal hemorrhaging that is repaired surgically. Three days after surgery the patient begins hemorrhaging again and the surgeon must perform the same repair again. Would you use the repeat procedure modifier on the second repair? Yes, assuming that the same procedure code was being reported. If a different physician had performed the second repair, he would use the "-77" modifier.

It may be necessary to send a special report with the claim explaining why the procedure needed to be repeated. This is appropriate where the need for the repeat may not be clear to the payer.

"–78"   Return to the Operating Room for a Related Procedure During the Postoperative Period

This and the next modifier ("-79") were developed to accommodate changes in reimbursement and billing policies that are part of the Medicare Fee Schedule. Medicare (and some other payers) will deny payment for treatment of postsurgical complications that arise during the surgical follow-up period *unless* treatment is performed in the operating room. For example, if the patient was initially treated for internal hemorrhaging and began hemorrhaging again necessitating a trip back to the operating room, Medicare would likely cover the service provided the "-78" modifier is listed with the CPT surgery code(s) related to treating the hemorrhage. Medicare policy limits payment to the intraoperative portion only (i.e., a fee not including pre- and postoperative services) when related procedures during a postoperative period are performed. As an example, if your normal charge for the procedure is $1,500, Medicare may reduce the payment to an amount less than $1,000.

"–79"   Unrelated Procedure or Service by the Same Physician During the Postoperative Period

If during the postoperative period for a surgery the patient develops a problem unrelated to the initial surgery which requires additional procedures or services, these should be reported separately and accompanied by the "-79" modifier. For example, if during the follow-up for a fracture of the arm, the patient falls and breaks her hip, the procedures and services related to treating the hip problem should be listed with the "-79" modifier. Note that this modifier should not be used with E/M services provided during a follow-up period; the "-24" modifier is provided for that purpose.

"–80"   Assistant Surgeon
"–81"   Minimum Assistant Surgeon
"–82"   Assistant Surgeon (Where Qualified Resident Not Available)

These modifiers are used to identify surgical services provided by assistants. A normal surgical assist is billed by reporting the appropriate CPT surgery code (that is, the code(s) used by the primary surgeon) plus the "-80" modifier. In cases where a second assistant surgeon is warranted, his surgery code(s) would list the "-81" minimum assistant surgeon modifier. It is important to note that assistant surgeons submit their charges on claims separate from those of the primary surgeon, even if both are from the same group practice or clinic. The reason is straightforward: each physician must submit under his own unique identification number, and by doing so, accept responsibility for the services he provided.

Many hospitals have surgical residency programs which provide qualified resident assistants. In hospitals where qualified residents are available, most payers will not reimburse for the services of a nonresident assistant surgeon arguing that the fees they pay for the patient's hospitalization, use of the surgical suite, etc., include the services of the resident assistant. With one exception, the non-resident assistant's services in such situations will usually not be covered. The exception exists when, for whatever reason, a qualified resident assistant was not available at the time of the patient's surgery. In these cases the non-resident assistant surgeon may bill for the assist by adding the "-82" modifier to the surgery code(s). However, and it's a big "however," the assistant needs a letter from the hospital's administration stating that a qualified resident was not available thus necessitating the services of the non-resident assistant surgeon. A copy of the note or letter should be submitted with the claim for the assistant surgeon's services. Of course, if a hospital does not have a surgical residency program, the assistant surgeon will use the "-80" modifier.

"–90" Reference (Outside) Laboratory

When the physician bills the patient for lab work that was performed by an outside (or "reference") lab, add the "-90" modifier to the lab procedure codes. Physicians should never bill Medicare or Medicaid patients for lab work done outside their office.

"–99" Multiple Modifiers

If two or more different modifiers are added to the same procedure code, a third modifier, "-99," can be added to alert the payer to the fact that two or more modifiers are associated with the procedure, though it is rarely required for payment.

For example, to report for the physician who assisted on a bilateral subcutaneous mastectomy (19182) you would code as shown below. Since the procedure is bilateral, you must list each procedure separately. In this case, each procedure will list the assistant surgeon modifier ("-82"), and the second, bilateral procedure requires the use of the "-50" modifier. Since there are two modifiers on the second procedure, the "-99" modifier is listed.

> 19182-82 (for the first procedure)
> 19182-99 ("-99" for multiple modifiers on second procedure)
> 19182-82 ("-82" for assist, qualified resident not available)
> 19182-50 ("-50" for the second, bilateral procedure)

Most payers require a charge for each line used on the claim form. Thus, you may want to string modifiers together on the same line on the claim form. Using the above example, you would code:

> 19182-82
> 19182-99 82/50

It is generally a good idea to list modifiers in numeric order. That is, the highest numbered modifier first, next highest second, etc. In any case, the "-99" multiple modifier, when used, must always be listed as the first modifier.

HCPCS National Modifiers

There are 150 modifiers listed in the 1997 HCPCS National coding system. These modifiers may be grouped as follows:

- Modifiers relevant to the provision and billing of medical and surgical services;
- Modifiers for use in describing and qualifying the provision of anesthesia;
- Modifiers for use in identifying services of "non-MDs";
- Modifiers related to provision of supplies and equipment (e.g., durable medical equipment);
- Modifiers for use in identifying the place of origin and destination of ambulance services.

In this chapter, the discussion is limited to the first three categories of modifiers. If you need more information about the other HCPCS National modifiers, you should obtain a copy of the HCPCS National coding system.

The National (and Local) modifiers are reported in the same manner that you report CPT modifiers: to the right of the code.

National modifiers are different from CPT modifiers in that they are alpha/numeric rather than numeric. They always consist of either one letter, a letter and a number, or two letters. The modifiers that you may have occasion to use are listed below along with their definitions, but they are not intended to be exhaustive.

"–AP"   *Determination of refractive state was not performed in the course of diagnostic ophthalmological examination*

Medicare (and possibly Medicaid) does not reimburse for refractions and the fees paid physicians under the Medicare Fee Schedule for general ophthalmology services (92002 through 92014) do not include refraction. If refraction is performed, it should be billed separately by use of code 92015 in addition to the eye examination.

"E1"   *Upper left, eyelid*
"E2"   *Lower left, eyelid*
"E3"   *Upper right, eyelid*
"E4"   *Lower right, eyelid*

These modifiers are to be listed with procedures performed on the eyelids. For example, the correction of trichiasis, with a free mucous membrane graft would be coded as follows:

   67835-E1

"–EP"   *Service Provided as Part of Medicaid Early Periodic Screening, Diagnosis and Treatment (EPSDT) Program*

This modifier was added to the HCPCS National system to use when reporting to Medicaid payers services that are part of an EPSDT program.

"F1" through "FA"   *Finger and Thumb Modifiers*

Each of the ten modifiers in this series is used to identify the particular finger (digit) or thumb on which a procedure was performed. As an example, drainage of the tendon sheath of the third digit on the right hand would be coded as:

   26020-F8

"–FP" Service Provided as Part of Medicaid Family Planning Program

Use of modifier "-FP" is limited to communicating to Medicaid that the service(s) being billed were related to a Family Planning program.

"-GC" *This Service Has Been Performed in Part by a Resident Under the Direction of a Teaching Physician*

"-GE" *This Service has been performed by a resident without the presence of a teaching physician under the primary care exception*

These two modifiers were added to the HCPCS National system in response to an initiative by Medicare's Office of the Inspector General whereby major teaching institutions were being penalized for billing services that were being provided by residents but being reported by the teaching physicians. Use of these modifiers, as described, will help clarify who performed the service and minimize misunderstandings between Medicare and teaching physicians.

"–LS"   FDA-monitored intraocular lens implant

Physicians performing intraocular lens implants as part of the FDA monitoring program would add this modifier to the appropriate implant code(s).

"–LT" *Left side   Used to identify procedures performed on the left side of the body*

When performing bilateral procedures, it is helpful to list this modifier next to the procedure which was performed on the left side of the body; for example, left breast, left eye, left kidney, etc.

"–RT" *Right side. Used to identify procedures performed on the right side of the body*

As with the "-LT" modifier, use this modifier on bilateral procedures to note the right side of the body, or in other situations where clarification of body side may be needed to expedite payment.

"-SF"   Second opinion ordered by a professional review organization (PRO) per section 9401, P.L. 99-272 (100% reimbursement -- no Medicare deductible or coinsurance)

If a second opinion is ordered by a professional review organization under contract with Medicare, the physician providing the opinion would use modifier "-SF" on the appropriate additional opinion consultation code. The "-SF" modifier is similar to CPT modifier 32 for mandated services, but is used expressly for PRO second opinion requests under the Medicare program.

"-TA" through "T9"   Toe modifiers

As with the digit and thumb modifiers discussed above, HCPCS provides modifiers to allow for identification of the specific toe upon which a procedure was performed.

"–VP" *Aphakic Patient*

Aphakia is a condition where part or all of the lens of the eye is missing. This modifier is used primarily by ophthalmologists (possibly optometrists) when reporting services provided to an aphakic Medicare patient.

National Modifiers for Anesthesia Services

Nine modifiers are listed in the National system for use by anesthesiologists. These modifiers are added to CPT Anesthesia Service codes as appropriate.

"-AA"   Anesthesia services performed personally by anesthesiologist
"-AB"   Medical direction of own employee(s) by anesthesiologist (not more than four employees)
"-AC"   Medical direction of other than own employees by anesthesiologist (not more than four employees)
"-AD"   Medical supervision by a physician: more than four concurrent anesthesia procedures
"-AE"   Direction of residents in furnishing not more than two concurrent anesthesia services—attending physician relationship met
"-AF"   Anesthesia complicated by total body hypothermia
"-AG"   Anesthesia for emergency surgery on a patient who is moribund or who has an incapacitating systemic disease that is a constant threat to life (may warrant additional charge)
"-QK"   Medical direction of two, three or four concurrent anesthesia procedures involving qualified individuals
"-QS"   Monitoring anesthesia care services

In addition to the modifiers listed above for anesthesiologists, some payers may accept the physical status modifiers shown in the CPT book. These modifiers range from "-P1" through "-P6." As a practical matter, most private payers will only accept the "-P4" and "-P5" modifiers which communicate that the patient was gravely ill when the anesthesia was provided.

National Modifiers for Non-MD Services

Several of the most important non-M.D. (and non-D.O.) modifiers are discussed below.

"–AH"   Clinical Psychologist
"–AJ"   Clinical Social Worker

Independently practicing licensed clinical psychologists and clinical social workers may provide services to Medicare patients. Such services are limited to those allowed by state law. In all cases the psychologists and social workers must accept assignment. These modifiers would be reported with services when billing Medicare.

"–AN"   PA services for other than assistant-at-surgery, nonteam member
"–AS"   PA services for assistant-at-surgery (nonteam member)
"–AU"   Physician Assistant for other than assistant-at-surgery, team member service

These modifiers are used for reporting covered services of licensed (or certified) physician assistants.

"-QX"   CRNA service: with medical direction by a physician
"-QZ"   CRNA service: without medical direction by a physician

Nurse anesthetists should list these modifiers, as appropriate, with anesthesia codes when billing Medicare for their services.

MEDICINE

In this section we will review key concepts related to proper use of codes in the Medicine section of CPT. The material in this section is by no means exhaustive, but focuses on issues that are likely to cause difficulty when coding. Specific topics covered in this section include:

- Immunization Injections
- Therapeutic and Diagnostic Injections
- Psychiatry
- Dialysis
- Ophthalmology
- Cardiovascular Services
- Allergy and Clinical Immunology
- Chemotherapy Administration
- Special Services and Reports

Immunization Injections (Codes 90700–90749)

It is surprising how few offices are aware that when a patient comes to the office to receive an immunization injection by the nurse or assistant, and the immunization is the only service rendered, a Level I established patient office visit charge may be added in addition to the charge for the immunization. Refer to the notes associated with immunization injections in the CPT book.

Therapeutic or Diagnostic Injections (Codes 90782– 90799)

These codes are used to report injections of therapeutic agents, such as antibiotics, as well as diagnostic agents. Until the relatively recent acceptance by many payers of the HCPCS National injection codes ("J" series in HCPCS), it was not uncommon for practices to bundle the charge for the supply of the injected substance with the injection. Alternatively, some practices would bill for both the injection and for the supply, the latter charge made by reporting CPT's all purpose supply code, 99070. Today it is more common for practices to bill for the injection from the code range 90782-90799 and for the substance with the appropriate HCPCS National or Local code.

As an example, a physician who administers dalteparin sodium subcutaneously to a Medicare patient would bill the service as follows:

90782   Therapeutic or diagnostic injection; subcutaneous

J1645   Supply of Dalteparin sodium

Alternatively, for those payers that do not utilize HCPCS, CPT's all purpose supply code 99070 would be listed instead of J1645. In these situations it may be necessary to provide basic information with the claim explaining what drug was administered in order for the payer to adjudicate the claim.

Medicare and many other payers do not allow therapeutic or diagnostic injection charges if the injection is provided in conjunction with an E/M service. In such cases you can bill for the E/M service and the supply of the injectable. If the injection is not performed in association with an E/M service, it may be itemized.

In addition to the above, there are four circumstances when these codes should not be reported. First, they are not used when reporting injections of dyes or other materials associated with diagnostic radiology procedures. The Surgery section of CPT provides codes for these types of injections. Second, they should not be listed for injections of chemotherapeutic agents. CPT provides a separate set of codes for chemotherapy injections. Third, these codes are not used when providing surgical injection services (such as an injection into an inflamed bursa) or for aspiration (such as aspirating blood from a ligament injury). You will also find codes for these injection and aspiration services in the Surgery section of CPT. Finally, you should not list these injections when performed in conjunction with prolonged services.

Psychiatry (Codes 90801–90899)

Careful reading of the psychiatry notes in the CPT book reveals several often overlooked billing opportunities. First, when appropriate, hospital E/M services can be billed in addition to psychotherapy for hospitalized patients. For example, if the psychiatrist reviews patient activity reports, orders tests, discusses patient management with ancillary staff, and provides psychotherapy, the psychiatrist may bill for both the psychotherapy and the hospital service. On days when the psychiatrist does not provide psychotherapy, but reviews records, orders tests, etc., for a patient, he can bill for the appropriate level of hospital service. Of course, the patient's medical record should show evidence of the services performed.

Second, psychiatrists often charge for the "General Clinical Psychiatric Diagnostic Or Evaluative Interview Procedures" (code 90801) when they could be billing for consultations. If another physician or other referring source asks the psychiatrist for his or her opinion regarding a patient's problem(s), it is likely that the service provided by the psychiatrist is consultative in nature. Refer to the discussion on consultations earlier in this chapter. If the referring source is transferring the management of the patient's psychiatric problems to the psychiatrist, then code 90801 may be the appropriate one to use when reporting the initial diagnostic or evaluative procedures.

Third, there are codes for various services which may go unreported and unbilled because psychiatrists are unaware of them. These include codes for environmental intervention (90882), interpretation or explanation of results of psychiatric tests (90887), and preparation of psychiatric reports (90889). Psychiatrists should familiarize themselves with these codes and their definitions.

Finally, psychiatrists may not be aware of how they can use the E/M service codes (office visits, hospital visits, etc.) to report such services as conferences with the parents of children with behavioral problems, reevaluation of hospital patients, and the like. A review of the examples associated with the definitions of the levels of E/M services provided for your reference with the E/M codes may help you better understand how the levels of services might be used under a variety of circumstances.

Dialysis (Codes 90918–90999)

Special attention should be paid to the notes appearing with the dialysis codes in CPT. Dialysis procedures (90935-90947) invariably include all evaluation and management services provided to the patient by the physician. And, if E/M services for conditions unrelated to the dialysis procedure are provided during the dialysis encounter, such services may not be billed separately. For example, if the physician is providing a hemofiltration service (90945) to a patient and also evaluates the patient's chest cold, a separate charge for the evaluation of the cold may not be made.

End stage renal disease services (ESRD) can be billed on a monthly basis (codes 90918-90921) or daily basis (codes 90922-90925). Billing by use of the daily service code should be limited to those instances when the physician is providing <u>less</u> than a full month's worth of ESRD services. Physicians and staff should also note that the monthly and daily ESRD codes are differentiated by patient age.

Ophthalmology (Codes 92002–92488)

The coding and reimbursement issues facing ophthalmologists are unique in several important ways. Of foremost importance, ophthalmologists provide levels of diagnostic and treatment services which have been viewed by the CPT editorial panel as requiring definitions distinct from those given for E/M codes. The complexities associated with proper use of these service codes are frequently overlooked by novice billers. To better understand these issues, turn your CPT book to the beginning of the ophthalmology notes.

Two types of information are provided in the notes. First, definitions for intermediate and comprehensive ophthalmological services, along with examples, are given for reference. These are discussed in detail below. Second, CPT provides guidance related to reporting special ophthalmological services. In general, if a special service, such as an extended color vision examination, is provided in addition to the normal ophthalmological service, it may be billed separately.

Definitions for intermediate and comprehensive ophthalmological services are outlined below.

Intermediate Ophthalmological Services

The key features of this service are:

1. The patient has either a new condition, or an existing condition complicated by a new diagnostic or management problem. The new problem may or may not be related to the existing condition.

2. The service includes the following:
    • History
    • General medical observation
    • External ocular and adnexal exam
    • Other diagnostic services (as needed)
    • Use of mydriasis (as needed)

Comprehensive Ophthalmological Services

The key features of this level of service include:

1. It may take more than one physician/patient encounter to complete the service.

2. The following will be performed:
    • History
    • General medical observation
    • External and ophthalmoscopic exam

- Gross visual fields exam
- Basic sensorimotor exam
- Initiation of diagnostic procedures and treatment as needed

3. As indicated, the service might include:
   - Biomicroscopy
   - Exam with cycloplegia or mydriasis

Ophthalmology offices which prescribe and supply contact lenses should be aware that the prescription of contacts is not considered part of the general ophthalmological service. It is charged separately. Furthermore, your charge for prescribing contacts will include fitting, and possibly the supply, of the lenses. If the physician chooses to charge separately for the supply of the contact lenses, code 92391 or 92396 should be used for the supply and the "-26" professional component modifier will be added to the prescription and fitting code (range 92310 - 92313).

To properly bill for the ophthalmology services described in the Medicine section of CPT, be sure to carefully read *all* the notes provided.

Cardiovascular (Codes 92950–93799)

The cardiovascular service codes are the largest group in the Medicine section of CPT. They include therapeutic services, cardiography, echocardiography, cardiac catheterization, intracardiac electrophysical procedures, other vascular studies, and other procedures. In addition to the recommendation that you carefully review all notes relevant to those cardiology codes reported by your practice, you may wish to observe the following related to echocardiography and cardiac catheterization.

Echocardiography services include:

1. Obtaining ultrasonic signals from the heart and great arteries with
   - two-dimensional image, and/or
   - Doppler ultrasonic signal documentation.

2. Interpretation and report.

If interpretation and report are performed separately, use the "-26" modifier on the echocardiography code.

Cardiac catheterization services include:

1. Introduction, positioning and repositioning of catheter(s), when necessary.

2. Recording of intracardiac and intravascular pressure.

3. Obtaining blood samples for measurement of blood gases and/or dye (or other) dilution curves.

4. Cardiac output measurements, with or without electrode catheter placement.

5. Final evaluation and report.

If multiple procedures from the cardiac catheterization section are performed on a patient on the same day, it is not appropriate to add the "-51" multiple procedure modifier to the additional procedures.

Allergy and Clinical Immunology (Codes 95000–95199)

There are two areas in this section which can lead to billing errors. First, be aware of the note associated with the title "Other Therapy." It informs you that when the physician has a conference with a patient regarding the use of " ... mechanical and electronic devices ... , climatotherapy, physical therapy, occupational and recreational therapy ... ," the appropriate E/M code should be reported.

Second, allergen Immunotherapy codes 95120 through 95170 include provision of the allergenic extracts by the physician whereas codes 95115 and 95117 do not. When billing these latter codes you may use the CPT code 99070 to report the supply of the extracts. All codes in this allergen immunotherapy section include those professional services related to providing the therapy. For example, you would not separately bill the patient for time spent by the physician and/or nurse observing the patient following administration of the extract, unless the services were prolonged as defined in the E/M section of this book.

Chemotherapy Injections (Codes 96500–96549)

Many physicians who bill for chemotherapy often overlook the notes associated with chemotherapy injections. They state that the injections are " ... independent of the patient's visit." However, an office visit should not be charged unless the physician provides services beyond the injection itself. Typically, physicians bill separately for the chemotherapeutic agents. Code 96545 is used for billing for the supply of chemotherapeutic drug(s). If the patient is a Medicare or Medicaid patient, refer to the chemotherapy drug codes listed in the HCPCS National system.

Special Services and Reports (Codes 99000–99090)

This is perhaps the most misunderstood and misused subsection of CPT. It contains codes which are to be added *in addition to* the basic service or procedure. To help you understand these codes and their uses, they are discussed in detail below.

Handling codes (99000 – 99002)

Codes 99000 and 99001 are used to report the handling and/or conveyance of a specimen from the doctor's office (99000) or from a location other than the doctor's office (99001) to an outside laboratory. Code 99002 is reserved for handling, conveyance and/or other ordering services related to devices, such as prostheses. These codes do not include collection services, such as blood draws, which may (depending upon carrier policy) be reported separately.

Postoperative Follow–Up Visits (99024)

This code is generally used to report visits when the patient is seen after surgery (hospital, office, home, etc.) but for which there is no charge because the visit is part of the normal surgical follow-up. Some practices always provide patients with a superbill or charge ticket showing proof of the visit (patients may need this proof to be able to deduct mileage, etc., from their taxes). Since code 99024 invariably has a $0 profile, you can list this code for the visit and not have to worry if the patient should mistakenly file the visit with their carrier.

New Patient — Starred Procedure (99025)

As you will learn in the next section on Surgery, if a new patient is seen by the physician and the major procedure performed is one of the starred surgical procedures, code 99025 may be used to describe the initial visit (history, exam, starting medical record, etc.) instead of the usual E/M code. If a payer rejects code 99025, consider using code 99201 or 99202 instead, as justified by the level of E/M service provided.

After Hour and Holiday Charges (99050 – 99054)

When a physician sees a patient after his normal office hours, late at night, or on a Sunday or holiday, the physician may wish to add charges for the inconvenience. The codes in this group can be used for this purpose. However, not all carriers reimburse for these codes, and in those cases alternative methods of reporting should be considered (e.g., use of the "-22" modifier, special reports, etc.).

Code 99050 is used when the physician sees a patient after his office has actually closed. If the physician normally closes the office at 5:00 p.m. but is still seeing patients at 5:45, the physician would not bill the after hour codes to those patients seen after 5:00 p.m. If, by contrast, the physician were to see a patient in the nursing home, hospital, emergency department, etc., after his office had closed and outside his normal hours, then the code might be considered.

To make an additional charge for seeing patients late at night (between 10:00 p.m. and 8:00 am), code 99052 would be appropriate. Also, for patients seen on Sundays or holidays, code 99054 could be reported. Free standing emergency clinics would not use these codes for late night, holiday or Sunday visits if the clinic is normally open at those times.

Remember that these codes are to be added in addition to the codes used to report other services, such as E/M, procedures, etc.

Other Location (99056)

Some patients may request that the physician provide services normally performed in the physician's office at a location more convenient to the patient. For example, a traveling corporate executive who becomes ill may ask that the physician perform an exam in the executive's hotel suite. In such cases this code could be used either in place of, or in addition to, the service charge for the exam. (It might be argued that the physician could bill a home visit plus the 99056 code, as the hotel was the patient's "home" at the time of the visit.)

Emergency Office Services (99058)

Both the use of code 99058 and its reimbursement will depend upon several factors. First, it should only be used when a patient is seen in the office and the patient's problem can be classified as an emergency. Second, some carriers pay in addition to the charges made for other services such as wound repair, fracture reduction, and the like. Other carriers will deny payment on the code. The key factor is the patient's diagnosis. Finally, some physicians may elect to use this code by itself to describe the services provided to the patient during the visit. That is, it is the only code reported.

Supplies (99070)

CPT is not a system for coding supplies. Apart from the occasional specific supply codes for such items as spectacles, contact lenses, chemotherapeutic agents and radioactive elements, the code you will use for items supplied to the patient will be 99070. Think of it as the all-purpose, generic supply code. When billing patients for supplies it will help to keep the following factors in mind.

Many payers are now accepting HCPCS National codes for supplies instead of CPT code 99070. There are advantages to using HCPCS codes. First, when listing 99070 you are invariably required to submit a special report describing the supply. You avoid this problem when billing with a HCPCS code that describes the supply you provided. Second, there are no specific payer allowed amounts associated with code 99070 and as such you may need to justify your charge for the supply each time you submit the code. Again, with HCPCS, the payer is likely to have established reasonable payment amounts for each code. Third, Medicare and most Medicaid programs require that you submit a HCPCS National or Local code when billing for supplies; code 99070 will simply not be accepted. Finally, Medicare and other payers that have adopted the Medicare fee schedule, generally bundle charges for surgical trays and related supplies with payment for procedures and services.

Educational Supplies (99071)

These are items such as books, video tapes, audio cassettes, pamphlets, etc., which are purchased by the physician and provided to the patient. If you or your patients expect to be reimbursed from carriers for these supplies, a special report may need to be sent to justify the supply.

Group Educational Services (99078)

When the physician provides educational services to a group of patients, each patient can be billed using code 99078. Patient group education is sometimes provided to patients who need help with regard to cardiac problems, diabetes, pregnancy, and dialysis.

Special Reports (99080)

Use this code when billing a patient for preparing insurance or other reports that go well beyond the standard communication. For example, if extensive documentation needs to be prepared to support a claim for a routinely performed procedure because the carrier is denying payment, you may wish to charge the patient for the time and effort involved. Obviously, carriers are reluctant to reimburse for preparation of reports unless they have specifically requested that they be prepared. The charge for billing such reports will likely have to be paid by the patient. Therefore, discretion should be used when reporting this code. Medicare does not permit billing of the patient for these services. The carrier may pay a fee if it requested that you prepare documentation.

Unusual Travel (99082)

If the physician escorts a patient, travels to a distant location to examine or treat a patient or transports a patient, code 99082 can be used to bill for the travel time. As with many other of the special service and report codes, justification (such as a KISS letter) may be required in order for the physician or patient to receive reimbursement from the insurance company.

SURGERY

The Surgery section of CPT is the longest and technically most difficult to use. Proper surgery coding requires more than just understanding the key concepts you will learn in this chapter—you need to have an understanding of the procedures being performed. As such, physicians should not depend exclusively on their staff to code surgical procedures unless the staff has extensive related experience (e.g., surgical nurses or certified physician assistants).

In this chapter, you will learn about the following topics:

- Organization of the Surgery section.
- Surgical package concept.
- Follow-up for diagnostic procedures.
- Separate procedure concept.
- Coding starred procedures.
- Add-on codes.

Other covered topics will include those related to lesions, wound repair, grafts, orthopedic services, injections, procedures, and maternity care. This section is not intended to be an exhaustive technical guide to the subtle variations between codes which describe similar procedures. Its purpose is to provide you with an overall understanding of the key Surgery concepts as well as insights into those coding areas most likely to cause you problems when billing.

Organization of the Surgery Codes

There is a logic to the presentation of codes in the Surgery section of CPT. Recall that you previously learned that surgery codes are first grouped by body system. For example, all procedures related to the skin and subcutaneous tissues are listed under the Integumentary System and procedures related to muscle and bone are grouped in the Musculoskeletal System. Within each of these body systems, the codes are further grouped by anatomic sites. It is important to note that the last code in each anatomic site is the unlisted procedure code. In those situations which require use of an unlisted procedure, the code you use will be the last one in the anatomic site related to the procedure performed by the physician.

As an example, suppose the physician performed a repair on a patient's esophagus. If, after searching the CPT Index and the codes listed under "Esophagus" in the Digestive System, you were unable to locate a code which described the procedure, the unlisted code you would report would be the last code under Esophagus, 43499.

Surgical Package Concept

According to CPT, physicians' charges for surgery include the following:

- The operation itself;
- Any local anesthetics, topical anesthetics, or metacarpal/digital blocks (if used);
- Normal, uncomplicated postoperative follow-up care.

Taken together these items comprise what is known as the "surgical package." It is considered improper for the physician to itemize and charge separately for these items, and virtually all third party payers will deny payment if these services are itemized. As you will learn further on in this section, Medicare has its own surgical package rules.

The idea behind package billing for surgery is the predictability of the components. Each surgical procedure defined in CPT is unique. The length of time and skill required varies from procedure to procedure. The normal period of follow-up will vary from procedure to procedure. And, the use of anesthetics will vary from procedure to procedure. Thus, physicians have different charges for different surgical procedures. However, for any particular procedure, the time and effort, follow-up, and anesthetics will generally be consistent each time the procedure is performed. Although there will be a few variations from one patient to another, the variations tend to balance out across patients. It is the predictability of these components which allows you to use the package when billing. From a practical standpoint, package billing is easier, both for the physician and the patient.

In reading through the three elements of the package defined above, you may have noticed that the package includes only the *normal* and *uncomplicated* follow-up care. This means that you can charge for treating complications and for "abnormal" follow-up. When doing so you should be aware of how these terms are commonly defined.

First, "normal" follow-up is typically defined as a period of time, expressed in days, following the surgery. The normal follow-up will vary from procedure to procedure. For some procedures, the normal follow-up might be seven days. For other procedures, it could be six months. Many offices use guides, such as the *Relative Values for Physicians* (RVP), or *Resource Based Relative Value Study* (RBRVS), to help them decide what the period of normal follow-up is considered to be for the procedures they perform. These publications list the number of follow-up days typically associated with surgical procedures. The importance of knowing the period of normal follow-up is that the physician has the option of billing the patient for visits related to the surgery that are made after the normal follow-up period. For example, suppose a diabetic patient is taking a long time to heal from a back surgery procedure which has a normal follow-up of 90 days. If the physician is still seeing the patient on day 91 as part of the surgical follow-up, the physician may wish to begin billing for the visits starting on day 91.

Uncomplicated follow-up is more straightforward in concept. It assumes the patient's recovery is routine. If it is not, and the physician needs to perform procedures or services related to the complications (e.g., incision and drainage of an infected incision site), then these items can be billed separately. When doing so, be sure to note the complicating diagnosis on the claim form, and add a modifier if necessary.

Conspicuously missing from the package concept definition is preoperative management. A review of the package definition given by the AMA in the Surgery Guidelines in the CPT book will show that preop is not listed as part of the package even though many physicians include preop in their surgical package charge. It is believed that the AMA did not include preop because there is great variation between physicians with regard to billing preop. Some physicians include it in their package, others do not. With the exception of conditions mandated by specific payers, there is no right or wrong way to bill preop; it really depends on how the physician chooses to handle the charge.

An unfortunate by-product of the AMA's decision not to specifically include or exclude the preop component from the surgical package definition is that it has allowed insurance companies to decide whether or not the preop charge will be included in the package. If you analyze the explanation of benefits received by your patients from their carriers (assuming you are billing the preop separately), you may find that some carriers will cover the preop charges and others will not. Furthermore, preop coverage may not only vary from carrier to carrier, but even from procedure to procedure. In some states, Medicaid and the Blues will not reimburse for services provided by the surgeon for a period as long as 14 days prior to the surgery if the listed diagnosis is the same (or related to) that used when reporting the surgical procedure.

Another aspect of preop billing to which you should be alert is the physician's past practice of charging for the preoperative management. If the physician's past billing practice was to include the preop in the surgery charge, and then he decides to begin billing for preop, you may find that some carriers will not pay for the preop — this is another example of unbundling. By contrast, some physicians who have always itemized the preop have found payment denials on these services by some other carriers. If proof of past billing and carrier payment exists, the physician is in an excellent position to argue either for payment of the preop, or if that is not possible, for an increase in the physician's charge for the surgical procedure. In the latter case, the physician would "make a deal" with the carrier: the physician would not itemize preop, but in exchange, would be allowed to charge more for the surgical package so that the increased fee reflects the inclusion of preop services. Unfortunately, if the physician's charge is already at the limit of the carrier's allowable charge, the "deal" will not have any affect on the physician's reimbursement unless these charges can be passed on to the patient.

Medicare's Major Surgery Package

Medicare's definition of the surgical package differs substantially from that discussed above. First, Medicare defines which specific preoperative services are allowed to be billed separately, and which are to be included in the surgery charge. Second, Medicare establishes a 90-day period of follow-up for all major surgical procedures. Finally, treatment of most complications related to the surgery are not to be billed.

Major surgery includes:

- All preoperative visits (in or out of the hospital) by the surgeon beginning the day before surgery.

- All usual and necessary intraoperative services and all additional medical or surgical services required to handle complications if they do not require an additional trip to the operating room.

- Ninety days of follow-up care related to the procedure. This includes treatment by the surgeon of *all* conditions related to the diagnosis for which the surgery was performed. Conditions would include treatment of *all* complications, except those which require taking the patient back to the operating room.

Medicare's major surgery package does not include the following:

- E/M services provided by the physician to the patient more than two days prior to surgery. Or, if the decision for surgery was made during an E/M visit the day of or day before surgery, it may be billed with the addition of the "-57" modifier.

- Medically necessary return trips to the operating room to treat a complication arising during the follow-up period. Modifier "-78" should be added to the surgical procedure code that describes treatment of the complication. Note that under such circumstances, Medicare's allowable will be limited to the intra-operative component of the procedure's fee schedule amount.

- Treatment of unrelated problems and conditions that arise during the surgical follow-up period. Codes for these services and/or procedures should include the appropriate modifier ("-24," "-25," or "-79") to alert Medicare that the services or procedures are unrelated to the surgery.

- Staged or related procedures performed during the follow-up period as defined for situations where use of the "-58" modifier is warranted. Since not all related procedures may be covered by Medicare, it may be necessary to submit a special report with the claim justifying these services.

Follow-Up for Diagnostic Procedures

The Surgery section lists many diagnostic procedures. These range from injections of contrast media for radiographs to endoscopies. When billing for these procedures, the charge should include any normal follow-up associated with the procedure. For example, if a hospitalized patient was given an injection of radioactive iodine for an intravenous pyelogram (IVP) and the physician who gave the injection stopped by to see the patient several hours after the procedure to make sure that there were no complications related to the injection, a hospital visit would not be charged.

Add-On Codes

You may have noticed that some surgical procedures have the following or similar descriptions as part of their definition:

- Each separate/additional
- More than four
- Each additional
- List separately in addition to primary procedure

These types of codes are termed add-on codes and as such they are not subject to the multiple procedure modifier, "-51." For example, suppose a dermatologist removes 25 skin tags from a patient. These would be coded as follows:

11200   Removal of skin tags, up to 15
11201   Removal of additional skin tags, ea 10

Note that the 51 modifier was not applied to code 11201 as it is considered to be an add-on code.

Separate Procedures

You may have noticed that some CPT surgical code descriptions contain the parenthetical remark "(separate procedure)." This notation signifies that the service is typically performed as a component of a more comprehensive, global procedure. In such situations, the procedure would not be separately identified. For example, consider the codes shown below related to cystourethroscopy:

52000   Cystourethroscopy (separate procedure)

52005   Cystourethroscopy, with ureteral catheterization, with or without irrigation,   instillation, or ureteropyelography, exclusive of radiologic service;

52010   with brush biopsy of ureter and/or renal pelvis

52020   Cystourethroscopy, with ejaculatory duct catheterization, with our without   irrigation, instillation, or duct radiography, exclusive of radiologic service

Procedures 52005, 52010 and 52020 include cystourethroscopy in addition to other surgical procedures and as such when reporting these services it would be inappropriate to also bill for code 52000. However, if the surgeon performs a cystourethroscopy either by itself or in conjunction with unrelated services, then it may be itemized separately on the claim.

Not all instances of the separate procedure concept are so straightforward: too often it may not be clear which procedures are and which procedures are not assumed to be included in a comprehensive service. As a rule, if more than one surgical procedure has been performed on the patient during a surgical session, and if one (or more) of the codes describing the procedures has the terms "separate procedure" as part of its description, then you may want to consider the following:

If the "separate procedure" is normally performed as component of a more global procedure that is also listed on the claim, then the "separate procedure" should not be itemized.

If the "separate procedure" was performed through a separate incision and/or is not directly related to other procedures performed, then it may be itemized and you may want to consider listing the distinct procedure modifier, "-53," with the code.

Starred Procedures

In the surgical package concept discussion above, you learned that charges for most surgical procedures include the surgery itself and the normal uncomplicated follow-up. Furthermore, you saw that the predictability of the components of the package allowed for billing surgeries in this manner. However, not all surgical procedures have well-defined postoperative management. For example, consider minor procedures related to removal of foreign bodies lodged in subcutaneous tissues, or the excision of small cysts. In many patients, these minor procedures require no follow-up. But in some patients, especially the elderly or those with existing systemic problems, even a minor procedure may require hospitalization or follow-up visits.

To deal with the unpredictable nature of the follow-up for these minor procedures, CPT lists stars next to those procedures for which the follow-up is usually nonexistent or varies with the patient's other underlying conditions. When a starred procedure is listed on a physician's bill, the charge for the starred procedure should be only for the procedure itself. Any pre- or postoperative management will be charged separately. Rules for using the starred procedures appear in the CPT Surgery Guidelines. The substance of these rules is:

1. When billing a starred procedure, the charge listed with the procedure should be for the surgery only; it should not include any pre- or postoperative services.

2. Preoperative management is charged based on the following:

    a. If the patient is new *and* the major procedure performed is a starred procedure, then charge for both the procedure and an initial visit. CPT recommends that you use code 99025 for billing the initial visit. If the patient's carrier rejects code 99025, for whatever reason, try using a Level I new patient visit instead, code 99201.

    b. If the patient is an established patient *and* the major procedure being performed is a starred procedure, then charge only for the starred procedure.

    c. If the starred procedure is *not* the major procedure or service being rendered during the visit, then list all procedures and services performed. For example, a patient may be seeing the physician for follow-up of hypertension, and during the visit the physician removes skin tags from the patient's neck (a starred procedure). In this case, the physician would list both the office visit and the starred procedure. When additional identifiable procedures or services are rendered, it does not matter whether the patient is new or established. Be sure to report the different diagnoses so as to support the provision of both services. And, it may be worthwhile to list the "-25" modifier with the E/M service to ensure that the payer understands that the E/M service was unrelated to the surgery.

    d. If the patient's condition requires that he be hospitalized in order for the starred procedure to be performed, the physician will charge for both the starred procedure and hospital visits. To give an example of a situation where the physician would bill both, suppose an elderly diabetic patient with other systemic problems needs to have an infected sebaceous cyst drained. Normally the physician performs the procedure in the office. But due to the patient's other problems, he decides to perform the procedure in the hospital and admits the patient. The code for removing the cyst is starred (code 10060) and thus, the physician would bill for: initial hospital care when admitting the patient; the incision and drainage of the cyst; and any other hospital visits related to the procedure.

3. Follow-up care related to the starred procedure, if any, is billed on a service-by-service basis. For example, if a patient had a simple wound repaired with sutures (assume it was a starred procedure), the physician could charge for the visit which involved the nurse removing the sutures (a Level I office visit).

4. As with all surgical procedures, if the patient develops complications related to the starred procedure, any services or procedures rendered to treat the complication(s) can be charged. List the complicating diagnosis on the claim to help insure reimbursement.

Medicare's Minor Surgery Package

Surgeries under this definition include CPT's starred surgical procedures and nonincisional endoscopic procedures.

Minor surgery includes:

- The visit on the day of the procedure, unless a documented, separately identifiable service is furnished.

- Zero or ten days of follow-up (on a code-by-code basis).

Medicare does not bundle the following with minor surgery:

- Follow-up on some services (on a code-by-code basis).
- Postoperative services for endoscopies performed through an existing body orifice.
- Services related to treating the patient's underlying condition.

Special care must be taken to understand these Medicare-specific billing rules. For example, if you perform a starred procedure on a patient and the patient requires follow-up related to the procedure, a commercial carrier may cover the follow-up visit in instances where Medicare will not.

To assist with the reader's understanding of what is and what is not included in the CPT and Medicare surgical package definitions, Figure 3.4 on the following page is provided for reference.

Now that you have a better grasp of the surgery coding fundamentals, we will turn our attention to a few areas of surgery coding which are likely to cause you confusion.

Excision of Lesions (Codes 11400–11646)

In the CPT Surgery section you will find codes for excising benign and malignant lesions. Listed along with these codes are brief notes which explain how they are to be reported. The notes for both the benign and malignant lesion codes have the following in common:

"Excision (including simple closure) ... "

The key is the parenthetical remark regarding the closure. When performing these excisions the physician invariably creates a wound which has to be closed. If the closure is a simple one, that is, a simple wound repair, the closure will not be itemized. However, if the wound made by the physician requires either an intermediate or complex closure, the closure can be billed in addition to the lesion excision code.

To clarify this point, imagine a patient who has a 1.8 cm lesion removed from his face. Because the lesion is on the face, the physician may need to make a plastic-type repair (a complex repair) in the area where the lesion was excised. The physician would bill for both the excision and the repair.

Figure 3.4: Surgical Package Definitions

SURGICAL PACKAGE DEFINITIONS*				
	CPT		MEDICARE	
	Major	**Minor**	**Major**	**Minor**
Types of Surgery	All non-starred CPT Surgery codes	Starred CPT Surgery codes	All non-starred CPT Surgery codes except nonincisional endoscopies	Starred CPT procedures and nonincisional endoscopies
Preoperative E/M Services	Not defined	Visit allowed for new patients on same day or if significant services unrelated to surgery provided	Not allowed on day of or day before surgery except if decision for surgery is made	Not allowed unless separately identifiable service provided
Operation	Included	Included	Included	Included
Complications During Surgery	Not defined	Not defined	Included	Not defined
Local, Topical, or Digital Anesthetics	Included	Included	Included	Included
Postoperative Time Period	"Normal" only included	None. Bill for follow-up visits	90 days	0 or 10 days (defined by code)
Treatment of Complications During Postoperative Period	Not included	Not included	Included unless performed in operating room	Included if code has 10 day follow-up period and treatment is during follow-up period
Treatment of Unrelated Conditions During Postoperative Period	Not included	Not included	Not included (modifiers required)	Not included (modifiers required)

* These definitions only apply to the surgeon providing the surgical services or to other physicians who perform a portion of the surgical package.

Repair (Codes 12001–13300)

There are extensive notes discussing both the classification and proper coding of repairs in the CPT book. Consider first the types of repairs described.

1. *Simple Repairs.* A simple repair is one that involves suturing of superficial tissues (primary dermis or epidermis and subcutaneous tissues in cases where there is not significant involvement of deeper tissues), and where the wound requires simple one layer closure with suturing. Local anesthetic is included in the repair charge. Note that if adhesive strips are used to close the wound, the closure would be included as part of an E/M service and not be listed separately. Heavily contaminated wounds that require extensive cleaning and simple closure would be reported using an intermediate repair code.

2. *Intermediate Repairs.* When a repair involves layer closure of one or more of the subcutaneous tissues and superficial fascia (i.e., in addition to the basic dermal or epidermal closure), then the repair can be listed by use of the intermediate repair codes.

3. *Complex Repairs.* As defined in CPT these repairs include " ... repairs of wounds requiring more than layered closure, viz., scar revision, debridement, (e.g., traumatic lacerations or avulsions), extensive undermining, stents or retention sutures." Note that these codes may include "creation of the defect and necessary preparation for repairs or the debridement and repair of contaminated lacerations or avulsions."

With regard to reporting wound repairs you should adhere to the following rules.

1. The length of a wound is always measured in centimeters, no matter what shape it may be.

2. When you have more than one wound within the same "classification," sum together the lengths of the repairs and report them as one repair. A classification is commonly accepted to mean a group of indented codes. For example, codes 12001 through 12007 are in the same indented group, or the same classification. If the patient had a 2.0 cm simple wound repair on the arm and a 5.0 cm simple repair on the neck, you would report code 12002. Since these wounds are both simple and described under the same indented group, you would sum together their lengths (2.0 + 5.0 = 7.0) and report the 7.0 cm simple repair code, 12002.

3. Neither debridement nor cleansing of wound sites are billed separately unless they are:

    a. Performed at a different time from the closure, or,
    b. Are very difficult or time consuming to perform.

4. Repairs involving nerves, blood vessels or tendons can be reported using codes found elsewhere in CPT. That is, find codes in the Nervous System to report nerve repairs, locate codes under the Musculoskeletal System to report tendon repairs, and the like. You should note that when charging for these other procedures, (e.g., nerve repair), the simple and intermediate wound repairs are considered to be included with your charge for the

major procedure (e.g., nerve repair). However, if the physician needs to make a *complex* repair of the wound site in addition to repairing the underlying structure (e.g., a nerve), then both repairs can be reported.

Grafts and Flaps (Codes 15000–15776)

Coders often overlook several billing opportunities when charging for grafts and flaps. First, you will find notes in CPT which state:

> "Repair of donor site requiring skin graft or local flaps is to be added as additional procedure"

The appropriate wound repair or other related procedure can be listed *in addition to* the graft.

Second, code 15000 should be used in addition to your graft charge when applicable. It is for reporting the "Excisional preparation or creation of recipient site by excision of intact skin ... ."

Finally, grafts are often performed following major procedures such as mastectomies and removal of deep tumors. The charge you make for the major procedure (e.g., mastectomy) does not include the graft. These should be itemized separately. Refer to the notes in your CPT book.

Musculoskeletal System (Codes 20000–29909)

In many respects this is the technically most difficult subsection in CPT. It lists codes used by orthopedic surgeons, oral surgeons, and other specialties. A few points need to be kept in mind when billing for casts, strappings and traction devices.

1. Many of the procedures involve the application of casts and traction devices. Your fee for the major procedure includes the *first* application of casts and traction.

2. If a cast or strapping is reapplied either during or immediately after the normal period of follow-up, you can charge for the casting or strapping procedure(s) by use of the codes found under the heading "Applications of Casts and Strapping."

3. The removal of a cast is *always* included in the charge for the procedure which involved applying the cast. It is only charged separately when the cast is removed by a physician other than the one who originally applied it. Refer to cast removal and repair codes.

4. Do not report office, hospital, nursing home, or similar visits as an additional charge when billing for reapplications of casts or strappings *unless* you can document significant additional services beyond the cast or strapping application.

CPT now also provides definitions for closed treatment, open treatment, and percutaneous skeletal fixation. *Closed treatment* applies to a fracture site that is not surgically opened. Treatment methods include without manipulation, with manipulation and with or without traction. For example, the following code is an example of the use of the term "closed treatment":

23570   Closed treatment of scapular fracture; without manipulation

Open treatment applies to a fracture site that is surgically opened. Both ends of the fractured bones are "visualized" by the surgeon, and internal fixation may be used. For example, the following code is an example of use of the term "open treatment":

24579   Open treatment of humeral condylar fracture, medial or lateral, with or without internal or external fixation

Percutaneous skeletal fixation describes treatment that has the following characteristics:

- Treatment is neither open nor closed.
- Fracture fragments are not directly visualized by the surgeon.
- Fixation (often pins) is placed across the fracture area, usually via X-ray imaging.

Note also that there is no correlation between the type of fracture (open, closed, or compound) and the type of treatment given (open, closed, or percutaneous). Definitions and other important information for skin traction, skeletal traction, grafts of bone and related tissues, re-reductions of fractures, and external fixation are provided in the Musculoskeletal System notes. If your practice utilizes these codes, you should take the time to thoroughly review these CPT notes.

Another important point regarding the use of the musculoskeletal codes relates to the "General" codes located at the beginning of the Musculoskeletal section. There will be times when you cannot locate a code in the musculoskeletal system which describes the procedure that was performed. In such cases, search the "General" codes. You might find a code which describes what was done. Make it a rule to use the unlisted musculoskeletal procedure codes *only* after you have unsuccessfully searched the "General" codes.

Vascular Injection Procedures (Codes 36000–37190)

Most physicians and their staff perform at least a few of the procedures listed in this subsection. Codes range from those for inserting an IV (36000) to catheterization. The most commonly used code is for routine venipuncture – 36415. However, if the physician is required to perform the venipuncture, use code 36410.

Notes associated with these codes remind you that when giving vascular injections, depending upon the type of procedure being performed, your charge should include:

- Local anesthetic;
- Introduction of needle or catheter;
- Injection of contrast media (with or without automatic power injection);
- Pre- or post-care related to the injection itself.

When injecting contrast media, the physician's charge should not include the charge for the contrast media. These codes do not include charges for the supply of drugs and catheters. If these items are provided by the physician, you can list them by use of code 99070 or the appropriate HCPCS code. If the patient is a Medicare or Medicaid beneficiary, use only the appropriate HCPCS National or Local code.

Maternity Care and Delivery (Codes 59000-59899)

Reporting the typical maternity case is easily handled by use of code 59400, total obstetric care. This is a global procedure and includes all antepartum care, the normal vaginal delivery, and postpartum care. It is when the maternity care or delivery becomes complicated that coding difficulties arise. Coding problems occur when one physician performs only a portion of the maternity care, or when there are complications leading up to or during the delivery.

When more than one physician is involved, there are several coding options depending upon the circumstances. Note that there are codes which allow the physician to bill that portion of the care which he performed. For example, to bill just for antepartum care, code 59425 or 59426 should be used. To bill for postpartum care as a separate procedure, list code 59430.

The specific procedures and services which are included with antepartum and postpartum care and delivery services are as follows:

1. Antepartum Care. This service includes:

  - Initial and subsequent histories
  - Physical examinations
  - Recording patient's weight, blood pressures and fetal heart tones
  - Routine urinalysis
  - Monthly visits up to 28 weeks gestation
  - Biweekly visits up to 36 weeks gestation
  - Weekly visits up to delivery

Services other than those specified above that are provided to the patient may be billed separately.

2. Delivery. This service includes:

  - Admitting the patient to the hospital
  - Admission history and physical
  - Management of uncomplicated labor
  - Vaginal delivery (with or without episiotomy, with or without forceps), or,
  - Cesarean delivery

Problems that complicate labor and delivery management can be billed separately by use of codes from the Medicine and E/M sections of CPT.

3. Postpartum Care. This service includes:

  - Hospital visits following delivery
  - Office visits following delivery

Complications occurring before delivery which necessitate additional visits, procedures, and tests (such as for diabetes, toxemia, hypertension, etc.) are not considered part of the normal care. The physician should list office visits, hospital visits, surgical procedures, and the like to describe these additional services.

ANESTHESIA

Obtaining appropriate reimbursement for anesthesia services may be complicated by several factors. First, the type of individual attracted to anesthesiology may prefer the more flexible schedule, predictable work hours, and other benefits associated with the specialty. Since these specialists are often hospital-based or members of a group practice, billing is typically handled by someone other than the physician, such as the hospital staff or a billing service. As a result, anesthesiologists are usually far removed from the coding and billing process and may have no or little interest in becoming involved. Lack of involvement can lead to significant reimbursement problems.

Second, anesthesiologists report CPT anesthesia codes when billing Medicare and CPT surgery codes when billing most other payers. This can result in confusion and coding inaccuracies. To inexperienced staff billing anesthesia services, it may be unclear which codes to submit to which payers: CPT anesthesia or CPT surgery codes. When the CPT surgery codes are used, the biller may have to wait until the surgeon reports his services before it is known which code the anesthesiologist should list. So, anesthesia billers often have to rely on the surgeon's operative report or claim to determine which code to report for the anesthesia services. Time delays may result, or worse, the biller may select a CPT surgery code which differs from that reported by the surgeon. This can lead to claim delays or denials.

A third factor affecting anesthesia reimbursement is the use of procedural and time units. Again, these vary with the type of payer. Most payers require that the anesthesiologist calculate total units based upon the sum of the procedure's units and time units. Medicare has anesthesiologists report time as a function of either 15- or 30-minute segments (and portions thereof), depending upon whether the anesthesiologist personally performed the anesthesia service or supervised others who performed the service. Other third party payers are billed on the basis of the procedure's units and, most typically, units consisting of 10-minute time segments. The different reporting methods for different payers also has the potential for causing confusion and mistakes.

Fourth, methods for noting delivery of anesthesia services (personally furnished or supervisory) vary from payer to payer. For example, Medicare requires that anesthesiologists' claims list HCPCS National modifiers from the "-AA" through "-AG" range. Other payers may not require the use of any modifiers for reporting normal anesthesia services.

A fifth complicating factor is the billing of anesthesia-related services. Many payers carriers will reimburse separately for the insertion of Swan-Ganz catheters by the anesthesiologist when the service is provided as part of the anesthesia service. They will also pay separately for the insertion of central venous pressure lines or intra-arterial lines. This may or may not be true of other payers. Again, the ability of the anesthesiologist to bill and expect to receive payment for special anesthesia services varies by payer.

Finally, most third party payers require anesthesiologists to report the *major* procedure performed by the surgeon using the CPT surgery code. Secondary procedures performed during the same operative session are not to be listed. (Time units make up the difference.) Thus, when receiving the operative report, it is often left to the anesthesiologist's biller to determine:

A.   The procedure(s) performed. This is an extraordinarily difficult task for the staff as a wide range of surgical services must be interpreted and coded. Even surgeons and their staff have difficulty coding outside their area of specialty.

B.   The major procedure, if more than one surgery was performed. Coding becomes increasingly difficult when more than one procedure is performed on a patient. The coder must code each procedure and then report the *major* procedure (the one with the most anesthesia units).

In addition to the above, another reimbursement problem may arise due to the anesthesiologist's dependency upon the surgeon's coding. The anesthesiologist's reported diagnosis should be virtually identical to that reported by the surgeon. As with CPT procedure codes, if the two physicians use very different diagnoses, the anesthesiologist's claim may be delayed or denied.

Specific steps can be taken by anesthesiologists to help ensure proper payment on their claims:

1.   Develop a working relationship with the surgeons' offices that allows you to obtain (in a timely manner) the relevant CPT surgery codes and ICD-9-CM diagnosis codes which are being reported on the surgeons' claims. However, do not always assume that the surgeon or his staff are better coders than you or your staff.

2.   Become familiar with payer policies related to the use of CPT surgery or anesthesia codes, time units and modifiers.

3.   Attempt to identify policies of payers related to the billing of specialized anesthesia services, such as for the insertion of intra-arterial lines.

RADIOLOGY

This brief section covers key topics related to billing radiology procedures, focusing primarily on the needs of non-radiologists. Radiology is one of the easiest sections of CPT to use, and for the most part, the coding is straightforward. After reviewing this section you will have a better understanding of:

- • The organization of the radiology codes.
- • Procedures involving injections.
- • Professional and technical components.
- • The miscellaneous codes.
- • Therapeutic radiology.

Organization

The Radiology section is divided into four subsections: Diagnostic Radiology (Diagnostic Imaging); Diagnostic Ultrasound; Radiation Oncology; and, Nuclear Medicine. The Diagnostic Radiology subsection is the most widely used portion of Radiology as it lists codes for commonly performed procedures including X-rays and CAT scans.

Within the Diagnostic Radiology, Diagnostic Ultrasound, and Nuclear Medicine subsections, the codes are grouped by anatomic areas. For example, codes in the Diagnostic Radiology subsection are grouped under the following headings:

- • Head and Neck
- • Chest

- Spine and Pelvis
- Upper Extremities
- Lower Extremities
- Abdomen
- Gastrointestinal Tract
- Urinary Tract
- Gynecological and Obstetrical
- Heart
- Aorta and Arteries
- Veins and Lymphatics
- Miscellaneous

This organization makes it easier for you to locate codes.

Coding Diagnostic Radiology Procedures

Most of the diagnostic radiology procedures can be viewed as being a member of one of two classes of codes. The first consists of those procedures which involve the injection of contrast (or other) materials. These procedures include two components: the supervision and interpretation, and the injection of the contrast or other materials. When these services are reported, two codes are utilized. The radiologist who performs the supervision and interpretation will select a code from the Radiology section of CPT. The physician (many times a radiologist) who performs the injection will report an appropriate code from the Surgery section of CPT. For example, suppose a patient's physician orders a sialogram, a radiological procedure involving an injection. If the radiologist performs both components of the procedure he would list the following codes on the claim:

70390	Sialography, radiological supervision and interpretation
42550-51	Injection procedure for sialography

Notice that reference to the appropriate injection code is listed in CPT as a parenthetical note appearing immediately below code 70390. These parenthetical reference notes are provided for all radiology codes that invariably have an injection component. In the above example you may have noticed use of the multiple procedure modifier ("-51") on the secondary procedure. Use of the modifier is optional with most third party payers.

If two physicians were involved in performing the procedure discussed above, a radiologist and internist, for example, their claims would be as follows:

Radiologist:	70390	Sialography, radiological supervision and interpretation
Internist:	42550	Injection procedure for sialography

The second class of diagnostic radiology codes are those which have both professional and technical components. The professional part, or professional component, consists of those aspects performed by the physician. These can include ordering the radiograph, supervising the "picture-taking," reading and interpretation of the results, and writing a report that contains the interpretation. On the other hand, the technical component consists of non-physician services and supplies needed to perform the radiograph. A technician who takes the radiograph, the cost of film and chemicals, and the use of the X-ray equipment are examples of what is meant by the technical part of the procedure.

Most of the codes in the Diagnostic Radiology subsection do not specify whether the charge for the code is assumed to include the professional, technical, or both components. Consider, for example, code 71010 for a single frontal view chest X-ray. Suppose the physician (or clinic) owns the X-ray equipment and a patient is given a chest X-ray. In this case the coder will want to make sure that the charge for the radiograph includes both the technical and professional components. To do so the coder would simply list 71010, and charge an amount which reflects the provision of both components. This concept applies to all radiographs taken in the physician's office which utilize the physician's radiographic equipment, supplies, and technicians.

Consider another example in which the radiograph was taken at the hospital, and you are to code for the physician who interpreted the X-ray. (Assume the hospital will bill the patient separately for the technical aspects.) Recall that we discussed the professional component modifier "-26." In this case, to charge for the interpretation only, the physician would list the "-26" modifier next to the radiograph code. If the procedure was a single view chest X-ray, the physician would report:

71010-26

The amount of the charge for the procedure would reflect the physician's professional services only.

In workshops, participants often ask how to bill for physicians who interpret radiographs in the ER or office when a radiologist has already, or will be, charging for the interpretation. An example will help clarify the issue. Suppose a patient is admitted to the emergency room complaining of severe pain in her side. A urologist is called in to consult with the ER physician. The urologist orders that an intravenous pyelogram (IVP) be performed stat. (An IVP is a series of X-rays of the urinary tract which involves an injection of contrast media). After the pictures have been taken, the urologist reviews them, and proceeds to schedule further tests and procedures. Since most states and hospitals require that a radiologist read the radiographs (IVP in this case), the patient's carrier will receive a bill from the hospital which may include the interpretation. If not, there will be two bills, one from the hospital for the technical component, and another from a radiologist for the professional component. The question becomes: how can the urologist charge for taking the time to review the series of radiographs?

As you may know, if confronted with two charges for the reading of the radiograph, most carriers will approve the charge made by the radiologist and reject the other physician's charge. Therefore, it would be a waste of time for the urologist to report a charge for reading the radiograph. Recall the discussion of evaluation and management services. The medical decision making component of E/M services includes the review and analysis of diagnostic tests, such as the IVP. If the amount of test data to be reviewed was moderate or extensive, it might affect the level of E/M service selected by the urologist. Depending upon the levels of history, examination, and other medical decision making components, the higher amount of data review might allow the urologist to report a higher level of service. In any case, the reading of the radiographs would be included as part of the urologist's E/M service and would not be itemized separately.

Other Procedures

At the end of the Diagnostic Radiology subsection you will find a group of codes under the subheading "Other Procedures." Many radiology coders tend to overlook these codes. It is a good place to look if you cannot find the diagnostic radiology code you need listed under the anatomic areas which precede these miscellaneous codes. The group contains descriptions for fluoroscopy, bone age studies, joint surveys, CAT scans, cineradiograms, consultations on X-rays made elsewhere, and magnetic resonance imaging, among others.

Radiation Oncology

As described in the notes at the beginning of the Radiation Oncology subsection, the codes listed for teletherapy and brachytherapy " ... include initial consultation, clinical treatment planning, simulation, medical radiation physics, dosimetry, treatment devices, special services, and clinical treatment management procedures." These services also include the normal follow-up both during and for three months after the completion of the treatment procedures.

However, if the radiologist provides an opinion or advice regarding the patient's condition or management, he may consider billing for consultation. Refer to the discussion on consultations in earlier in this section.

Radiology coders should be careful to take note of and read the definitions of the simple, intermediate and complex levels given for planning, management, and brachytherapy.

PATHOLOGY AND LABORATORY

In this section you will be given a brief overview of several key reimbursement concepts associated with effective use of laboratory and pathology procedure codes. For labs and physicians who specialize in these areas, coding is relatively easy (or certainly easy when compared to the complexities associated with use of the E/M and Surgery sections of CPT). As you will see, several of the problems you are likely to encounter when using codes from this section are due either to lack of familiarity with the codes, or strict reimbursement policies of insurance carriers.

Specific topics which are covered in this section include:

- Medicare regulations regarding in-office lab work.
- Multichannel and group tests.
- Individual chemistry and toxicology tests.
- Pathology consultation.
- Surgical pathology.

Medicare Lab Regulations

On January 1, 1987, Medicare began requiring that physicians and groups accept assignment on all clinical diagnostic laboratory tests performed in the office. This regulation applies only to Medicare claims. Both participating and nonparticipating physicians are subject to the regulation. Medicare will reimburse 100 percent of the allowable for the service; there is no copayment. The amount paid by Medicare for the lab work is to be considered payment-in-full.

Coders in nonparticipating physician offices have been confused as to how to file claims when there are both lab and non-lab services rendered for the Medicare patient on the same day. Problems arise when the physician does not want to accept assignment on the non-lab services, but must do so for the lab work. There are two solutions:

1.   Under these circumstances (and these circumstances only) the physician can submit two claims to Medicare for services provided to the patient on that day. One claim will list the lab work, and the physician will note that he is accepting assignment on the claim. The second claim will list the non-lab services, and the physician will note that he does not accept assignment on the claim.

2.   The physician can put both lab and non-lab services on the same claim. However, the box for assignment should be checked as *not* accepting assignment. In the area where the physician signs his name he should write the following statement:

       "I accept assignment for the clinical laboratory tests only."

       Your local Medicare carrier may make other provisions if you submit your claims electronically.

Multichannel Tests (Codes 80002–80019)

Automated multichannel tests are the first codes listed in the Pathology and Laboratory section of CPT. These tests are typically performed by reference labs, although a few larger group practices may have the automated equipment required to perform these tests. (For the uninitiated, an example of an automated multichannel test is the SMA-12.) The importance of these codes to the typical physician's office is not in that they will be used, but rather that they may appear on the Explanation of Benefits received by your patients. To understand the issue, consider the situation where a physician performs four different tests on a patient's blood in the office. Each test is performed individually and each is reported separately by use of a chemistry test code. (These codes are listed in CPT under the Chemistry and Toxicology subsection.) If the insurance carrier believes that these tests could have been performed at substantially less expense by an outside lab using multichannel equipment, they may deny individual lab charges submitted by the physician. Furthermore, they may recode the four individual chemistry test codes you submitted and list one code, a multichannel code, on the Explanation of Benefits form and reimburse at the same rate they would have paid an outside lab to perform the multichannel test. In this way, carriers discourage physicians from performing lab work in the office that can be handled more cost effectively by reference labs. If, however, the tests were performed in the office on a "stat" basis, that is the patient's condition was such that the physician could not wait for a lab to perform the tests, then a payer may reimburse on the basis of each individual test. In such cases you should submit a note with the claim that includes the lab tests and notes the urgent need for immediate test results.

Organ or Disease Oriented Panels (Codes 80050–80092)

These panel codes are provided to allow physicians and labs to utilize one code for a group of tests frequently performed for a specific purpose. Panels listed include those for general health, obstetrics, liver function, lipid, arthritis, TORCH antibody and thyroid function. With each panel code is listed those tests that must be included as part of the panel. Note that if additional tests not listed with the panel are performed, those tests may be billed separately.

Individual Chemistry Tests (Codes 82000–84999)

To report an individual chemistry or toxicology test you should use codes from the series 82000 through 84999. Upon reviewing these codes you should note that the tests are listed alphabetically by the *type* of substance being analyzed. Specific techniques for analyzing substances are also listed.

When trying to locate tests from the chemistry and toxicology group you should follow these guidelines:

1.   Look under the name of the substance for which the test is being performed.
2.   If the code is not listed alphabetically, check codes 80150 through 80299.
3.   If you are reporting a molecular diagnostic test, review codes 83890-83912.
4.   If that doesn't work, look under the miscellaneous codes at the end of the Pathology and Laboratory section, codes 89050-89399.
5.   If you still have not located the code, try looking under the name of the technique used to analyze the substance.
6.   Finally, if all else fails, use the unlisted procedure code 84999 and send a KISS letter with the claim.

Surgical Pathology and Consultations

The codes in this section are organized into surgical pathology examinations, consultation and other analytic procedures, such as immunocytochemistry and immunofluorescent studies. Determining which surgical pathology procedure to select (from codes in the range 88300 - 88309) is relatively straightforward—they are based on the specimen being examined. The specimens which apply to a code are listed for each code. For example, the gross and microscopic evaluation of the kidney biopsy would be reported using code 88305 as the kidney biopsy is specified for this code. The only exception to this rule is when only gross examination (not microscopic) of the specimen is needed. In this case, code 88300 should be reported regardless of the specimen being examined.

Pathologists occasionally perform consultative services. CPT contains special codes to describe the pathologist's consulting activities. First, you will find clinical pathology consultation codes (80500-80502) listed. Two levels are described: limited and comprehensive. These codes should only be used when:

1.   The services have been requested by an attending physician, and
2.   The test results require "additional medical interpretive judgment."

The key distinction between the limited and comprehensive clinical pathology consultation is in whether the patient's history and medical records are reviewed by the pathologist. The comprehensive consult requires the review. Furthermore, the comprehensive consult code is reserved for use with patients who have a complex diagnostic problem(s).

In addition to the consult codes discussed above, there are several consult codes specifically related to surgical pathology, codes 88321-88332. These codes describe consultations on referred material and consultations during surgery.

PROBLEM SET: SECTION THREE

Suggested solutions to the problems below can be found in Appendix A.

Mark the following statements true or false.

		True	False
1.	Unless stated otherwise in an E/M code's definition, time is to be used as the key component driving code selection when the face-to-face encounter with the patient exceeds 30 minutes.	_____	_____
2.	When reporting emergency department services, selection of codes is not based on whether the patient is new or established.	_____	_____
3.	To report physician standby services, the standby services must be requested by either the patient or a qualified healthcare professional.	_____	_____
4.	You can report up to a maximum of three initial inpatient consultation services on a patient during the course of his/her stay in the hospital.	_____	_____
5.	To bill for two-way voice communication direction of EMS services, the physician must have been in either the hospital's emergency department or critical care department.	_____	_____
6.	The history component of E/M services does not include documenting the examination of an affected body area or organ system.	_____	_____
7.	The number of diagnosis or management options under consideration is an integral aspect of the medical decision making component of E/M services.	_____	_____
8.	A physician providing E/M services to a patient in a free-standing urgent care facility between the hours of 8:00 pm and 6:00 am should report the emergency department service codes instead of office/outpatient visit codes.	_____	_____
9.	You would only report observation care discharge services when they are performed on a day subsequent to initial observation care.	_____	_____
10.	Depending upon circumstances, you can report office visit E/M codes even if you did not perform the history, examination, and medical decision making components.	_____	_____

11. The "-21" modifier for prolonged E/M services should be _____ _____
     listed with E/M service codes 99354 through 99357.

12. HCPCS Local modifiers are reported in the same manner as _____ _____
     HCPCS National modifiers.

13. With one exception (the unusual services modifier "-22"), _____ _____
     CPT modifiers may not be listed with HCPCS national codes.

14. Only the primary surgeon would report "-62" or "-66" _____ _____
     modifiers for two surgeons and surgical team, respectively.

15. The "-82" modifier is to be used by qualified residents _____ _____
     performing a surgical assist in a nonteaching hospital.

16. There are no circumstances that would allow you to use _____ _____
     the "-54," surgery only modifier, on E/M codes.

17. There are no situations where you would list the "-21" _____ _____
     modifier on radiology codes.

18. The following code and modifier combination could be _____ _____
     correct: 93042-26

19. Between CPT and the HCPCS National systems there are _____ _____
     approximately 180 modifiers.

20. You should not use the "-53" discontinued procedure _____ _____
     modifier for services canceled prior to surgical preparation
     of the patient.

21. The primary purpose of the reduced service modifier "-52" _____ _____
     is to provide a legitimate means of reducing charges for a
     service.

22. "09999" is a CPT modifier. _____ _____

23. For Medicare, you would list the "-QI" modifier instead of _____ _____
     modifier "-57."

24. If one surgeon performs surgery on a patient and then a _____ _____
     second surgeon performs a different surgical procedure on
     the same patient during the global period for the first
     procedure, the second surgeon should list the "-79" modifier
     next to the surgery code(s) on his/her claim.

25. The "-T3" modifier would be added to procedures _____ _____
     performed on a Medicare patient's third thoracic vertebra.

26. You can never bill for giving an immunization injection as _____   _____
     it is always included in the E/M service; however, you can
     bill separately for the supply of the immunization drug.

27. There are invasive surgical-type procedures listed in the _____   _____
     CPT Medicine section of codes.

28. The physician provides an intramuscular injection of 10 mg _____   _____
     of furosemide (Lasix) during a E/M visit with a Medicare
     patient. You may bill separately for the E/M visit, injection,
     and the supply of the Lasix.

29. A physician may bill for end-stage renal disease related _____   _____
     services on a daily basis, but only if such services are
     provided for no more than 14 days (two weeks) in any
     given month.

30. Routine ophthalmoscopy is never reported separately. It is _____   _____
     always part of either a general or special ophthalmologic
     service.

31. Physicians who provide chemotherapeutic agents when _____   _____
     giving a chemotherapy injection should, in addition to listing
     the administration code, use code 99070 to charge for the
     agent (drug).

32. Osteopathic manipulative treatment of the lumbosacral area _____   _____
     would be reported by code 97260 (and 97261 as appropriate).

33. Injection procedures performed in conjunction with cardiac _____   _____
     catheterization services do not include the introduction of
     catheters.

34. Depending upon payer requirements and local custom, it is _____   _____
     possible that a psychiatrist's bill for individual medical
     psychotherapy might occasionally include use of the "-52"
     modifier.

35. It is generally acceptable to bill for handling and/or _____   _____
     conveyance of a lab specimen even if the specimen if
     transferred from the physician's examination area to a lab
     within the physician's office.

36. To locate an appropriate unlisted surgical procedure code _____   _____
     always refer to the last code listed under the affected body
     system.

37. Prior to closing a laceration on the back of a patient's head _____ _____
with three sutures, the surgeon applies an topical anesthetic
agent. The surgeon may not bill for the anesthetic agent in
addition to the would repair.

38. With rare exception, the normal follow-up for surgical _____ _____
procedures is usually considered to be 60 days.

39. The CPT book does not define preoperative management _____ _____
when describing the components of the surgical package.

40. The normal follow-up related to the injection of contrast _____ _____
media, such as radioactive iodine, should be included in the
charge for the injection.

41. A "separate procedure" is defined as a procedure which is _____ _____
often mistaken for being a component of a global procedure
and may, therefore, be billed separately when performed in
addition to the global procedure.

42. Starred procedures can be found in the Surgery, Radiology, _____ _____
and Medicine sections of CPT.

43. Medicare's major surgical package rules do not allow billing _____ _____
for treatment by incision and drainage of an abscess that
develops in the patient's incision site.

44. The billing of wound closures associated with lesion _____ _____
excisions apply only to malignant lesions.

45. When coding simple wound repairs, if there is more than _____ _____
one repair, sum together the length of all the simple wounds
and report them as one repair.

46. When billing for radical mastectomy procedures, the charge _____ _____
should include any grafts needed to cosmetically repair the
excision area.

47. In situations where a physician removes a cast that was _____ _____
applied by another physician, he should use a surgery code
to report the removal.

48. You would never list the "-51" modifier with an "add-on" _____ _____
code.

49. A VBAC (Vaginal Birth After Cesarean) could be reported _____ _____
by use of code 59400.

50.   Anesthesiologists bill the CPT anesthesia codes to Medi-   _____   _____
       care, and the CPT surgery codes to most other payers, when
       billing for anesthesia services.

51.   If an anesthesiologist provides anesthesia services for   _____   _____
       multiple surgical procedures on a non-Medicare patient,
       payment is based on total time (converted to units) plus the
       number of units for the major surgical procedure, plus any
       physical status units, if applicable. Units associated with the
       secondary surgical procedures are not taken into account.

52.   The Radiology section of CPT is divided into the five   _____   _____
       following subsections:

       *   Diagnostic Radiology
       *   Diagnostic Ultrasound
       *   Radiation Oncology
       *   Nuclear Medicine
       *   Cyclotronic Imaging

53.   The bilateral bronchography code (71060) includes super-   _____   _____
       vision and interpretation, injection of contrast material, and
       provision of contrast material (if performed in an outpatient
       setting).

54.   It is not uncommon for radiologists to bill using CPT   _____   _____
       surgery codes.

55.   Unless otherwise specified, most diagnostic radiology   _____   _____
       procedures are assumed to include both professional and
       technical components.

56.   Payers will generally allow payment for the rereading of a   _____   _____
       radiograph, but only when a non-radiologist (such as an
       emergency room physician) bills for the first reading, and a
       radiologist the second reading (as a confirmation of the
       non-radiologist's interpretation).

57.   A radiologist is asked by an insurance company's medical   _____   _____
       review department to provide an opinion regarding the
       appropriateness of treating a patient's cancer with a specific
       radiation therapy procedure. The radiologist would report
       the service using a consultation code from the E/M section
       of CPT.

58.   A radiologist is asked by an insurance company's medical
        review department to provide a written opinion about a
        radiograph previously taken and interpreted by another
        physician. The radiologist would report the service using the
        code which describes the radiological procedure and add the
        "-26" modifier for the professional component (writing the
        report).

59.   Federal law requires that physicians must accept assignment _____   _____
        on <u>all</u> lab work performed in the office (that is, not by an
        outside lab), regardless of who is the third party payer.

60.   Although Medicare billing regulations require that all   _____   _____
        services provided to a patient on the same day be put on the
        same claim form, there are instances where this is not true.
        This would include situations where in-office lab services
        that require assignment are being billed in conjunction with
        other services that are not being taken on an assigned basis.

61.   CPT identifies six individual chemistry tests that, though   _____   _____
        normally part of a multichannel lab code, may be billed
        separately when performed after hours or on Sundays.

62.   In the case of organ or disease oriented lab panel codes, if, _____   _____
        in addition to tests included in a specific panel, the physician
        orders tests not defined in the panel, the panel code may not
        be used and each individual test must be itemized on the
        claim.

63.   The morphometric analysis of a tumor would be included as _____   _____
        part of a Level IV surgical pathology service (code 88305).

The following are multiple choice questions. Select the most correct answer(s).

64.   With regard to proper documentation of E/M services, which of the following is NOT
        relevant?

        a.   Identification of appropriate health risk factors.

        b.   Ability to infer rationale for ordering diagnostic tests.

        c.   Signature of nurse or qualified medical assistant attesting to accuracy of physician's
               documentation.

        d.   Noting revisions to diagnosis in instances where the initial or previous diagnosis was
               either incomplete or inaccurate.

        e.   All of the above are relevant.

The following information applies to problems 65 through 67.

Dr. Daniels, an otorhinolaryngologist, sees a 35 year-old patient in his office to evaluate her chronically draining ear, imbalance, and likely cholesteatoma. He performs a complete ear, nose, mouth, and throat exam on the patient, takes a history of her chief complaints, an extended history of the illness, and reviews related body systems. During the course of the examination he asks pertinent questions about the patient's work, family, and social life. Although the number of diagnostic and treatment options are multiple and the risk of complications moderate, the amount of information and data to be reviewed was limited.

65. Assuming that Dr. Daniels previously saw the patient for another problem two years ago, this service would be billed as:

    a. 99214

    b. 99204

    c. 99224

    d. 99205

    e. 99215

66. If the patient had not been previously seen by Dr. Daniels, but had been seen three and one-half years ago by Dr. Daniels' partner, who is also an otorhinolaryngologist, the services would be billed as:

    a. 99204

    b. 99205

    c. 99213

    d. 99214

    e. 99215

67. Assuming that the patient was referred to Dr. Daniels by the patient's internist for an opinion and advice, and Dr. Daniels sent his findings and recommendations to the internist in a word processing document via electronic mail, the service would be billed as:

    a. 99214

    b. 99215

    c. 99204

    d. 99244

    e. 99245

68.   Which of the following statements is true about billing initial hospital observation care?

a.   The service cannot be billed if the patient is not subsequently admitted to the hospital.

b.   The service cannot be reported if the day after providing the initial hospital observation service the physician admits the patient to the hospital.

c.   Charges for services performed in the physician's office related to, and in conjunction with, the patient's initial observation care should be billed either instead of or in addition to initial observation care.

d.   Charges for services performed in the physician's office related to, and in conjunction with, the patient's initial observation care should not be billed in addition to initial observation care.

e.   None of the above are true.

69.   A physician provides prolonged services with direct (face-to-face) patient contact for two hours. The correct coding for this service is?

a.   99356 with 2 units

b.   99356 with 1 unit
       99357 with 2 units

c.   99357 with 4 units

d.   99354 with 1 unit
       99355 with 2 units

e.   99356 with 1 unit
       99357 with 4 units

70.   Dr. Ganz is managing a patient in the critical care unit of a hospital. Over the course of the day he spends two and one-half hours directly caring for the patient. Other services he performs for the patient that day include an arterial puncture to collect blood, interpretation of a bilateral chest x-ray, ventilator management, and a wound closure. Dr. Ganz could bill the following:

a.   99291 with 2 units
       99292 with 1 unit
       71020-26
       12002
       36600
       94660

b.   99291 with 1 unit
       99292 with 3 units
       71020-26

12002
36600
94660

c. 99292 with 5 units
    71020-26
    12000
    36600
    94660

d. 99291 with 1 unit
    99292 with 3 units
    12002
    94660

e. None of the above.

71. Which of the following is not required in order to bill for consultation services?

a. The doctor must communicate his or her findings and/or recommendations to the physician requesting the opinion or advice.

b. The request for the opinion or advice must be documented by the consultant in the patient's medical record.

c. If a patient initiates the consultation, the physician must be aware that she is confirming or denying the opinion of another physician.

d. With the exception of confirmatory consultations, the referral must originate from a physician.

e. None of the above.

72. On a Thursday, a physician discharges a patient form the hospital and admits him to a skilled nursing facility. The patient had been in the hospital under the physician's supervision for the past two weeks. The physician completes the patient's hospital discharge papers, performs a detailed interval history and comprehensive examination, and medical decision making is of low complexity. The physician also spends 30 minutes discussing with the patient and the patient's children the care he will be receiving in the nursing home. At the nursing home the physician completes the appropriate admission paperwork. How would you code for the doctor's services?

a. 99238
    99301

b. 99303

c. 99239

d. 99239
99301

e. None of the above.

73. Suppose in problem 72 above that the patient was not in the hospital, but was seen in the physician's office on the day of admission to the nursing facility. Assuming the same levels of history, examination, and medical decision making were provided and that counseling the patient and patient's children dominated the office service, how would you code the services?

a. 99301

b. 99214

c. 99302

d. 99301
99214

e. None of the above.

74. The surgeon removes an embedded foreign body from the upper right eyelid of a Medicare patient. What is the correct way of coding this service?

a. 67938

b. 67938-E3

c. 67938-77

d. 67930

e. None of the above.

75. A Medicare patient is being treated in a teaching hospital. A resident performs a level two subsequent hospital visit on the patient without the presence of a teaching physician. How would you code this service?

a. It cannot be billed as the teaching physician was not present.

b. 99232

c. 99232-RP

d. If it is being billed under the primary care exception rule, it would be reported as 99232-GE.

e. None of the above.

76.   A second surgical opinion is ordered by a Medicare approved PRO. The reporting physician might list which of the following on his/her claim?

   a.   99262-YY

   b.   99263-ZZ

   c.   99252-YY

   d.   99273-YY

   e.   None of the above.

77.   Which of the following code and modifier combinations could be correct?

   a.   99216-24

   b.   99213-21

   c.   99203-24

   d.   99213-22

   e.   99213-56

78.   Which of the following code and modifier combinations could be correct?

   a.   31576-50

   b.   21406-50

   c.   56315-50

   d.   65710-50

   e.   None of the above.

79.   Which of the following code and modifier combinations could be correct?

   a.   31512
        31505-51

   b.   97260
        97261-51

   c.   59510
        59525-51

   d.   40490
        40801-51

   e.   None of the above.

80. Which of the following code and modifier combinations could be correct?

    a. 99233-56
       58240-54

    b. 58240-54
       99233-55

    c. 58240-54/56

    d. 58240-54/55

    e. None of the above.

81. Which of the following code and modifier combinations could be correct?

    a. 99343-57

    b. 99385-57

    c. 67901-Q1

    d. 78584-53

    e. None of the above.

82. Which of the following code and modifier combinations could be correct?

    a. 26615-79/78

    b. 71020-26

    c. 83775-77

    d. 80053-22

    e. None of the above.

83. Which of the following code and modifier combinations could be correct?

    a. 12004-80

    b. 12004-81

    c. 12032-82

    d. 12004-80/52

    e. None of the above.

84.   An ophthalmologist examines and prescribes treatment for a patient she last saw three and one-half years ago. The ophthalmologist's services include obtaining a history, basic sensorimotor examination, external examination, general medical observation, gross field examination, ophthalmoscopic examination, and biomicroscopy. In addition, the physician prescribes spectacles for the patient. These services would be coded using:

    a.   92012
          92340

    b.   92004
          92340

    c.   92002

    d.   92004

    e.   None of the above.

85.   Dr. Vincent, a cardiologist, writes a report related to his interpretation of a real-time transesophageal two-dimensional echogram that he performed in the hospital on the patient earlier in the day. Because the echogram included probe placement and image acquisition, it would be coded using:

    a.   93312-26

    b.   93314-26

    c.   93317

    d.   93314

    e.   None of the above.

86.   A psychiatrist has a formal conference with the nurses and residents regarding a hospital patient's progress and management, examines the patient, and updates the patient's history. During the same day the psychiatrist provides psychotherapy to the patient. The psychiatrist would:

    a.   Charge for hospital-based environmental intervention services and psychotherapy.

    b.   Charge only for the psychotherapy as the hospital services are included in the psychotherapy service.

    c.   Charge only for the hospital visit because a hospital visit and psychotherapy cannot both be billed for the patient on the same day and the hospital visit charge is usually higher than that for the psychotherapy.

    d.   Charge for both the psychotherapy and hospital visit.

    e.   None of the above.

87.   Dr. Greene performs a right heart catheterization. Which of the following services, if performed in conjunction the catheterization, could be billed separately?

   a.   Injection for pulmonary angiography.

   b.   Positioning of catheter.

   c.   Recording intravascular pressure.

   d.   Electrode catheter placement.

   e.   None or the above.

88.   Dr. Norman is called from home to see a patient in the E.R. on a Thursday night at 11:00 pm In addition to charges for procedures and services she renders, Dr. Norman might also bill for:

   a.   99052

   b.   99054

   c.   99050 and 99054

   d.   99052 and 99054

   e.   a or b

   f.   a or b or d

89.   Dr. Swanson provides 50 minutes of diet counseling to a group of six patients at his office. This is the second of three sessions being provided to these patients. He should bill each patient as follows:

   a.   99204

   b.   99214

   c.   99215

   d.   There are no CPT codes for diet counseling, thus code 99499 for unlisted E/M services, along with a special report, should be listed.

   e.   None of the above.

90.   When deciding whether or not it is appropriate to bill a patient for supplies used in the performance of a procedure, the physician should consider which of the following factors?

    a.   Whether or not the patient is a Medicare beneficiary.

    b.   The impact of unbundling on audit liability.

    c.   Patient satisfaction.

    d.   If he previously billed for the supply when providing the service.

    e.   All of the above.

91.   Which of the following items are not included in Medicare's rules for billing major surgical procedures?

    a.   Treatment of complications that arise during performance of the surgical procedure.

    b.   Treatment of complications that arise during the postoperative period which require a trip to the operating room.

    c.   Treatment of related conditions 100 days post-surgery.

    d.   Treatment of related conditions 11 days post-surgery.

    e.   Treatments involving nonincisional endoscopies.

92.   For which of the following surgical procedures, if any, could you charge separately for the normal follow-up services?

    a.   60100

    b.   67820

    c.   50574

    d.   30100

    e.   Each of the above.

93.   The physician is treating an obstetrics patient. Assuming that the physician reports code 59510, which of the following codes could NOT also be reported on the claim?

    a.   59525

    b.   59000

    c.   81000

    d.   59025

    e.   58925

94. A surgeon performs an exploration of a patient's retroperitoneal area (code 49010). Under which circumstances could the physician charge for the exploration?

    a. The exploration is performed by itself.

    b. In addition to the exploration, the surgeon performs a biopsy through the exploration incision site.

    c. In addition to the exploration, through the exploration incision the physician stops internal hemorrhaging.

    d. In addition to the exploration, through the exploration incision the physician performs an incidental appendectomy.

    e. In addition to the exploration, through a different incision, the physician excises a malignant tumor.

95. Which of the following code combinations are not appropriate?

    a. 17000
       17001-51

    b. 20205
       20200-51

    c. 12035
       12031-51

    d. 29820
       29815-51

    e. All of the above are appropriate.

96. The surgeon repairs the following wounds:

       2.7 cm layer closure, left foot
       4.9 cm simple closure, right foot
       2.5 cm layer closure, face
       2.8 cm simple closure, right armpit

The repairs would be coded as?

    a. 12042
       12004-51

    b. 13300

c. 12042
   12051-51
   12002-51
   12002-51

d. 12051
   12042-51
   12004-51

e. 12053
   12004-51

97. An anesthesiologist provided anesthesia services on a Medicare patient who underwent a cholecystostomy (code 47480). Which of the following regarding billing of the anesthesia services might apply?

   a. The anesthesiologist would bill the appropriate CPT anesthesia code and report total time in minutes in the units column on the claim form.

   b. The anesthesiologist would bill the CPT surgery code (47480) and report total time in minutes in the units column of the claim form.

   c. The anesthesiologist would bill the appropriate CPT anesthesia code and list in the units column of the claim form, total units. (That is, the units associated with the reported anesthesia CPT codes added to the units associated with time—total time in minutes divided by 15 minutes per unit.)

   d. None of the above.

CHAPTER FOUR:
PROVEN TECHNIQUES
FOR OPTIMIZING
REIMBURSEMENT

Reporting physician services to obtain proper reimbursement involves more than just listing the correct codes on the claim and submitting additional information when appropriate. As you will soon see, the method you use to report services, the style you use when writing special reports, the way you deal with payers, and your diagnosis coding can all have a significant impact on your and your patients' reimbursement.

In past chapters, the focus was on helping you better understand how to code properly. In this chapter you will learn some very powerful techniques for insuring optimal reimbursement. Specifically, you will learn:

I.   The steps for properly identifying reportable services and diagnoses.
II.   Why clean claims are important.
III.   The importance of frequent billing.
IV.   How to deal effectively with third party payers.
V.   The value of KISS letters.
VI.   How to use EOBs to your advantage.

GENERAL REPORTING RULES

No matter what your specialty, you should observe the following six steps when coding and filing insurance claim forms.

1. Identify Procedures, Services, and Supplies Provided.

The first step is to identify what was done for the patient during the physician/patient encounter. In most cases this is an easy task because you will be identifying commonly performed services and procedures such as office visits, hospital visits, routine surgical procedures, and the like. However, you should be aware of two issues that can lead to reimbursement problems.

First, many physicians feel strongly that they did not go into the field of medicine in order to spend time dealing with coding and billing issues. As a result, they tend not to involve themselves with reimbursement issues and remain generally unaware of the procedures, services, and supplies which can be billed. This is especially true of physicians who work in large clinics, universities, hospitals, and nonprofit organizations. The result of the physician's inattention to coding and billing issues is both lower reimbursement and increased audit liability.

Unfortunately, it is not only the physicians and institutions who suffer. The patient may be put in a difficult financial situation by the physician's ignorance. Consider the patient who seeks treatment at a prestigious clinic or university and must pay a substantial portion of the physician's charges out-of-pocket because the physician inappropriately coded and as a result the carrier would not fully cover the services provided. For the patient, what began as a physical illness could result in an economic problem worse than the ailment for which he sought treatment. (Perhaps one of the reasons that prestigious clinics and universities have a reputation for being expensive derives not from their being all that expensive, but rather, that the physicians attracted to these organizations may be so disinterested in billing matters that the financial burden shifts to the patient.)

It takes surprisingly little time for physicians to learn the basics of properly coding the procedures and services they perform. Even if the physician spends just 15 minutes a day for two or three weeks, the results in increased reimbursement and decreased audit liability can be substantial.

The second issue is best illustrated through an example. During the course of a day a physician may see many patients in settings outside the office, such as in the hospital. In addition to patients who require only routine hospital services, there will be some patients for which he performs procedures, and others for which he provides major services such as a formal conference with the staff regarding patient management. Upon returning to the office, the physician's staff inquires about which patients were seen and for what they are to be billed. After a long day and many patient encounters, the physician does not recall several procedures and services rendered, and as a result they go unbilled.

This example was provided by a psychiatrist's office manager. She purchased a note pad for the psychiatrist and strongly encouraged him to take notes of whom he saw and what he did. Within six months the psychiatrist had doubled his gross revenue. *The importance of noting who was seen and what services were provided cannot be overemphasized for those physicians who see patients outside the office.*

2. Code the Billable Procedures, Services, and Supplies.

Once you have identified what was provided to the patient, your next step is to code the *billable* elements. This is a difficult step because it requires a working knowledge of both the coding systems and carrier policies. There are two issues you need to keep in mind: locating the correct code(s) and determining whether or not the item is billable.

To find the correct code you first need to know which coding system(s) should be used — CPT, HCPCS National, or HCPCS Local. Next, locating the code may involve use of the coding system's Index as well as reading the notes associated with the code you have selected. If you are not a physician and do not understand the procedure, a medical dictionary may be of help to you. Also, do not hesitate to ask the physician who performed the service to help you locate the proper code. There may be subtle differences between procedures and services that you cannot be expected to know even if you have a strong background in clinical medicine. Furthermore, the physician is legally responsible if the wrong procedure is billed. Incorrect billing of procedures and services could lead to charges of *fraud* against the physician.

Next, you need to determine which codes can and should be billed. Some procedures are considered to be a component of another procedure and are therefore not billable as separate entities. Examples include: hospital and office visits following surgery that are considered to be part of the surgical package; surgical procedures that are identified with the words "separate procedure" when other procedures are also performed through the same incision; and supplies which were previously included in service charges.

One way to determine the "billability" of a procedure, service, or supply is to read the notes associated with the code. You should also check the carrier's policy. There is a movement among insurance companies to have physicians "bundle" their charges; that is, to have one charge that includes a variety of services and supplies, rather than itemizing each component charge.

3. Identify and Code Patient Illness(es).

It is becoming increasingly important that you properly identify and code patient illnesses. Third party payers routinely delay the processing of, or worse, deny payment on claims that do not list diagnosis codes. Claims that list vague diagnoses, such as an unspecified disorder or condition, may also be delayed or denied.

To code diagnoses you must first identify the patient's specific illnesses. In some practices this is handled by billing staff or nurses who "translate" the physician's diagnosis statement into ICD-9-CM codes. As with procedure coding, if you have difficulty locating codes which match the physician's terminology, *ask for help*. It is not uncommon for physicians to use terms which they are most familiar with but which may differ from those in the code manuals. When this occurs you may want to write down the physician's term and its matching code manual term so that you will not have to repeat the code identification process again in the future.

In other practices the doctor may check a pre-printed diagnosis from a superbill or routing ticket. Beware that it is rarely possible for practices to pre-print all potentially relevant diagnoses on the form. As a result, physicians have a tendency to check the "closest" diagnosis rather than locating the specific diagnosis. It may be helpful for practices which pre-print diagnosis codes on their billing forms to put a special symbol by codes that require fifth digits or greater specificity. In this way the staff will know to locate the code which most accurately describes the patient's problem.

4. Rank Procedures by Importance.

Once you have identified and coded the billable procedures, list them in order of importance by date of service. The ranking is usually from highest to lowest charge. Note that this ranking is done for each day's codes. The items listed on the claim, if for more than one day, should be listed first by date. *Within each date* the billable items are ranked by *charge*. The claim shown in Figure 4.1 has been prepared incorrectly. A proper listing of the same services is shown in Figure 4.2.

There are two reasons for listing the items in order of importance. First, you want to make sure that surgical procedures performed on the same date are ranked by charge because the carriers will usually reduce the secondary surgical charges. Therefore, your highest charge needs to be listed first, followed by the next highest charge, etc. Second, some carriers (especially Medicaid programs) have policy limitations which state that they will only pay for one service provided to a patient per day. Thus, the first charge you list for that day should be your highest. Beginning coders often believe that the services should be listed in the sequence that they were performed by the physician. This is not the case and can have an adverse impact on reimbursement.

Figure 4.1: Ranking Procedures Within Each Date—Incorrect

HEALTH INSURANCE CLAIM FORM

APPROVED OMB-0939-0008

PLEASE DO NOT STAPLE IN THIS AREA

PICA | PICA

1. MEDICARE	MEDICAID	CHAMPUS	CHAMPVA	GROUP HEALTH PLAN	FECA BLK LUNG	OTHER	1a. INSURED'S I.D. NUMBER (FOR PROGRAM IN ITEM 1)
[X] (Medicare #)	(Medicaid #)	(Sponsor's SSN)	(VA File #)	(SSN or ID)	(SSN)	(ID)	B12345678

2. PATIENT'S NAME (Last Name, First Name, Middle Initial)
Kahn, Lori

3. PATIENT'S BIRTH DATE MM DD YY **06 12 23** SEX M [ ] F [X]

4. INSURED'S NAME (Last Name, First Name, Middle Initial)
Same

5. PATIENT'S ADDRESS (No., Street)
123 Dresden Lane

6. PATIENT RELATIONSHIP TO INSURED
Self [X] Spouse [ ] Child [ ] Other [ ]

7. INSURED'S ADDRESS (No., Street)
Same

CITY **Cherry Hill** STATE **ID**

8. PATIENT STATUS
Single [X] Married [ ] Other [ ]

CITY | STATE

ZIP CODE **60789** TELEPHONE (Include Area Code) **(123) 555-3323**

Employed [ ] Full-Time Student [ ] Part-Time Student [ ]

ZIP CODE | TELEPHONE (Include Area Code)

9. OTHER INSURED'S NAME (Last Name, First Name, Middle Initial)

10. IS PATIENT'S CONDITION RELATED TO:

11. INSURED'S POLICY GROUP OR FECA NUMBER

a. OTHER INSURED'S POLICY OR GROUP NUMBER

a. EMPLOYMENT? (CURRENT OR PREVIOUS) YES [ ] NO [ ]

a. INSURED'S DATE OF BIRTH MM DD YY SEX M [ ] F [ ]

b. OTHER INSURED'S DATE OF BIRTH MM DD YY SEX M [ ] F [ ]

b. AUTO ACCIDENT? YES [ ] NO [ ] PLACE (State)

b. EMPLOYER'S NAME OR SCHOOL NAME

c. EMPLOYER'S NAME OR SCHOOL NAME

c. OTHER ACCIDENT? YES [ ] NO [ ]

c. INSURANCE PLAN NAME OR PROGRAM NAME

d. INSURED PLAN NAME OR PROGRAM NAME

10d. RESERVED FOR LOCAL USE

d. IS THERE ANOTHER HEALTH BENEFIT PLAN? YES [ ] NO [ ] If yes, return to and complete item 9 a–d.

READ BACK OF FORM BEFORE COMPLETING & SIGNING THIS FORM.
12. PATIENT'S OR AUTHORIZED PERSON'S SIGNATURE I authorize the release of any medical or other information necessary to process this claim. I also request payment of government benefits either to myself or to the party who accepts assignment below.
SIGNED *Lori Kahn* DATE *1-29-97*

13. INSURED'S OR AUTHORIZED PERSON'S SIGNATURE I authorize payment of medical benefits to the undersigned physician or supplier for services described below.
SIGNED *Lori Kahn*

14. DATE OF CURRENT: MM DD YY ◄ ILLNESS (First symptom) OR INJURY (Accident) OR PREGNANCY (LMP)

15. IF PATIENT HAS HAD SAME OR SIMILAR ILLNESS, GIVE FIRST DATE MM DD YY

16. DATES PATIENT UNABLE TO WORK IN CURRENT OCCUPATION MM DD YY FROM TO MM DD YY

17. NAME OF REFERRING PHYSICIAN OR OTHER SOURCE
Heather Strewn, M.D.

17a. I.D. NUMBER OF REFERRING PHYSICIAN
115-54-6678

18. HOSPITALIZATION DATES RELATED TO CURRENT SERVICES MM DD YY FROM TO MM DD YY

19. RESERVED FOR LOCAL USE

20. OUTSIDE LAB? YES [ ] NO [ ] $ CHARGES

21. DIAGNOSIS OR NATURE OF ILLNESS OR INJURY. (RELATE ITEMS 1,2,3 OR 4 TO ITEM 24E BY LINE)

1. **217**   3. |___.___
2. **706 2**   4. |___.___

22. MEDICAID RESUBMISSION CODE | ORIGINAL REF. NO.

23. PRIOR AUTHORIZATION NUMBER

24. A. DATE(S) OF SERVICE From MM DD YY	To MM DD YY	B. Place of Service	C. Type of Service	D. PROCEDURES, SERVICES OR SUPPLIES (Explain Unusual Circumstances) CPT/HCPCS	MODIFIER	E. DIAGNOSIS CODE	F. $ CHARGES	G. DAYS OR UNITS	H. EPSDT Family Plan	I. EMG	J. COB	K. RESERVED FOR LOCAL USE
11 25 97		11		19100		1	225 00	1				
11 23 97		11		76091	26	1	50 00	1				
11 23 97		11		10160		2	95 00	1				
11 23 97		11		99243		1,2	145 00	1				

25. FEDERAL TAX I.D. NUMBER **123-45-6789** SSN [ ] EIN [X]

26. PATIENT'S ACCOUNT NO.

27. ACCEPT ASSIGNMENT? (For govt. claims, see back) YES [X] NO [ ]

28. TOTAL CHARGE $ **515 00**

29. AMOUNT PAID $ **0 00**

30. BALANCE DUE $ **515 00**

31. SIGNATURE OF PHYSICIAN OR SUPPLIER INCLUDING DEGREES OR CREDENTIALS (I certify that the statements on the reverse apply to this bill and are made a part thereof.)
SIGNED *H. Stern* DATE *11/25/97*

32. NAME AND ADDRESS OF FACILITY WHERE SERVICES WERE RENDERED (If other than home or office)

33. PHYSICIAN'S SUPPLIER'S BILLING NAME, ADDRESS, ZIP CODE & PHONE #
Heather Stern, M.D.
33 Empire Way
Hordsville, ID 60789
PIN# **1234567890** GRP#

(APPROVED BY AMA COUNCIL ON MEDICAL SERVICE 8/88)   **PLEASE PRINT OR TYPE**

FORM HCFA-1500 (12-90)
FORM OWCP-1500   FORM RRB-1500

CARRIER — PATIENT AND INSURED INFORMATION — PHYSICIAN OR SUPPLIER INFORMATION

Figure 4.2: Ranking Procedures Within Each Date—Correct

APPROVED OMB-0939-0008

PLEASE DO NOT STAPLE IN THIS AREA

PICA

HEALTH INSURANCE CLAIM FORM

PICA

1. MEDICARE	MEDICAID	CHAMPUS	CHAMPVA	GROUP HEALTH PLAN	FECA BLK LUNG	OTHER	1a. INSURED'S I.D. NUMBER (FOR PROGRAM IN ITEM 1)
[X] (Medicare #)	(Medicaid #)	(Sponsor's SSN)	(VA File #)	(SSN or ID)	(SSN)	(ID)	B12345678

2. PATIENT'S NAME (Last Name, First Name, Middle Initial)
Kahn, Lori

3. PATIENT'S BIRTH DATE MM | DD | YY **06 | 12 | 23** SEX M [ ] F [X]

4. INSURED'S NAME (Last Name, First Name, Middle Initial)
Same

5. PATIENT'S ADDRESS (No., Street)
123 Dresden Lane

6. PATIENT RELATIONSHIP TO INSURED
Self [X] Spouse [ ] Child [ ] Other [ ]

7. INSURED'S ADDRESS (No., Street)
Same

CITY **Cherry Hill**   STATE **ID**

8. PATIENT STATUS
Single [X] Married [ ] Other [ ]

CITY   STATE

ZIP CODE **60789**   TELEPHONE (Include Area Code) **(123) 555-3323**

Employed [ ] Full-Time Student [ ] Part-Time Student [ ]

ZIP CODE   TELEPHONE (Include Area Code)

9. OTHER INSURED'S NAME (Last Name, First Name, Middle Initial)

10. IS PATIENT'S CONDITION RELATED TO:

11. INSURED'S POLICY GROUP OR FECA NUMBER

a. OTHER INSURED'S POLICY OR GROUP NUMBER

a. EMPLOYMENT? (CURRENT OR PREVIOUS) [ ] YES [ ] NO

a. INSURED'S DATE OF BIRTH MM | DD | YY   SEX M [ ] F [ ]

b. OTHER INSURED'S DATE OF BIRTH MM | DD | YY   SEX M [ ] F [ ]

b. AUTO ACCIDENT? PLACE (State) [ ] YES [ ] NO [ ]

b. EMPLOYER'S NAME OR SCHOOL NAME

c. EMPLOYER'S NAME OR SCHOOL NAME

c. OTHER ACCIDENT? [ ] YES [ ] NO

c. INSURANCE PLAN NAME OR PROGRAM NAME

d. INSURED PLAN OR PROGRAM NAME

10d. RESERVED FOR LOCAL USE

d. IS THERE ANOTHER HEALTH BENEFIT PLAN? [ ] YES [ ] NO If yes, return to and complete item 9 a–d.

READ BACK OF FORM BEFORE COMPLETING & SIGNING THIS FORM.
12. PATIENT'S OR AUTHORIZED PERSON'S SIGNATURE I authorize the release of any medical or other information necessary to process this claim. I also request payment of government benefits either to myself or to the party who accepts assignment below.

SIGNED *Lori Kahn*   DATE **1-29-97**

13. INSURED'S OR AUTHORIZED PERSON'S SIGNATURE I authorize payment of medical benefits to the undersigned physician or supplier for services described below.

SIGNED *Lori Kahn*

14. DATE OF CURRENT: ILLNESS (First symptom) OR INJURY (Accident) OR PREGNANCY (LMP) MM | DD | YY

15. IF PATIENT HAS HAD SAME OR SIMILAR ILLNESS. GIVE FIRST DATE MM | DD | YY

16. DATES PATIENT UNABLE TO WORK IN CURRENT OCCUPATION MM | DD | YY   FROM   TO   MM | DD | YY

17. NAME OF REFERRING PHYSICIAN OR OTHER SOURCE
Heather Strewn, M.D.

17a. I.D. NUMBER OF REFERRING PHYSICIAN
115-54-6678

18. HOSPITALIZATION DATES RELATED TO CURRENT SERVICES MM | DD | YY   FROM   TO   MM | DD | YY

19. RESERVED FOR LOCAL USE

20. OUTSIDE LAB? [ ] YES [ ] NO $ CHARGES

21. DIAGNOSIS OR NATURE OF ILLNESS OR INJURY. (RELATE ITEMS 1,2,3 OR 4 TO ITEM 24E BY LINE)
1. **217**
2. **706 2**
3. _____
4. _____

22. MEDICAID RESUBMISSION CODE   ORIGINAL REF. NO.

23. PRIOR AUTHORIZATION NUMBER

24. A DATE(S) OF SERVICE From MM DD YY	To MM DD YY	B Place of Service	C Type of Service	D PROCEDURES, SERVICES OR SUPPLIES (Explain Unusual Circumstances) CPT/HCPCS	MODIFIER	E DIAGNOSIS CODE	F $ CHARGES	G DAYS OR UNITS	H EPSDT Family Plan	I EMG	J COB	K RESERVED FOR LOCAL USE
11 23 97		11		99243		1,2	145 00	1				
11 23 97		11		10160		2	95 00	1				
11 23 97		11		76091	26	1	50 00	1				
11 25 97		11		19100		1	225 00	1				

25. FEDERAL TAX I.D. NUMBER **123-45-6789** SSN [ ] EIN [X]

26. PATIENT'S ACCOUNT NO.

27. ACCEPT ASSIGNMENT? (For govt. claims, see back) [X] YES [ ] NO

28. TOTAL CHARGE $ **515 00**

29. AMOUNT PAID $ **0 00**

30. BALANCE DUE $ **515 00**

31. SIGNATURE OF PHYSICIAN OR SUPPLIER INCLUDING DEGREES OR CREDENTIALS (I certify that the statements on the reverse apply to this bill and are made a part thereof.)

SIGNED *H. Strewn*   DATE **11/25/97**

32. NAME AND ADDRESS OF FACILITY WHERE SERVICES WERE RENDERED (If other than home or office)

33. PHYSICIAN'S SUPPLIER'S BILLING NAME, ADDRESS, ZIP CODE & PHONE #
Heather Stern, M.D.
33 Empire Way
Hordsville, ID 60789
PIN# **1234567890** GRP#

(APPROVED BY AMA COUNCIL ON MEDICAL SERVICE 8/88)   **PLEASE PRINT OR TYPE**

FORM HCFA-1500 (12-90)
FORM OWCP-1500   FORM RRB-1500

5. Associate Diagnoses to Procedures.

This is a critical step to ensuring proper reimbursement. Each procedure, service or supply you report must be justified by the patient's condition or payment will be delayed or denied. It is imperative that you list the primary diagnosis justifying the service or supply, and any additional diagnoses that directly affect the care you are providing. As shown in Figure 4.2, each diagnosis is appropriately associated with each procedure or service. In the case of the consultation, both diagnoses are listed.

6. Modify as Necessary.

You will not know if modifiers are required and to which codes they are to be linked until you have completed the first three steps. For example, suppose the physician performed three surgical procedures during the same operative session on a patient. Reporting the procedures requires that you add the "-51" multiple procedure modifier to the secondary procedures. You cannot do this until you have identified, coded, and ranked the services by charge.

DAILY REPORTING AND LINKING DIAGNOSES TO PROCEDURES

There are two things you can do that will have a significant and immediate impact on your level of reimbursement. First, in situations which require additional documentation it may be helpful to include a special report using the KISS principle (discussed later in this chapter). Second, whenever the physician has several high-charge procedures that were performed on a patient over a short period of time, each day's procedures should be submitted on separate claims, and as a appropriate, under different diagnosis codes. In this chapter, you are provided with insights into why daily reporting can be important to reimbursement. And as you will see, understanding requires insights into the workings of the claims processing departments at insurance companies.

Insurance carriers, whether commercial for-profit carriers, the Blues, or Medicare and Medicaid, generally pay low wages to the people who process claims. The typical claims processor has a high school education, is female, in her late teens or early twenties, and earns minimum wage or slightly better. Most carriers do not provide training to claims processors in the areas of medical terminology, clinical medicine or coding. The turnover rate in claims processing personnel is very high.

When the patient's claim arrives at the carrier or at the office of a third party payer administrator that processes claims for the payer, the people who open the mail immediately remove any attachments so that the claim and attachments can be microfilmed. Many carriers have people whose full-time employment involves removing staples from claims and separating any attachments. As such, it is a good idea to note the physician's name, patient's name, patient's policy number, date, etc., on any attachments you submit with the claim. Some physician offices have had rubber stamps made which allow them to put the words, "PLEASE DO NOT SEPARATE ATTACHMENTS," on the claim form.

The claim you submitted is then forwarded to the claims processors who usually work in large open office areas and spend their day entering claims at a computer terminal. The computer terminals are linked to a computer which has software that allows the claims processors' supervisor to keep track of how many claims are processed. Invariably, the supervisor has assigned quotas to each claims processor, and if the quotas are not met, the claims processor may lose her job. It is under this pressure to meet quotas that mishaps occur with greater frequency. These mishaps associated with meeting quotas are called "Friday Afternoon Specials."

It is Friday afternoon and the claims processor is woefully behind in her work. She had a great week with her friends, staying out late a few nights, and did not work as quickly as she should have Monday through Thursday. (Remember when you were in your late teens and early twenties?) Faced with a huge pile of claims and a deadline she discovers a "dirty" claim; that is, a problem claim which requires that it be returned to the physician's office and "fixed" before it can be paid. Processors like "dirty" claims because they can be "processed" very quickly. In fact, if working at a frenzied pace, the claims processor can "process" as many as ten "dirty" claims a minute, in contrast to the two to three minutes it takes to process a "clean" claim.

Suppose the claims processor in this story were to realize that the only way to achieve her quota for the week was by treating many of the claims in the huge pile as "dirty" claims. Since the processor knows that her supervisor counts a returned claim as a processed claim, she decides to treat some of the claims as "dirty" whether or not they actually are. In this way she meets her quota and keeps her job. Thus, the next time you have a claim returned because it was "lacking information" that was really there, you may have been a victim of a Friday Afternoon Special. Of course, there are many reasons why your claim may be wrongfully returned, which may have nothing to do with willful acts on the part of the claims processor. They make mistakes like the rest of us, especially when under a great deal of pressure.

This story teaches us two important lessons. First, whenever possible, submit routine claims electronically to the carrier. Most electronic claims are processed automatically and bypass the claims processor. Second, when you submit claims manually, do not put many high charge procedures that were performed on different days on the same claim. An example will help illustrate why.

Refer to the claim shown in Figure 4.3. The patient came to the physician's office on a Monday with blood in the urine. The physician performed a Level III examination and urinalysis. On the next day the patient returned to the physician's office for a cystoscopy. (This involves the use of a scope to look inside the patient's bladder.) Several medium size tumors were discovered. The next day the patient was admitted to the hospital, and on the following day the bladder tumors were removed. Biopsy determined that the tumors were malignant.

Note that all these services and procedures are being reported on one claim. If this claim were to become a Friday Afternoon Special, it could take as long as six months before payment would be made to the physician or patient. In cases such as this, where there are many high-charge procedures in a short period of time, it would probably be better to submit a claim for each day's services. That is, one claim for the office visit and urinalysis performed on Monday, another claim for the cystoscopy performed on Tuesday, etc., as illustrated in Figures 4.4 through 4.7.

Although this process requires more work on your part, there is another benefit to submitting each day's services on different claims. Note in Figure 4.3 that the physician listed malignant neoplasms of the bladder as the diagnosis associated with the services and procedures. The physician was correct in doing so, but he might have been equally correct if he submitted a claim after seeing the patient on Monday and listed hematuria (blood in the urine) as the diagnosis; this is shown in Figure 4.4. Furthermore, if he submitted a claim on the day he did the cystoscopy, he could list unspecified neoplasms of bladder as the diagnosis for that day's services, since that was the best

Figure 4.3: Several Days of Service on One Claim

PLEASE DO NOT STAPLE IN THIS AREA

APPROVED OMB-0939-0008

CARRIER

HEALTH INSURANCE CLAIM FORM

PICA   PICA

1. MEDICARE MEDICAID CHAMPUS CHAMPVA GROUP HEALTH PLAN FECA BLK LUNG OTHER	1a. INSURED'S I.D. NUMBER (FOR PROGRAM IN ITEM 1)
[X] (Medicare #) (Medicaid #) (Sponsor's SSN) (VA File #) (SSN or ID) (SSN) (ID)	123456789B

2. PATIENT'S NAME (Last Name, First Name, Middle Initial)	3. PATIENT'S BIRTH DATE MM DD YY SEX	4. INSURED'S NAME (Last Name, First Name, Middle Initial)
Carlson, Richter	5 10 28 M [X] F	Same

5. PATIENT'S ADDRESS (No., Street)	6. PATIENT RELATIONSHIP TO INSURED	7. INSURED'S ADDRESS (No., Street)
345 Park Place	Self [X] Spouse Child Other	Same

CITY	STATE	8. PATIENT STATUS	CITY	STATE
Naperville	IL	Single Married [X] Other		

ZIP CODE	TELEPHONE (Include Area Code)		ZIP CODE	TELEPHONE (Include Area Code)
60543	(630)654-8800	Employed Full-Time Student Part-Time Student		

9. OTHER INSURED'S NAME (Last Name, First Name, Middle Initial) | 10. IS PATIENT'S CONDITION RELATED TO: | 11. INSURED'S POLICY GROUP OR FECA NUMBER

a. OTHER INSURED'S POLICY OR GROUP NUMBER | a. EMPLOYMENT? (CURRENT OR PREVIOUS) YES [X] NO | a. INSURED'S DATE OF BIRTH MM DD YY   SEX M F

b. OTHER INSURED'S DATE OF BIRTH MM DD YY SEX M F | b. AUTO ACCIDENT? PLACE (State) YES [X] NO | b. EMPLOYER'S NAME OR SCHOOL NAME

C. EMPLOYER'S NAME OR SCHOOL NAME | c. OTHER ACCIDENT? YES [X] NO | c. INSURANCE PLAN NAME OR PROGRAM NAME

d. INSURED PLAN NAME OR PROGRAM NAME | 10d. RESERVED FOR LOCAL USE | d. IS THERE ANOTHER HEALTH BENEFIT PLAN? YES NO *If yes, return to and complete item 9 a–d.*

READ BACK OF FORM BEFORE COMPLETING & SIGNING THIS FORM.

12. PATIENT'S OR AUTHORIZED PERSON'S SIGNATURE I authorize the release of any medical or other information necessary to process this claim. I also request payment of government benefits either to myself or to the party who accepts assignment below.

SIGNED **On File**   DATE **8/19/97**

13. INSURED'S OR AUTHORIZED PERSON'S SIGNATURE I authorize payment of medical benefits to the undersigned physician or supplier for services described below.

SIGNED **On File**

14. DATE OF CURRENT: ILLNESS (First symptom) OR INJURY (Accident) OR PREGNANCY (LMP) MM DD YY	15. IF PATIENT HAS HAD SAME OR SIMILAR ILLNESS, GIVE FIRST DATE MM DD YY	16. DATES PATIENT UNABLE TO WORK IN CURRENT OCCUPATION FROM MM DD YY TO MM DD YY
8 17 97		

17. NAME OF REFERRING PHYSICIAN OR OTHER SOURCE	17a. I.D. NUMBER OF REFERRING PHYSICIAN	18. HOSPITALIZATION DATES RELATED TO CURRENT SERVICES FROM MM DD YY TO MM DD YY

19. RESERVED FOR LOCAL USE	20. OUTSIDE LAB? YES [X] NO $ CHARGES

21. DIAGNOSIS OR NATURE OF ILLNESS OR INJURY. (RELATE ITEMS 1,2,3 OR 4 TO ITEM 24E BY LINE)

1. **188.9 M-Lesion,Bladder Wall**
2.
3.
4.

22. MEDICAID RESUBMISSION CODE   ORIGINAL REF. NO.

23. PRIOR AUTHORIZATION NUMBER

24. A. DATE(S) OF SERVICE						B. Place of Service	C. Type of Service	D. PROCEDURES, SERVICES OR SUPPLIES (Explain Unusual Circumstances) CPT/HCPCS MODIFIER	E. DIAGNOSIS CODE	F. $ CHARGES		G. DAYS OR UNITS	H. EPSDT Family Plan	I. EMG	J. COB	K. RESERVED FOR LOCAL USE
From MM	DD	YY	To MM	DD	YY											
8	18	97				11		99213	1	55	00	1				
8	18	97				11		81000	1	15	00	1				
8	19	97				11		52204	1	400	00	1				
8	20	97				21		99221	1	110	00	1				
8	22	97				21		52235	1	1250	00	1				

25. FEDERAL TAX I.D. NUMBER SSN EIN	26. PATIENT'S ACCOUNT NO.	27. ACCEPT ASSIGNMENT? (For govt. claims, see back)	28. TOTAL CHARGE	29. AMOUNT PAID	30. BALANCE DUE
987-65-4321 [X]		[X] YES NO	$ 1830 00	$ 0 00	$ 1830 00

31. SIGNATURE OF PHYSICIAN OR SUPPLIER INCLUDING DEGREES OR CREDENTIALS (I certify that the statements on the reverse apply to this bill and are made a part thereof.)	32. NAME AND ADDRESS OF FACILITY WHERE SERVICES WERE RENDERED (If other than home or office)	33. PHYSICIAN'S SUPPLIER'S BILLING NAME, ADDRESS, ZIP CODE & PHONE #
John Brieski 8/22/98 SIGNED DATE	St. Tammaras 674 Highland Naperville, IL 60543	John Brieski, M.D. 6453 Santa Fe Drive Clarendon Hills, IL 65432 PIN# 123456965 GRP#

(APPROVED BY AMA COUNCIL ON MEDICAL SERVICE 8/88)   **PLEASE PRINT OR TYPE**

FORM HCFA-1500 (12-90) FORM OWCP-1500   FORM RRB-1500

PATIENT AND INSURED INFORMATION

PHYSICIAN OR SUPPLIER INFORMATION

Figure 4.4: Single Day of Service on One Claim

APPROVED OMB-0939-0008

PLEASE DO NOT STAPLE IN THIS AREA

CARRIER

HEALTH INSURANCE CLAIM FORM

PICA PICA

1. MEDICARE MEDICARD CHAMPUS CHAMPVA GROUP HEALTH PLAN FECA BLK LUNG OTHER
[X] (Medicare #) [ ] (Medicard #) [ ] (Sponsor's SSN) [ ] (VA File #) [ ] (SSN or ID) [ ] (SSN) [ ] (ID)

1a. INSURED I.D. NUMBER (FOR PROGRAM IN ITEM 1)
123456789B

2. PATIENT'S NAME (Last Name, First Name, Middle Initial)
Carlson, Richter

3. PATIENT'S BIRTH DATE MM | DD | YY SEX
5 | 10 | 28   M [X] F [ ]

4. INSURED'S NAME (Last Name, First Name, Middle Initial)
Same

5. PATIENT'S ADDRESS (No., Street)
345 Park Place

6. PATIENT RELATIONSHIP TO INSURED
Self [X] Spouse [ ] Child [ ] Other [ ]

7. INSURED'S ADDRESS (No., Street)
Same

CITY **Naperville** STATE **IL**

8. PATIENT STATUS
Single [ ] Married [X] Other [ ]

CITY   STATE

ZIP CODE **60543** TELEPHONE (Include Area Code) **(630)654-8800**

Employed [ ] Full-Time Student [ ] Part-Time Student [ ]

ZIP CODE   TELEPHONE (Include Area Code)

9. OTHER INSURED'S NAME (Last Name, First Name, Middle Initial)

10. IS PATIENT'S CONDITION RELATED TO:

11. INSURED'S POLICY GROUP OR FECA NUMBER

a. OTHER INSURED'S POLICY OR GROUP NUMBER

a. EMPLOYMENT? (CURRENT OR PREVIOUS) [ ] YES [X] NO

a. INSURED'S DATE OF BIRTH MM | DD | YY SEX M [ ] F [ ]

b. OTHER INSURED'S DATE OF BIRTH MM | DD | YY SEX M [ ] F [ ]

b. AUTO ACCIDENT? PLACE (State) [ ] YES [X] NO

b. EMPLOYER'S NAME OR SCHOOL NAME

c. EMPLOYER'S NAME OR SCHOOL NAME

c. OTHER ACCIDENT? [ ] YES [X] NO

c. INSURANCE PLAN NAME OR PROGRAM NAME

d. INSURED PLAN NAME OR PROGRAM NAME

10d. RESERVED FOR LOCAL USE

d. IS THERE ANOTHER HEALTH BENEFIT PLAN? [ ] YES [X] NO If yes, return to and complete item 9 a–d.

READ BACK OF FORM BEFORE COMPLETING & SIGNING THIS FORM.
12. PATIENT'S OR AUTHORIZED PERSON'S SIGNATURE I authorize the release of any medical or other information necessary to process this claim. I also request payment of government benefits either to myself or to the party who accepts assignment below.

SIGNED **On File** DATE **8/18/97**

13. INSURED'S OR AUTHORIZED PERSON'S SIGNATURE I authorize payment of medical benefits to the undersigned physician or supplier for services described below.

SIGNED **On File**

14. DATE OF CURRENT: MM | DD | YY ILLNESS (First symptom) OR INJURY (Accident) OR PREGNANCY (LMP)
8 | 17 | 97

15. IF PATIENT HAS HAD SAME OR SIMILAR ILLNESS, GIVE FIRST DATE MM | DD | YY

16. DATES PATIENT UNABLE TO WORK IN CURRENT OCCUPATION MM | DD | YY FROM   TO

17. NAME OF REFERRING PHYSICIAN OR OTHER SOURCE

17a. I.D. NUMBER OF REFERRING PHYSICIAN

18. HOSPITALIZATION DATES RELATED TO CURRENT SERVICES MM | DD | YY FROM   TO

19. RESERVED FOR LOCAL USE

20. OUTSIDE LAB? [ ] YES [X] NO $ CHARGES

21. DIAGNOSIS OR NATURE OF ILLNESS OR INJURY. (RELATE ITEMS 1,2,3 or 4 TO ITEM 24E BY LINE)
1. **599.7 Hematuria**
2.
3.
4.

22. MEDICAID RESUBMISSION CODE   ORIGINAL REF. NO.

23. PRIOR AUTHORIZATION NUMBER

24.

A. DATE(S) OF SERVICE From MM DD YY To MM DD YY	B. Place of Service	C. Type of Service	D. PROCEDURES, SERVICES OR SUPPLIES (Explain Unusual Circumstances) CPT/HCPCS MODIFIER	E. DIAGNOSIS CODE	F. $ CHARGES	G. DAYS OR UNITS	H. EPSDT Family Plan	I. EMG	J. COB	K. RESERVED FOR LOCAL USE
8 18 97	11		99213	1	55 00	1				
8 18 97	11		81000	1	15 00	1				

25. FEDERAL TAX I.D. NUMBER SSN EIN
987-65-4321 [X]

26. PATIENT'S ACCOUNT NO.

27. ACCEPT ASSIGNMENT? (For govt. claims, see back) [X] YES [ ] NO

28. TOTAL CHARGE $ **70 00**

29. AMOUNT PAID $ **0 00**

30. BALANCE DUE $ **70 00**

31. SIGNATURE OF PHYSICIAN OR SUPPLIER INCLUDING DEGREES OR CREDENTIALS (I certify that the statements on the reverse apply to this bill and are made a part thereof.)
SIGNED *John Brieski* 8/22/98 DATE

32. NAME AND ADDRESS OF FACILITY WHERE SERVICES WERE RENDERED (If other than home or office)

33. PHYSICIAN'S SUPPLIER'S BILLING NAME, ADDRESS, ZIP CODE & PHONE #
John Brieski, M.D.
6453 Santa Fe Drive
Clarendon Hills, IL 65432
PIN# **123456965** GRP#

(APPROVED BY AMA COUNCIL ON MEDICAL SERVICE 8/88) *PLEASE PRINT OR TYPE*

FORM HCFA-1500 (12-90) FORM OWCP-1500 FORM RRB-1500

PATIENT AND INSURED INFORMATION | PHYSICIAN OR SUPPLIER INFORMATION

information he had at the time he submitted the claim. This is illustrated in Figure 4.5. The same diagnosis could be reported for the initial hospital care (Figure 4.6). The diagnosis for the tumor excisions, malignant neoplasms of the bladder, would be the correct diagnosis for the procedure performed on Thursday (Figure 4.7).

Some carriers (especially Medicare and Medicaid) may have restrictions on the number of services they will reimburse under a particular diagnosis or during the surgical package. For example, refer again to Figure 4.3, the claim on which all the patient's services are listed under the same diagnosis. The claims processor may deny the office visit on Monday and the hospital visit on Wednesday because they are under the same diagnosis as the surgery. Or, she may question the necessity of two surgeries under the same diagnosis and possibly reject the cystoscopy or the cystourethroscopy. Remember, the person who processes your claim and her immediate boss probably know little or nothing about medicine, and may not realize that a cystoscopy is a diagnostic, not a therapeutic, procedure. Also, the claims processor can get in trouble for overpaying you, but will rarely get in trouble for underpaying you. So when in doubt, they tend to deny payment.

If the services are listed on separate claims and mailed in on separate days, the chances are quite good that different claims processors will process each of the claims. Furthermore, and most importantly, although there is a good chance that the computer will show procedures and services you recently billed, if they are listed under a different diagnosis code, the processor may not realize that the diagnoses are related, and thus pay your claim. If the recent charges had been listed under the same diagnosis code, your current charge might have been rejected.

Now that you have a better understanding of why it is in your, and your patients' best interest to use separate claim forms for each day's services when you have several high charges in a short period of time, and to list different diagnoses whenever legitimately possible, you will learn why it is equally important for you to understand how to write special reports.

Over the next few years as payers begin embracing new computer and software technologies that allow for higher quality claims adjudication, the relevance of the issues discussed above will diminish. Improvements in software and electronic submission of claims will reduce the number of people involved in handling claims and thereby reduce errors, such as the Friday Afternoon Special type problems. Furthermore, when claims adjudication software identifies a specific problem on a claim it will be able to direct the claim to an individual at the payer who has expertise in dealing with the specific problem. These and other improvements will ultimately lead to faster, more accurate, and fairer adjudication of your claims.

Finally, it is worth noting that some payers, rather than returning problem claims for additional information or correction, will simply pay them in order to meet filing deadlines. This is especially true with Workers' Compensation programs that have strict payment deadlines. In the case of claims involving small payments, it may be less expensive for the payer to pay the claim than ask you to submit additional information.

KISS LETTERS

CPT, HCPCS, and ICD-9-CM codes provide a "shorthand" method of communicating with insurance carriers. Instead of describing at length what was done for the patient and the nature of the patient's illness, by use of just codes, the majority of claims can be processed quickly and

Figure 4.5: Single Day of Service on Claim

		APPROVED OMB-0939-0008

PLEASE
DO NOT
STAPLE
IN THIS
AREA

HEALTH INSURANCE CLAIM FORM

PICA		PICA

1. MEDICARE	MEDICARD	CHAMPUS	CHAMPVA	GROUP HEALTH PLAN	FECA BLK LUNG	OTHER	1a. INSURED'S I.D. NUMBER (FOR PROGRAM IN ITEM 1)
X (Medicare #)	(Medicard #)	(Sponsor's SSN)	(VA File #)	(SSN or ID)	(SSN)	(ID)	123456789B

2. PATIENT'S NAME (Last Name, First Name, Middle Initial)
Carlson, Richter

2. PATIENT'S BIRTH DATE MM 5 | DD 10 | YY 28   SEX M X F

4. INSURED'S NAME (Last Name, First Name, Middle Initial)
Same

5. PATIENT'S ADDRESS (No., Street)
345 Park Place

6. PATIENT RELATIONSHIP TO INSURED Self X Spouse Child Other

7. INSURED'S ADDRESS (No., Street)
Same

CITY **Naperville** STATE **IL**

8. PATIENT STATUS Single Married X Other

CITY STATE

ZIP CODE **60543** TELEPHONE (Include Area Code) **(630)654-8800**

Employed Full-Time Student Part-Time Student

ZIP CODE TELEPHONE (Include Area Code)

9. OTHER INSURED'S NAME (Last Name, First Name, Middle Initial)

10. IS PATIENT'S CONDITION RELATED TO:

11. INSURED'S POLICY GROUP OR FECA NUMBER

a. OTHER INSURED'S POLICY OR GROUP NUMBER

a. EMPLOYMENT? (CURRENT OR PREVIOUS) YES X NO

a. INSURED'S DATE OF BIRTH MM | DD | YY   SEX M F

b. OTHER INSURED'S DATE OF BIRTH MM | DD | YY   SEX M F

b. AUTO ACCIDENT? PLACE (State) YES X NO

b. EMPLOYER'S NAME OR SCHOOL NAME

C. EMPLOYER'S NAME OR SCHOOL NAME

c. OTHER ACCIDENT? YES X NO

c. INSURANCE PLAN NAME OR PROGRAM NAME

d. INSURED PLAN NAME OR PROGRAM NAME

10d. RESERVED FOR LOCAL USE

d. IS THERE ANOTHER HEALTH BENEFIT PLAN? YES X NO *If yes, return to and complete item 9 a–d.*

READ BACK OF FORM BEFORE COMPLETING & SIGNING THIS FORM.
12. PATIENT'S OR AUTHORIZED PERSON'S SIGNATURE I authorize the release of any medical or other information necessary to process this claim. I also request payment of government benefits either to myself or to the party who accepts assignment below.
SIGNED **On File** DATE **8/19/97**

13. INSURED'S OR AUTHORIZED PERSON'S SIGNATURE I authorize payment of medical benefits to the undersigned physician or supplier for services described below.
SIGNED **On File**

14. DATE OF CURRENT: MM 8 | DD 17 | YY 97 ILLNESS (First symptom) OR INJURY (Accident) OR PREGNANCY (LMP)

15. IF PATIENT HAS HAD SAME OR SIMILAR ILLNESS, GIVE FIRST DATE MM | DD | YY

16. DATES PATIENT UNABLE TO WORK IN CURRENT OCCUPATION FROM MM | DD | YY TO MM | DD | YY

17. NAME OF REFERRING PHYSICIAN OR OTHER SOURCE

17a. I.D. NUMBER OF REFERRING PHYSICIAN

18. HOSPITALIZATION DATES RELATED TO CURRENT SERVICES FROM MM | DD | YY TO MM | DD | YY

19. RESERVED FOR LOCAL USE

20. OUTSIDE LAB? YES X NO $ CHARGES

21. DIAGNOSIS OR NATURE OF ILLNESS OR INJURY. (RELATE ITEMS 1,2,3 OR 4 TO ITEM 24E BY LINE)
1. **239.4 Neoplasm-Unspec.-Bladder**
2.
3.
4.

22. MEDICAID RESUBMISSION CODE ORIGINAL REF. NO.

23. PRIOR AUTHORIZATION NUMBER

24. A DATE(S) OF SERVICE From MM DD YY To MM DD YY	B Place of Service	C Type of Service	D PROCEDURES, SERVICES OR SUPPLIES (Explain Unusual Circumstances) CPT/HCPCS MODIFIER	E DIAGNOSIS CODE	F $ CHARGES	G DAYS OR UNITS	H EPSDT Family Plan	I EMG	J COB	K RESERVED FOR LOCAL USE
8 19 97	11		52204	1	400 00	1				

25. FEDERAL TAX I.D. NUMBER SSN EIN
987-65-4321 X

26. PATIENT'S ACCOUNT NO.

27. ACCEPT ASSIGNMENT? (For govt. claims, see back) X YES NO

28. TOTAL CHARGE $ **400 00**

29. AMOUNT PAID $ **0 00**

30. BALANCE DUE $ **400 00**

31. SIGNATURE OF PHYSICIAN OR SUPPLIER INCLUDING DEGREES OR CREDENTIALS (I certify that the statements on the reverse apply to this bill and are made a part thereof.)
SIGNED *John Brieski 8/22/98* DATE

32. NAME AND ADDRESS OF FACILITY WHERE SERVICES WERE RENDERED (If other than home or office)

33. PHYSICIAN'S SUPPLIER'S BILLING NAME, ADDRESS, ZIP CODE & PHONE #
John Brieski, M.D.
6453 Santa Fe Drive
Clarendon Hills, IL 65432
PIN# **123456965** GRP#

(APPROVED BY AMA COUNCIL ON MEDICAL SERVICE 8/88) **PLEASE PRINT OR TYPE**

FORM HCFA-1500 (12-90)
FORM OWCP-1500 FORM RRB-1500

CARRIER — PATIENT AND INSURED INFORMATION — PHYSICIAN OR SUPPLIER INFORMATION

Figure 4.6: Single Day of Service on Claim

PLEASE DO NOT STAPLE IN THIS AREA

APPROVED OMB-0939-0008

CARRIER

| | PICA | HEALTH INSURANCE CLAIM FORM | PICA | |

1. MEDICARE ☒ (Medicare #) MEDICAID ☐ (Medicaid #) CHAMPUS ☐ (Sponsor's SSN) CHAMPVA ☐ (VA File #) GROUP HEALTH PLAN ☐ (SSN or ID) FECA BLK LUNG ☐ (SSN) OTHER ☐ (ID)

1a. INSURED'S I.D. NUMBER (FOR PROGRAM IN ITEM 1)
123456789B

2. PATIENT'S NAME (Last Name, First Name, Middle Initial)
Carlson, Richter

3. PATIENT'S BIRTH DATE MM 5 | DD 10 | YY 28 SEX M ☒ F ☐

4. INSURED'S NAME (Last Name, First Name, Middle Initial)
Same

5. PATIENT'S ADDRESS (No., Street)
345 Park Place

6. PATIENT RELATIONSHIP TO INSURED Self ☒ Spouse ☐ Child ☐ Other ☐

7. INSURED'S ADDRESS (No., Street)
Same

CITY **Naperville** STATE **IL**

8. PATIENT STATUS Single ☐ Married ☒ Other ☐

CITY   STATE

ZIP CODE **60543** TELEPHONE (Include Area Code) **(630)654-8800**

Employed ☐ Full-Time Student ☐ Part-Time Student ☐

ZIP CODE   TELEPHONE (Include Area Code)

9. OTHER INSURED'S NAME (Last Name, First Name, Middle Initial)

10. IS PATIENT'S CONDITION RELATED TO:

11. INSURED'S POLICY GROUP OR FECA NUMBER

a. OTHER INSURED'S POLICY OR GROUP NUMBER

a. EMPLOYMENT? (CURRENT OR PREVIOUS) YES ☐ NO ☒

a. INSURED'S DATE OF BIRTH MM | DD | YY SEX M ☐ F ☐

b. OTHER INSURED'S DATE OF BIRTH MM | DD | YY SEX M ☐ F ☐

b. AUTO ACCIDENT? YES ☐ NO ☒ PLACE (State)

b. EMPLOYER'S NAME OR SCHOOL NAME

c. EMPLOYER'S NAME OR SCHOOL NAME

c. OTHER ACCIDENT? YES ☐ NO ☒

c. INSURANCE PLAN NAME OR PROGRAM NAME

d. INSURED PLAN NAME OR PROGRAM NAME

10d. RESERVED FOR LOCAL USE

d. IS THERE ANOTHER HEALTH BENEFIT PLAN? YES ☐ NO ☐ If yes, return to and complete item 9 a-d.

READ BACK OF FORM BEFORE COMPLETING & SIGNING THIS FORM.
12. PATIENT'S OR AUTHORIZED PERSON'S SIGNATURE I authorize the release of any medical or other information necessary to process this claim. I also request payment of government benefits either to myself or to the party who accepts assignment below.
SIGNED **On File** DATE **8/20/97**

13. INSURED'S OR AUTHORIZED PERSON'S SIGNATURE I authorize payment of medical benefits to the undersigned physician or supplier for services described below.
SIGNED **On File**

14. DATE OF CURRENT: MM 8 | DD 17 | YY 97 ILLNESS (First symptom) OR INJURY (Accident) OR PREGNANCY (LMP)

15. IF PATIENT HAS HAD SAME OR SIMILAR ILLNESS. GIVE FIRST DATE MM | DD | YY

16. DATES PATIENT UNABLE TO WORK IN CURRENT OCCUPATION FROM MM | DD | YY TO MM | DD | YY

17. NAME OF REFERRING PHYSICIAN OR OTHER SOURCE

17a. I.D. NUMBER OF REFERRING PHYSICIAN

18. HOSPITALIZATION DATES RELATED TO CURRENT SERVICES FROM MM | DD | YY TO MM | DD | YY

19. RESERVED FOR LOCAL USE

20. OUTSIDE LAB? YES ☐ NO ☒ $ CHARGES

21. DIAGNOSIS OR NATURE OF ILLNESS OR INJURY. (RELATE ITEMS 1,2,3 OR 4 TO ITEM 24E BY LINE)

1. **239.4 Neoplasm-Unspec.-Bladder**
2. ___.___
3. ___.___
4. ___.___

22. MEDICAID RESUBMISSION CODE   ORIGINAL REF. NO.

23. PRIOR AUTHORIZATION NUMBER

24.

A. DATE(S) OF SERVICE						B. Place of Service	C. Type of Service	D. PROCEDURES, SERVICES OR SUPPLIES (Explain Unusual Circumstances) CPT/HCPCS	MODIFIER	E. DIAGNOSIS CODE	F. $ CHARGES		G. DAYS OR UNITS	H. EPSDT Family Plan	I. EMG	J. COB	K. RESERVED FOR LOCAL USE
From MM 8	DD 20	YY 97	To MM	DD	YY	21		99221		1	110	00	1				

25. FEDERAL TAX I.D. NUMBER **987-65-4321** SSN ☐ EIN ☒

26. PATIENT'S ACCOUNT NO.

27. ACCEPT ASSIGNMENT? (For govt. claims, see back) ☒ YES ☐ NO

28. TOTAL CHARGE $ **110** | **00**

29. AMOUNT PAID $ **0** | **00**

30. BALANCE DUE $ **110** | **00**

31. SIGNATURE OF PHYSICIAN OR SUPPLIER INCLUDING DEGREES OR CREDENTIALS (I certify that the statements on the reverse apply to this bill and are made a part thereof.)
SIGNED *John Briesk* DATE *8/22/98*

32. NAME AND ADDRESS OF FACILITY WHERE SERVICES WERE RENDERED (If other than home or office)
St. Tammaras
674 Highland
Naperville, IL 60543

33. PHYSICIAN'S SUPPLIER'S BILLING NAME, ADDRESS, ZIP CODE & PHONE #
John Brieski, M.D.
6453 Santa Fe Drive
Clarendon Hills, IL 65432
PIN# **123456965** GRP#

(APPROVED BY AMA COUNCIL ON MEDICAL SERVICE 8/88)   *PLEASE PRINT OR TYPE*   FORM HCFA-1500 (12-90) FORM OWCP-1500 FORM RRB-1500

PATIENT AND INSURED INFORMATION

PHYSICIAN OR SUPPLIER INFORMATION

inexpensively. But there will be many times when the code does not suffice. On these occasions, you need to send supplementary documentation to further explain the "what" and "why" of your charges. This is always true when submitting the unlisted procedure codes, and in many cases, when submitting modifiers.

For the typical physician's office, support documentation consists of attaching an operative report, consult report, or lab findings to the claim. Sometimes this information is adequate to ensure proper payment. But not always.

It is important for you to realize that the person who first reviews your claim and support documentation is likely to have the same background as the typical claims processor described above, i.e., high school education, no knowledge of medical terminology, and low wages. This claims examiner will make one of four decisions based on the information you submit.

1. Because of their limited knowledge in the areas of medicine and medical terminology, there is a good possibility they may not understand what was done or why it was done. In such a case they are likely to return your claim for additional documentation. An example will help clarify what can go wrong. Suppose a physician performs an emergency appendectomy on a severely diabetic patient. Because of the patient's diabetes, what is normally a 30-minute procedure takes two hours to perform and the follow-up is extensive. As a result, the physician adds the "-22" unusual service modifier to the appendectomy code, triples his charge, and sends a copy of the operative report with the claim. If the operative report is written in highly technical language it is quite possible that justification for the increased charge will not be apparent to the examiner, and thus the claim will either be paid at the physician's usual fee or returned for additional information.

2. If the claims examiner does not understand what was done or why, instead of returning it to you he may put the claim in a file for later review. Such claims have a tendency to disappear, and if you inquire about what happened to the claim you are likely to be told that it was "never received."

3. If the medical necessity of the claim is obvious to the examiner, it is likely that he will authorize payment.

4. Sometimes the claims examiner may not understand what was done, but if it appears that the claim might be justifiable, the examiner will forward it to a nurse or physician for review. That is, it will be sent to someone who knows something about medicine and can make sense of your support documentation.

Ideally, you want the claims examiner to make one of the latter two decisions.

As you may have noticed in reading the above, problems are most likely to occur *when the examiner does not understand* what was done or why. In fact, several former claims examiners have confided to this author that company policy was to deny any claim for which the medical necessity was not stated in the first few sentences of the support documentation. Furthermore, they also admitted to having very little understanding of what was being described in the operative and consult reports they reviewed.

Figure 4.7: Single Day of Service on Claim

PLEASE DO NOT STAPLE IN THIS AREA

APPROVED OMB-0939-0008

CARRIER

HEALTH INSURANCE CLAIM FORM

PICA ▯▯ | PICA ▯▯

| 1. MEDICARE (Medicare #) [X] | MEDICAID (Medicaid #) | CHAMPUS (Sponsor's SSN) | CHAMPVA (VA File #) | GROUP HEALTH PLAN (SSN or ID) | FECA BLK LUNG (SSN) | OTHER (ID) | 1a. INSURED I.D. NUMBER (FOR PROGRAM IN ITEM 1) 123456789B |

| 2. PATIENT'S NAME (Last Name, First Name, Middle Initial) Carlson, Richter | 3. PATIENT'S BIRTH DATE MM DD YY 5 10 28 SEX M [X] F | 4. INSURED'S NAME (Last Name, First Name, Middle Initial) |

5. PATIENT'S ADDRESS (No., Street) **345 Park Place** | 6. PATIENT RELATIONSHIP TO INSURED Self [X] Spouse Child Other | 7. INSURED'S ADDRESS (No., Street)

CITY **Naperville** STATE **IL** | 8. PATIENT STATUS Single ☐ Married [X] Other ☐ | CITY STATE

ZIP CODE **60543** TELEPHONE (Include Area Code) **(630)654-8800** | Employed ☐ Full-Time Student ☐ Part-Time Student ☐ | ZIP CODE TELEPHONE (Include Area Code)

9. OTHER INSURED'S NAME (Last Name, First Name, Middle Initial) | 10. IS PATIENT'S CONDITION RELATED TO: | 11. INSURED'S POLICY GROUP OR FECA NUMBER

a. OTHER INSURED'S POLICY OR GROUP NUMBER | a. EMPLOYMENT? (CURRENT OR PREVIOUS) YES ☐ NO [X] | a. INSURED'S DATE OF BIRTH MM DD YY SEX M ☐ F ☐

b. OTHER INSURED'S DATE OF BIRTH MM DD YY SEX M ☐ F ☐ | b. AUTO ACCIDENT? YES ☐ NO [X] PLACE (State) | b. EMPLOYER'S NAME OR SCHOOL NAME

c. EMPLOYER'S NAME OR SCHOOL NAME | c. OTHER ACCIDENT? YES ☐ NO [X] | c. INSURANCE PLAN NAME OR PROGRAM NAME

d. INSURED PLAN NAME OR PROGRAM NAME | 10d. RESERVED FOR LOCAL USE | d. IS THERE ANOTHER HEALTH BENEFIT PLAN? YES ☐ NO [X] If yes, return to and complete item 9 a–d.

READ BACK OF FORM BEFORE COMPLETING & SIGNING THIS FORM.
12. PATIENT'S OR AUTHORIZED PERSON'S SIGNATURE I authorize the release of any medical or other information necessary to process this claim. I also request payment of government benefits either to myself or to the party who accepts assignment below. SIGNED **On File** DATE **8/22/97**

13. INSURED'S OR AUTHORIZED PERSON'S SIGNATURE I authorize payment of medical benefits to the undersigned physician or supplier for services described below. SIGNED **On File**

14. DATE OF CURRENT: MM DD YY **8 17 97** ILLNESS (First symptom) OR INJURY (Accident) OR PREGNANCY (LMP) | 15. IF PATIENT HAS HAD SAME OR SIMILAR ILLNESS, GIVE FIRST DATE MM DD YY | 16. DATES PATIENT UNABLE TO WORK IN CURRENT OCCUPATION FROM MM DD YY TO MM DD YY

17. NAME OF REFERRING PHYSICIAN OR OTHER SOURCE | 17a. I.D. NUMBER OF REFERRING PHYSICIAN | 18. HOSPITALIZATION DATES RELATED TO CURRENT SERVICES FROM MM DD YY TO MM DD YY

19. RESERVED FOR LOCAL USE | 20. OUTSIDE LAB? YES ☐ NO [X] $ CHARGES

21. DIAGNOSIS OR NATURE OF ILLNESS OR INJURY (RELATE ITEMS 1,2,3 OR 4 TO ITEM 24E BY LINE)
1. **188.9 M-Neoplasm,Bladder Walls**
2. ___
3. ___
4. ___

22. MEDICAID RESUBMISSION CODE ORIGINAL REF. NO.

23. PRIOR AUTHORIZATION NUMBER

24. A DATE(S) OF SERVICE From MM DD YY To MM DD YY	B Place of Service	C Type of Service	D PROCEDURES, SERVICES OR SUPPLIES (Explain Unusual Circumstances) CPT/HCPCS MODIFIER	E DIAGNOSIS CODE	F $ CHARGES	G DAYS OR UNITS	H EPSDT Family Plan	I EMG	J COB	K RESERVED FOR LOCAL USE
8 22 97	21		52235	1	125 00	1				

| 25. FEDERAL TAX I.D. NUMBER SSN EIN **987-65-4321** [X] | 26. PATIENT'S ACCOUNT NO. | 27. ACCEPT ASSIGNMENT? (For govt. claims, see back) YES [X] NO ☐ | 28. TOTAL CHARGE $ **1250 00** | 29. AMOUNT PAID $ **0 00** | 30. BALANCE DUE $ **1250 00** |

31. SIGNATURE OF PHYSICIAN OR SUPPLIER INCLUDING DEGREES OR CREDENTIALS (I certify that the statements on the reverse apply to this bill and are made a part thereof.) SIGNED *John Brieski* DATE *8/22/98*

32. NAME AND ADDRESS OF FACILITY WHERE SERVICES WERE RENDERED (If other than home or office)
**St. Tammaras
674 Highland
Naperville, IL 60543**

33. PHYSICIAN'S SUPPLIER'S BILLING NAME, ADDRESS, ZIP CODE & PHONE #
**John Brieski, M.D.
6453 Santa Fe Drive
Clarendon Hills, IL 65432**
PIN# **123456965** GRP#

(APPROVED BY AMA COUNCIL ON MEDICAL SERVICE 8/88) *PLEASE PRINT OR TYPE*

FORM HCFA-1500 (12-90)
FORM OWCP-1500 FORM RRB-1500

PATIENT AND INSURED INFORMATION

PHYSICIAN OR SUPPLIER INFORMATION

In light of this insight it is perhaps not surprising to learn that those physicians who have the fewest denials are those who take the time to include a *brief* letter which explains in clear, layperson's language the "why's" and "what's"; in other words, a one or two paragraph letter, in addition to the technical documentation, written primarily for the claims examiner. These brief reports have been labeled KISS letters — Keep It Simple S——-.

The importance and purpose of the brief KISS letter is straightforward. You want the claims examiner to understand:

1.   The medical necessity of the procedure or service the physician rendered. Medical necessity should always be listed in the first paragraph of the letter.
2.   What was wrong with the patient.
3.   What was done to the patient.
4.   When appropriate, the amount of time and effort needed to perform the service(s).
5.   When appropriate, any special equipment that was used.

To help clarify the KISS letter concept and its importance, take a moment to read the operative report shown in Figure 4.8. If you are familiar with operative reports you will see that this example is well written and to the point. However, the report is laden with highly technical terms such as "epicondyle," "anconeus," "brachioradialis," and "extensor carpi ulnaris," many of which are probably beyond the comprehension of the claims processor. It is likely that the claims processor will not understand what was being done or why.

Compare the operative report in Figure 4.8 to the KISS letter in Figure 4.9. Upon reading the KISS letter the procedure described in the operative report becomes immediately understandable, as does the need for the surgery. Hopefully you now have a better insight into the relevance and importance of taking the time to prepare KISS letters.

Another point needs to be made regarding the reporting of unlisted procedures. One of the difficulties encountered by carriers is trying to decide if the charge you are reporting for an unlisted procedure is appropriate. To help the carrier understand that your charge is appropriate, give them an equivalency code. That is, explain that are charging, say $1,000, for the procedure because it takes about the same amount of time and effort as another procedure you perform (give them the code number) for which you charge $1,000. In this way you will give the claims examiners something they can directly relate to — an equivalent procedure — and they are therefore more likely to approve payment on the claim.

In some cases it may be more desirable to have the physician's staff rather than the physician prepare the KISS letter, as the staff may be less caught up in medical terminology. Furthermore, it is recommended that the letter be written as if you were writing to a friend who knows nothing about medicine, but who nonetheless needs to know what was done to the patient and why. Of course, the physician should review the letter for accuracy before it is submitted along with the claim and other support documentation. Although there will be many times when the KISS letter provides enough information to ensure proper payment, it is not a substitute for operative reports, consult reports, and the like. It is a *supplement* which helps insure that the claim is either paid immediately or that the other formal medical documentation reaches a nurse or physician who can approve payment.

Figure 4.8: Sample Operative Report

OPERATIVE REPORT

Patient Name: Olga Opal
Hospital/Account Number: S23-89777
Date of Operation: 7/5/91
Preoperative Diagnosis: Post-traumatic synostosis left distal humerus and proximal ulna, secondary to fracture-dislocation, left elbow
Postoperative Diagnosis: Same

Surgeon: B. Smith, M.D.
Assistants: A. Jones, M.D.

Operation: Arthrotomy with resection of bony bridge exostosis between the distal humerus and proximal ulna
Anesthesia: General

Procedure: After satisfactory general endotracheal anesthesia, left upper extremity was prepped and draped in the usual manner and a pneumatic tourniquet was applied to the left upper extremity. A large lateral incision was then made extending over the lateral epicondyle, down over the interval laterally of the forearm between the anconeus and the extensor carpi ulnaris, and proximally between the brachioradialis and the triceps. Brachioradialis and the muscles in the anterior aspect of the lateral epicondyle were retracted and dissected anteriorly and the triceps posteriorly. The capsule was opened and the radial head was exposed. The exostosis evident on X-ray in the anterior aspect of the elbow was isolated with the use of a periosteal elevator and, with an osteotome, this large bone bridge was removed from the distal humerus. Dissection was then carried down to the coronoid process and the bone was also released from this area. Rongeuring was then performed to smooth the ends of the distal humerus anteriorly where the exostosis and synostosis had occurred, as well as in the proximal coronoid process of the ulna. Then, the capsule anteriorly which had tightened was resected. Following this procedure, one could extend the elbow to 180 degrees and flex it above a right angle. The wound was irrigated and bone wax was placed in the wound anteriorly where the bone had been resected as well as over the coronoid area. Hemovac suction drain was inserted and the wound was closed, suturing the fascia anteriorly and posteriorly to the periosteum and suturing the capsular structures over the radial head and closing the fascia over the anconeus and extensor ulnaris. The brachioradialis and triceps fascias were sutured together laterally. Subcutaneous fat was then closed with plain and the skin with polyethylene. Sterile dressing was applied and posterior type splint applied with the elbow at 90 degrees. Circulation was satisfactory on release of the tourniquet prior to closure of the wound and following application of the cast remained satisfactory. The patient left the surgical suite in satisfactory condition.

Figure 4.9: Sample KISS Letter

Patient Name: Olga Opal
I.D. Number: S23-8977
Group Number: 45678
Date of Service: 7/5/91
Surgeon: B. Smith, M.D.
                  111 Overlook Drive
                  Springfield, Illinois xxxxx

Provider I.D. #:
Phone:

Dear Sir or Madam:

Ms. Opal had fractured and dislocated her left elbow last year while on vacation in Idaho. The fracture healed, but during the process, excess bone tissue grew out from the ends of the bone of the upper arm (the humerus) and the long bone of the lower arm (the ulna) thus joining them together. Since these bones are not normally held together by bone, the joint became rigid and Ms. Opal was not able to move it at all. Therefore, it was medically necessary to remove the excess bone so that she could once again move her left elbow normally.

We made an incision over the elbow and exposed the area where the bones of the upper and lower arm had grown together abnormally. Then we removed the bony connection, or "bridge," between them with a special tool for that purpose. The ends of the bones were smoothed of any rough areas and then we closed the wound with sutures (stitches).

(For additional, complete details of the operative procedure, please see the attached operative report.)

Thank you for your consideration.
Sincerely,

B. Smith, M.D.

Without a doubt, the KISS letter is the most valuable tool you have for ensuring proper reimbursement in those cases which require extra information. Several clients and workshop participants have claimed near 100 percent success rates on claims when KISS letters are used.

CLEAN VERSUS DIRTY CLAIMS

Nearly one-third of claims submitted to third party payers by physician practices have errors or problems that can result in payment delays or denials. Claims with such problems are called "dirty claims." The major types of mistakes, and tips for eliminating them, are discussed below.

Technical Errors

Errors in this category typically arise from the use of improper, incomplete, or out-of-date information related to the noncoding areas of the claim. Examples include:

- Missing or invalid patient date-of-birth
- Missing or invalid patient policy number
- Missing or invalid provider identification number
- Missing or invalid place of service
- Date(s) of service inconsistent with units billed
- Invalid or missing ZIP Code
- Failure to list hospital when hospital services provided
- Lack of referring provider when required
- Patient no longer covered by policy

Of course, the above list is not exhaustive, it is intended to be representative of the types of technical reporting problems that can lead to needless denials. If you are submitting claims through a clearinghouse or if you are using a quality practice management system, chances are that these types of errors will be minimal as your system (or notification by your claims clearinghouse that you failed payer-specific clearinghouse edits) should prompt you to make sure that required data elements are present and appropriate.

Some of these technical errors result from lack of current patient information. For example, you should regularly update patient insurance information to ensure that the patient's payer and policy information is current and accurate, that dependents are listed, etc.

Coding Errors

There is nothing so embarrassing to a practice as to have claims rejected because the codes being submitted are out-of-date, or worse, nonexistent. Coding errors account for a substantial number of the claims errors received by payers. A sample of the types of errors commonly found on claims include:

Out-of-date CPT, HCPCS, or ICD-9-CM codes

These may arise because the practice has either not obtained or implemented new codes. This author has seen egregious examples including practices that in an effort to save a few hundred dollars printed several years worth of charge tickets (or superbills) at one time. After a few years, many of the codes on the charge tickets no longer existed. Other examples include codes created by staff to describe services not listed in a coding system which become submitted to payers. Clearly, keeping up-to-date with codes is one of the most important undertakings of a practice.

Codes that are inappropriate for the patient's gender or age

Although not as common as non-existent codes, claims that list male diagnoses for a female patient (or vice-versa), services inappropriate for a patient's age, and other related problems are another source of dirty claims.

Lack of diagnosis code specificity

Failure to list required fourth or fifth digits on ICD-9-CM codes is a common coding error that can lead to a claims delay or denial. Medicare can now fine practices for failing to report required fourth and fifth digits.

Inappropriate use of Modifiers

Problems claims also result from modifiers being listed inappropriately. For example, you should not use the surgery only modifier, "-54", on an E/M service. As another example, the "-51" modifier is generally not to be listed with add-on codes.

Again, the above listing is not exhaustive, but should help you be sensitive to the types of problems that can lead to a claims denial or payment delay.

Utilization Violations

Errors in this category occur when the practice bills for services beyond those either included with another charge or beyond those allowed for a particular patient condition. Examples include:

Surgical package violations

Billing for services that are included in the surgery, such as normal, uncomplicated postoperative care, are examples. Unfortunately, this error is relatively common as it may be difficult for a practice's billing staff to keep track of which services are and are not to be included with the surgery. For example, if a patient sees the physician 85 days following a major surgery for an unrelated condition and the staff fails to list the appropriate modifier, the payer may assume that the service is included with the surgery and deny it as a result.

Service limitations

Payers may have specific utilization limitations for certain services. For example, a state Workers' Compensation rule may limit physical therapy treatments to six per month for specific diagnoses. Alternatively, payers may limit how many or what level of E/M services may be performed on a patient over a given period of time.

Unbundling

Unbundling is generally defined as the billing of the components of a comprehensive procedure either instead of, or in addition to, the comprehensive procedure. If you have ever seen Medicare's 2,000 plus pages of Correct Coding Initiative (CCI) guidelines, you will understand what is meant by unbundling. This document primarily defines which services are considered to be components of other services. That is, it lists a primary service code and those other service codes that are included. An example is provided below for perirectal injection of sclerosing solution of prolapse (code 45520) taken from the 1997 CCI.

Comprehensive Code:

45520   Perirectal injection of sclerosing solution of prolapse

Component Codes:

45900	Reduction of procidentia (separate procedure) under anesthesia
45905	Dilation of anal sphincter (separate procedure) under anesthesia other than local
45910	Dilation of rectal sphincter (separate procedure) under anesthesia other than local
46211	Cryptectomy; multiple (separate procedure)
46220	Papillectomy or excision of single tag, anus (separate procedure)
46600	Anoscopy, diagnostic, with or without collection of specimen(s) by brushing or washing (separate procedure)
46940	Curettage or cauterization of anal fissure, including dilation of anal sphincter (separate procedure); initial
46942	Curettage or cauterization of anal fissure, including dilation of anal sphincter (separate procedure); subsequent

It is becoming increasingly common for payers to utilize sophisticated software that identifies unbundling and then rebundles services into the appropriate comprehensive code. Why? There are two reasons. First, the sum of the fees for the components of a comprehensive service are usually more than the fee for the comprehensive service itself. Second, in instances where one or more component of a comprehensive service is billed in addition to the comprehensive service, services are being double billed. As you may be aware, this might be construed as insurance fraud by the payer.

There are many other errors that can cause a claim to be considered "dirty." These range from illegible handwriting (yes, this author has even witnessed physicians handwriting claims on airplanes) to failing to supply required support documentation when reporting unlisted service codes. Remember that the vast majority of payment delays and denials result from errors made before the claim is submitted, something over which you have the potential to minimize.

DEALING WITH CARRIERS

In addition to the tips offered above, there are specific things you can do to smooth your relationship with insurance carriers. (Some of these tips were covered in Chapter One also.)

Be kind to the people at the insurance companies—no matter how angry or frustrated you become.

Two stories told by participants at workshops illustrate the importance of treating the individuals at the carriers with kindness. The first story is of a physician who was having difficulty obtaining information he needed from Medicare. After several unsuccessful calls and letters, he finally got in contact with an individual in professional relations. The physician was so upset at that point that he became irate and abusive with the Medicare representative. The next day, a Medicare auditor showed up at the physician's office. When all was said and done, he ended up having to pay tens of thousands of dollars in "overcharges" back to Medicare. For this physician, losing his temper was very expensive and he never did obtain the information he needed.

The other story concerns an office manager who took the opposite approach with the people she dealt with at insurance companies. She made an effort to befriend the people—she learned about their families, their interests, and their work. As a result, when she had a question or needed information, she knew who to call and her requests were handled quickly and accurately. Because of the friendships she developed, the representatives often gave her helpful tips (inside information) on how to get her physician's and patients' claims paid. In turn, the people at the carriers sometimes asked the office manager for assistance, such as helping answer questions asked by staff at other physicians' offices in her area.

Too many times physicians and their staff think of the insurance companies as the enemy—especially the Medicare and Medicaid carriers. They dread having to call or write because of past frustrations when trying to do so. This "us against them" attitude is counterproductive. The people at the carriers are just like you, and they appreciate kindness and respect just as you do in your dealings with other individuals.

Put it in writing.

There will be many times when you receive specific information from carriers over the phone regarding billing and reporting procedures. For example, you may be told that for a certain procedure performed by the physician, instead of using CPT code such-and-such which describes what the physician did, you should use a different CPT code to ensure proper payment. Obviously, you should be concerned about reporting a code which does not describe what the physician did, but which the carrier prefers you to submit. In these and similar cases, get the name of the person you spoke with. Follow-up your phone conversation with a kind letter thanking them for their help. In this letter you should restate what they advised you to do, and if there is any misunderstanding on your part you would appreciate their letting you know as soon as possible as you will be billing according to their recommendations.

By sending a letter you accomplish three objectives. First, you have an opportunity to begin developing a contact at the carrier which could help you again in the future. Second, you are protecting yourself against the possibility that the information you received over the phone was inaccurate. Third, in the event of an audit, you have written documentation, including a person's name, to prove the source of your information should it turn out to be incorrect.

When necessary, have the patient request a review of a problem claim.

There will be times when insurance carriers severely mishandle a patient's claim. Examples include claims for which clearly appropriate procedures and services are denied, and cases where the claim is grossly underpaid. If your efforts to resolve the problem are unsuccessful, you should consider having the patient request a review of the claim. Carriers tend to be more responsive to the requests of patients than of physicians. You may need to assist the patient with the paperwork, but inevitably, the patient's request will get results when you cannot.

FEEDBACK

Feedback is critical to ensuring that you are coding and billing properly. To illustrate the point consider the story of a major university on the East coast. Like many other large teaching institutions, the university had a staff that handled the paperwork of the physicians who saw patients in the university's hospital and offices. The billing staff submitted claims directly to the third party payers. Payments and explanation of benefits (EOBs) were received by another group located two blocks away from the office which sent out the bills. Until they attended a seminar on coding and reimbursement issues, the staff in the two offices had never met. The people who submitted the claims never saw if the claims were paid or denied. The people who received payment never saw what went out on the original claims. As you might suspect, the level of reimbursement received by this university was frightfully low.

It is relatively easy to keep track of payments, delays and denials on the claims you submit. If you routinely accept assignment from Medicare and other major payers, make it a habit to review the EOBs returned with payment. Compare approvals, paid amounts, etc., against a copy of the original claim. If you do not often accept assignment, you may want to obtain EOBs from your patients. This can be handled by providing a select group of patients with a postage-paid return envelope. When the patient receives payment and the EOB, ask them to mail you a copy of the EOB. Explain to them that you are interested in helping make sure they are being properly reimbursed by their insurance company. In this way you will be able to obtain the EOBs needed to ensure your billing is proper.

PROBLEM SET

Suggested solutions to the problems below can be found in Appendix A.

Mark the following statements true or false.

		True	False
1.	Once properly trained, staff can take responsibility for virtually all coding and regulatory compliance issues, allowing the physician to focus exclusively on practicing medicine.	_____	_____
2.	Using out-of-date procedure or diagnosis codes could lead to charges of fraud against the physician.	_____	_____
3.	When providing services for patients outside the office, the physician should keep detailed notes of whom he saw, when, and what he did.	_____	_____
4.	If you have more than one day's worth of services listed on the same claim form, rank each day's services by dollar amount from the highest to lowest charge.	_____	_____
5.	There will be many instances where more than one ICD-9-CM and CPT code will be reported on the same claim. In such cases, make sure that the diagnosis listed first for each CPT code is the primary reason or justification for the service.	_____	_____
6.	Despite the hype about electronic claims submission, with the exception of claims listing surgical services, you can expect to receive higher reimbursement when submitting paper rather than electronic claims.	_____	_____
7.	To simply get claims paid in a timely manner, a payer may make payment for services that it would deny on other occasions.	_____	_____
8.	KISS letters should be written using straightforward, easy-to-understand words and concepts so that claims processors with limited understanding of medical terminology can obtain an understanding of what was done and why.	_____	_____
9.	To ensure payment, an equivalency code is required by Medicare and other payers on claims listing services provided to nonresident aliens.	_____	_____
10.	Unbundling is defined as the reporting of services on	_____	_____

different claims that should be listed together on the same
claim in the hope of receiving higher payment.

11. Dirty claims are those which contain errors that may lead to _____   _____
rejection or a payment delay.

12. In the case of questionable payment denials, third party   _____   _____
payers tend to be more responsive to requests for review
made by the patient rather than the physician.

13. Most states have laws which require that insurance   _____   _____
company's medical claims processors receive a minimum
three months training in medical terminology and procedures.

14. Using out-of-date codes is one of the major factors that   _____   _____
leads to claim payment delays and denials.

The following are multiple choice questions. Select the most correct answer(s).

15. Which of the following options regarding reporting is in the correct order?

   a. Identify, rank by charge, code, modify

   b. Identify, modify, code, rank by charge

   c. Code, rank by charge, modify, identify

   d. Identify, code, modify, rank by charge

   e. Identify, code, rank by charge, modify

16. A patient is seen by the physician in the office. The patient is suffering from minor rectal
bleeding and the doctor suspects intestinal tumors based on his examination and patient
complaints. The physician orders tests and based on the results admits the patient to the
hospital the next day where he performs initial hospital care services. The following day,
the physician performs a colonoscopy and discovers tumors. The pathology report shows
that the tumors are benign. Which of the following combinations of services and
diagnoses are correct for reporting these services?

   a. Day 1   Office Visit / Dx = Rectal bleeding
      Day 2   Initial hospital care / Dx = Benign tumors
      Day 3   Colonoscopy / Dx = Benign tumors

   b. Day 1   Office Visit / Dx = Benign tumors
      Day 2   Initial hospital care / Dx = Benign tumors

| | Day 3 | Colonoscopy / Dx = Benign tumors |

c.   Day 1   Office Visit / Dx = Rectal bleeding
     Day 2   Initial hospital care / Dx = Rectal bleeding
     Day 3   Colonoscopy / Dx = Benign tumors

d.   None of the above.

17. Technical billing errors do not include which of the following:

      a.   Date(s) of service inconsistent with units billed.

      b.   Missing or invalid patient date of birth.

      c.   Missing or invalid provider SSD number.

      d.   Missing or invalid patient insurance information.

      e.   Missing or invalid ZIP Code.

      f.   Each of the above are examples of technical billing errors.

CHAPTER FIVE:
FEE AND REIMBURSEMENT MANAGEMENT, INCLUDING MANAGED CARE CONTRACTS

The vast majority of physicians and staff have only a vague understanding of how to properly utilize relative value systems, negotiate reimbursement schedules with managed care organizations, or make adjustments to the practice's standard fee schedule. For example, when desiring to raise practice fees, too often the physician will simply increase fees across-the-board by some percentage without giving thought to those services that may already be grossly overpriced or to services that may be substantially underpriced. With increased competition, the need to control costs, and the need to intelligently negotiate fees with managed care and managed competition organizations, fee management is a critical element to your practice's financial success. In this chapter you will learn the basics of relative value systems, how payers establish reasonable amounts for your fees, how to establish fees for new or rarely reported services, and tips on negotiating fee schedules with managed care and managed competition organizations. Specific topics include:

- Why relative values were created.
- How payers reimburse for services.
- The three types of relative value systems in use today.
- Using relative value systems to establish and adjust fees.
- How commercial fee databases are developed and implemented by payers.
- Using commercial fee reports to establish and adjust fees.
- Negotiating fee schedules with payers from a position of strength.
- The limitations of relative value systems and fee reports.

By applying the information contained in this chapter you are more likely to be able to maintain financial stability during a time when there is tremendous pressure to limit physician fees and income.

HISTORY OF VALUING SERVICES

Physician reimbursement has changed drastically over the past 100 years. Prior to health insurance physicians would often accept whatever they could get for their services, whether cash or a few jars of preserves. In urban areas standard fees for certain types of services were established, but for the most part the charge and payment system was informal and certainly primitive compared to today's complex system.

The institution of more modern fee schedules began in the 1930s when insurance began being offered by what were to become the first Blue Cross plans. Based on the concept of risk sharing, individuals would pool money into a fund that covered the hospital costs should one of the fund members become ill. During World War II, the government imposed wage freezes but did allow

---

employers to increase employee's benefits through the provision of tax deductible health insurance. This led to a rapid expansion of health insurance and by the 1950s most working individuals in the United States had both hospital and physician insurance. The advent of the third party payment necessitated the development of set fees for services and procedures.

Concurrent with the institutionalization of health insurance was an explosion in the development of new medical technology and procedures. This explosion gave rise to the need for a formal system that could be used to define procedures and services (both existing and new ones) and to determine the reasonableness of physicians' charges. The first such system to achieve national recognition was the *California Relative Value System* published by the California Medical Association in 1956. Known as the CRVS, this publication listed code numbers and terminology for each procedure and service, and provided relative values for each procedure. The relative values were established via a survey of the members of the California Medical Association. Among other questions, the survey asked members to rank procedures and services from the most to least difficult, thus establishing a sense of the relative worth, or value, of the various procedures listed in the system. Key features of the CRVS include:

Relative values are not dollar amounts, but reflect the relative difficulty of one procedure compared to another. For example, if one procedure has a relative value of 10 and another a relative value of 15, the one with the relative value of 15 would be considered one and one-half times more difficult than the procedure with the relative value of 10, and should be priced accordingly.

- To establish fees a conversion factor (or multiplier) is used. The conversion factor is a dollar amount that is multiplied times the relative value to establish a fee. For example, if a procedure has a relative value of 3.5 and the conversion factor is $200.00, then the fee should be $700.00 (3.5 x $200 = $700).

- Each physician has a conversion factor unique to his practice. For example, a doctor practicing in an urban area might have a conversion factor of $250, whereas a doctor in a rural area might utilize a factor or $175.

- Each section of codes (surgery, radiology, etc.) has its own conversion factor. For example, a physician might have a conversion factor of $35.75 for medical services and another of $210.35 for surgical procedures.

- Follow-up days are listed for most surgical procedures. These follow-up days are used to determine the number of days following a surgery during which the physician would not bill the patient for hospital visits, office visits, suture removal, or other surgery-related services.

Due to pressure from the Federal Trade Commission which was claiming that physicians were using the CRVS for price fixing, the California Medical Association "voluntarily" withdrew the publication in 1974. Ironically, 18 years after publication of the CRVS ceased, the federal government implemented its own relative value system, the Resource Based Relative Value Scale (RBRVS).

It is interesting to note that CRVS was the precursor to the American Medical Association's CPT book. CPT was first published in 1966 and was identical to CRVS with two exceptions: It did not list relative values or surgery follow-up days.

HOW PAYERS REIMBURSE FOR SERVICES

The methods used by third party payers to reimburse a physician for his services vary greatly and range from a percentage of the amount actually charged by the physician to what are called capitation rates—a fixed amount per year per patient. Each of the major payment methodologies in use today is discussed below.

Fee-Based

Under the fee-based system, the payer simply reimburses the physician (or patient) on the basis of the amount charged by physician. For example, the payer may set reimbursement at an amount of 80 percent of the physician's charge. Virtually all payers that use a fee-based reimbursement system also set caps, or maximums, on the amount they will reimburse for any particular procedure or service. UCRs, discussed below, are frequently used to establish these cap amounts.

UCR-Based

Really a component of fee-based, the UCR payment methodology traditionally consisted of establishing allowable charges on the basis of the lower of the following:

A.   Usual Charge — This is the average amount charged by the physician for the code over a previous period of time, such as a year. For example, if during the past year a physician's average submitted charge for an EKG service was $43.78, the physician's usual charge would be $43.78.

B.   Customary Charge — The customary charge is the average amount charged for a code by all physicians (usually in the same specialty) in the same geographic area. For example, if the average charge submitted for the EKG procedure by all physicians in the same specialty in the same area is $41.23, then the customary fee would be $41.23.

C.   Reasonable Charge — This is the amount appearing on the physician's current claim for the procedure. Continuing the above example, suppose the physician reported a charge of $45.00 for the EKG service, the reasonable charge would be $45.00. Since payers usually select the lowest of the usual, customary and reasonable charges, in the above example, the $41.23 would be the amount allowed by the insurance company. Prior to 1992, Medicare used a UCR payment system. Medicare called its methodology the CPR (customary, prevailing, and reasonable) payment system but it was virtually identical to the UCR payment system.

Today, most third party payers and third party administers purchase fee databases from firms that accumulate national fee information, analyze it, and offer it for sale. As such, with the exception of the very largest payers, such as some of the Blues plans, payers do not develop internal fee schedules or monitor provider charges. The submitted charges are compared against fee percentile amounts selected by the payer from the fee database they license. If the charged fee is higher than the ceiling fee for the service established by the payer, the amount allowed will be the ceiling fee. If the charged fee is lower than the ceiling fee, the charged amount will be allowed.

How UCR-based fee schedules are developed and implemented will discussed in more detail later in this chapter.

RBRVS-Based

Medicare's current payment system utilizes the Resource Based Relative Value Scale (RBRVS) developed at Harvard University. Under the RBRVS system, payments are a function of the resources that go into providing a procedure or service, along with other factors, such as the physician's geographic area. This system will be discussed in more detail below.

Contract-Based

Health maintenance organizations (HMOs), preferred provider organizations (PPOs), independent physician associations (IPAs) and other organizations typically negotiate fees for physician services. This is handled by a contract between the physician and payer. Payment rates vary from a percentage of the physician's usual charges, to sliding payment scales, to capitated rates.

It is anticipated that RBRVS and contract-based fee schedules will increasingly become the dominate payment systems in the late 1990s and after the turn of the century.

TYPES OF RELATIVE VALUE SYSTEMS

The types of relative value systems currently employed by physicians and payers may be seen as falling into one of three groups: consensus, fee-based, and resource-based. Each type of relative value system is discussed below.

Consensus Relative Value Systems

Both the CRVS and the St. Anthony's *Relative Values for Physicians* (formerly the McGraw-Hill *RVP*) relative value systems would be members of this group in which relative values are determined primarily by a consensus of physicians and others who participate in development of the system. The types of issues assessed in the development of these systems include:

- Interviews with or polling of select providers regarding the relative difficulty of procedures and services.
- An assessment of the relative risk to the patient and/or provider for the various procedures and services being analyzed.
- Analysis of the amount of time and skill required to perform procedures and services.
- A review of the amounts historically charged for procedures and services.

Consensus systems tend to be biased toward the viewpoint of the creators and the particular methodologies employed in the assessment and analysis of data. A sample page from the St. Anthony's *Relative Values for Physicians* is shown in Figure 5.1.

Fee-Based Relative Value Systems

Relative values in the fee-based systems are a direct function of the actual amounts charged by physicians. The following methodology is typically employed in the development of fee-based values:

- Fees are collected on a code-by-code basis.
- For each code an average (or mean) fee is determined.

Figure 5.1: Sample Page from *Relative Values for Physicians*

SURGERY/ANESTHESIA (43227-43258)
Digestive System

UPD	CPT	DESCRIPTION	UNITS	FUD	ANES
	43227	with control of bleeding, any method	5.7	0	5
	43228	with ablation of tumor(s), polyp(s), or other lesion(s), not amenable to removal by hot biopsy forceps, bipolar cautery or snare technique	5.7	0	5
		(Surgical endoscopy always includes diagnostic endoscopy)			
	43234	Upper gastrointestinal endoscopy, simple primary examination (eg, with small diameter flexible endoscope) (separate procedure)	3.1	0	5
	43235	Upper gastrointestinal endoscopy including esophagus, stomach, and either the duodenum and/or jejunum as appropriate; diagnostic, with or without collection of specimen(s) by brushing or washing (separate procedure)	4.2	0	5
	43239	with biopsy, single or multiple	4.3	0	5
	43241	with transendoscopic tube or catheter placement	4.2	0	5
	43243	with injection sclerosis of esophageal and/or gastric varices	7.0	0	5
	43244	with band ligation of esophageal and/or gastric varices	(I) 7.0	0	5
	43245	with dilation of gastric outlet for obstruction, any method	5.2	0	5
	43246	with directed placement of percutaneous gastrostomy tube	7.1	0	5
		(For radiological supervision and interpretation, see 74350)			
	43247	with removal of foreign body	5.2	0	5
		(For radiological supervision and interpretation, see 74235)			
	43248	with insertion of guide wire followed by dilation of esophagus over guide wire	(I) 5.0	0	5
94.2	43249	with balloon dilation at esophagus (less than 30mm diameter)	(I) 4.5	0	5
	43250	with removal of tumor(s), polyp(s), or other lesion(s) by hot biopsy forceps or bipolar cautery	(I) 5.3	0	5
	43251	with removal of tumor(s), polyp(s), or other lesion(s) by snare technique	5.4	0	5
	43255	with control of bleeding, any method	6.8	0	5
	43258	with ablation of tumor(s), polyp(s), or other lesion(s) not amenable to removal by hot biopsy forceps, bipolar cautery or snare technique	7.0	0	5
		(For injection sclerosis of esophageal varices, use 43204 or 43243)			

238

- Within each section of CPT (E/M, Surgery, etc.), codes are sorted from highest to lowest average charge.
- Relative values are established by using a ratio scale of highest to lowest charge.

Because fee-based relative value systems are derived from actual physician charges, they tend to be more realistic than consensus-based systems. Accuracy is a function of the size and diversity of the population of actual physician fees used to establish values, as well as the specific methodologies selected by the developers to generate values. The key weakness of the fee-based system is that relative values for new procedures and services cannot be compiled with any reasonable accuracy until many months after a new procedure or service code appears in CPT.

Resource-Based Relative Value Scale (RBRVS)

Developed at Harvard University in the 1980s through a study funded by the federal government, the RBRVS system is at the foundation of the Medicare Fee Schedule. The RBRVS system differs from the consensus and fee-based approaches in that it attempts to define the actual resources (work, practice costs, and malpractice costs) associated with each service, and as such, provides a more complete measure of a service's actual worth. Each relative value in the RBRVS system is composed of the following three underlying relative values:

- Work. This value indicates the amount of time, service intensity, training, etc., required to perform a service.
- Practice Cost. This value is for the practice costs, such as rent, overhead, personnel, etc., associated with the service.
- Malpractice Cost. The third and final value is an assessment of malpractice costs associated with the service.
- Summed together, the above three components yield the service's RBRVS value.

To generate a fee under the Medicare Fee Schedule, Medicare also takes into consideration regional or geographic variations in the work, practice cost, and malpractice cost components. That is, each underlying value is adjusted by a geographic index. There are currently (in 1997) 91 Medicare geographic regions. To arrive at a fee (called the fee schedule amount), the geographically adjusted value is multiplied by a conversion factor, or dollar amount. Medicare maintains separate conversion factors for surgery, primary care, and nonsurgery services. This is discussed below.

The following factors also affect Medicare fees:

A. *Conversion Factors*: Medicare currently applies three separate conversion factors to the geographically-adjusted RBRVS values. One conversion factor is for surgical procedures, one is for primary care services, and the third is for non-surgical procedures.

B. *Underserved Location Adjustments:* Physicians who practice in areas defined by Medicare as underserved (some rural and inner city areas) receive a higher level of reimbursement under the Medicare RBRVS fee schedule.

C. *Participating vs. Nonparticipating Physicians' Fees*: In 1992 Medicare eliminated paying different amounts for the same service to different medical specialists. As a result, physicians practicing in the same geographic area receive the same allowed fees regardless of their specialty.

Physicians who participate with Medicare receive the current fee schedule allowable amounts for their services. However, nonparticipating physicians' allowed fees depend upon whether or not the physician accepts assignment on a claim. When a nonparticipating physician accepts assignment on a claim, he will receive 95 percent of the amount allowed by Medicare to a participating physician who bills for the same service. For example, if Medicare allows a fee of $400 to a participating doctor for a service, an amount of $380 will be allowed to a nonparticipating physician who accepts assignment. When a nonparticipating physician does not accept assignment on a claim, the physician's charge is set at what is called the "limiting charge." The limiting charge is 115 percent of the amount that would be allowed had the nonparticipating physician accepted assignment. If you were to calculate the nonparticipating physician's limiting charge for a service it would be 109.25 percent of the amount allowed to a participating physician who bills the same service.

D. *Work Adjuster:* In 1997, Medicare began applying a work adjuster which has the effect of reducing the work component by a fee by 8.3 percent.

Payers other than Medicare who are beginning to implement the RBRVS system may or may not utilize the above types of adjustments when establishing fees for physicians.

USES OF RELATIVE VALUE SYSTEMS

Unless you have spent a substantial amount of time working with your fee schedule, it is likely that your fees have inconsistencies and other problems that can lead to the following:

Lower reimbursement
- Lower third party payer UCRs
- Overpricing for your market
- Higher patient out-of-pocket costs
- Increased audit liability
- Patient dissatisfaction
- Losses due to procedure costs exceeding income

Understanding how to appropriately use a relative value system can minimize these types of problems. In this chapter you will learn how to use a relative value system to set fees for a new or infrequently performed procedure, use the RBRVS system to establish fees for payers other than Medicare, use a relative value system to develop fee consistency, and use a relative value system to increase fees.

Later in this chapter you will learn how to use commercially available fee reports to accomplish the same ends.

To Establish Fees

Consider a situation where you have to determine a fee for a procedure which you have never before performed or which you infrequently perform. Specifically, suppose that you want to establish a fee for surgery code 12345 (a hypothetical procedure), which, according to the relative value guide you choose to use has a relative value of 14.0. (Note, this and the following examples are purely hypothetical. The codes, relative values, and fees are provided for illustrative purposes only.) To establish a fee, perform the following steps:

A. Locate the relative value for the procedure (in this example, the value is 14.0).
B. List your most frequently performed surgical procedures (select a minimum of 10 to 20 procedures).
C. List your current charges for each procedure.
D. Locate the relative values for each procedure in your relative value guide.

For simplicity's sake, five hypothetical procedures are provided below.

Procedure	Current Charge	Relative Value
#1	$950	19.5
#2	$1,500	26.0
#3	$800	18.2
#4	$300	5.8
#5	$600	10.9
Total	$4,150	80.4

E. Sum your current charges ($4,150) and the relative values (80.4).
F. Divide the total charges by the number of procedures listed ($4,150 / 5 = $830).
G. Divide the total relative values by the number of procedures listed (80.5 / 5 = 16.08).
H. Divide the average charge by the average relative value to establish a conversion factor (or multiplier, if you prefer) for the surgery codes ($830 / 16.08 = $51.61).
I. Multiply the conversion factor by the new procedure's relative value to establish your fee ($51.62 x 14.0 = $722).

Thus, you may consider charging an amount between $700 and $750 for the procedure. Note that the purpose of performing the above steps is to determine a conversion factor that can be used to establish fees. You should recall that *each section of CPT codes has its own unique conversion factor.* You would not use the $51.61 conversion factor for E/M, Anesthesia, Radiology, Path and Lab, or Medicine sections' codes; it is for Surgery codes only. Using the above methodology you can establish a conversion factor for each section of CPT.

An alternative to the above methodology is as follows (note that steps A through D are the same as above):

A. Locate the relative value for the procedure (in this example, the RV is 14.0).
B. List your most frequently performed surgical procedures (select a minimum of 10 to 20 procedures).
C. List your current charges for each procedure.
D. Locate the relative values for each procedure in your relative value guide.
E. Divide each fee by its associated relative value as shown below.

Procedure	Current Charge	Relative Value	Fee/RV
#1	$950	19.5	$48.72
#2	$1,500	26.0	$57.69
#3	$800	18.2	$43.96
#4	$300	5.8	$51.72
#5	$600	10.9	$55.05
Total			$257.14

F.   Divide the total Fee/RV by the number of procedures listed. The division provides you with the conversion factor ($257.14 / 5 = $51.43).

G.   Multiply the conversion factor by the new procedure's relative value to establish a fee ($51.43 x 14.0 = $720).

Although this alternative method yielded a slightly lower conversion factor is this example, neither method consistently leads to lower or higher conversion factors.

To Establish Non-Medicare Payer Fees

The RBRVS can also be used to establish fees, and may be especially helpful in determining fees for very new procedures for which consensus or fee-based relative values have not yet been developed. To utilize the RBRVS you will need to obtain a copy of RBRVS values from a healthcare administration text publisher such as PMIC, or the federal government. The most current RBRVS values are provided in the *Federal Register*.

Suppose you want to determine a fee for a Level III hospital service, code 99233, which has a RBRVS value of 2.16. To do so, follow the steps outlined below.

A.   List 10 to 20 of your most frequently performed <u>non-surgical</u> procedures.

B.   List your current standard (non-Medicare) fees for the services.

C.   List the RBRVS values for each service listed. (For accuracy you may want to adjust the RBRVS values for your geographic area.)

Procedure	Current Charge	RBRVS	Fee/RBRVS
70320	$45.00	1.14	$39.47
99202	$40.00	1.38	$28.99
99203	$50.00	1.92	$26.04
99222	$100.00	3.27	$30.58
99242	$70.00	2.15	$32.56
Total			$152.64

D.   Divide each fee by its associated RBRVS value as shown above.

E.   Sum the Fee/RBRVS column ($157.64).

F.   Divide the total in the Fee/RBRVS column by the number of services. This is your conversion factor for non-surgical services ($157.64 / 5 = $31.53).

G.   Multiply the conversion factor by the service's RBRVS value to establish a fee for code 99233 ($31.53 x 2.16 = $68.10 or $68.00).

Because it is likely that many payers will be converting to RBRVS-based payment schedules over the next few years you may want to take the time to familiarize yourself with the RBRVS system.

To Establish Fee Consistency

Do you know which of your fees are too low or which are too high? It is not uncommon for practices to have fees that are inconsistent with amounts being allowed by payers. Unfortunately (or fortunately, however you view the matter), it is illegal for you to discuss fees with your colleagues. Therefore, in theory, you can not know how much your colleagues charge or if your fees are too high or too low. (In reality, commercial fee reports, discussed later in this chapter, can provide you with reasonably accurate information about what other providers in your area charge for services.) You can, however, achieve what is called "internal consistency" with your fees. This means setting your fees so that they are consistent with a relative value system. (Under the next heading, "Changing Your Fee Schedule," you will learn how to estimate payer allowables and in the process get a sense of how your charges compare to those of others in your area.)

To develop a consistent fee schedule, consider the following steps:

A.   Determine a conversion factor for each section of CPT using one of the methodologies discussed above.

B.   List your procedures, relative values, conversion factor and the conversion factor multiplied by the relative value as shown below.

Procedure	Current Charge	RV	CF	CF x RV
#1	$950	19.5	$51.43	$1,003
#2	$1,500	26.0	$51.43	$1,337
#3	$800	18.2	$51.43	$936
#4	$300	5.8	$51.43	$298
#5	$600	10.9	$51.43	$561

C.   Subtract the conversion factor-derived fee from your current charge for each procedure as shown below. This shows you how your current charges compare to relative value system-derived fees.

Procedure	Current Charge	CF x RV	Difference
#1	$950	$1,003	-$53
#2	$1,500	$1,337	$163
#3	$800	$936	-$136
#4	$300	$298	$2
#5	$600	$561	$39

D.   Identify differences which are negative. These may be opportunities for you to increase fees. For example, you may wish to raise your fee for procedure #1 to $975 or $1000, and your fee for procedure #3 to $900 or $930. However, if you increase your fees pay attention to how your major payers respond. If your increased fee is above a payer's allowable, your overall charges (conversion factor) may be high.

E.   Identify differences that are positive. For these you may want to consider reducing your fees, especially if the difference is substantial and if many payers are not allowing the full amount of your charge. An outcome of using the above might be:

Procedure	Old Charge	New Charge
#1	$950	$1,000
#2	$1,500	$1,400
#3	$800	$925
#4	$300	$300
#5	$600	$575

Of course, you need to take the volume of services into consideration to assess the impact on your income before making fee changes.

To Change Your Fee Schedule

For most practices the process of making changes to their overall fee schedule involves simply raising fees across-the-board by a fixed amount, say three, five, seven, etc., percent. Unfortunately, by using this method you run the risk of raising already too high fees to a higher amount, and leaving too low fees at too low of an amount. One of the more rational methods involves raising, perhaps substantially, those fees that are too low, and slightly lowering those fees that are too high in a manner that leads to an overall increase in fees.

To make changes to your entire fee schedule it is important that you take your volume of services into consideration. It does you little good to raise fees on under-priced services that are infrequently performed while slightly lowering fees on overpriced, frequently performed services. Consider the following example which continues the discussion from above.

Procedure	Current Charge	Annual Volume	Income
#1	$950	23	$21,850
#2	$1,500	14	$21,000
#3	$800	32	$25,600
#4	$300	95	$28,500
#5	$600	57	$34,200
			$131,150

Note that the annual volume (number of times performed over the last year) has been added for each procedure and the old charges are listed. Using the approach of increasing undervalued and modestly decreasing overvalued fees, something like the following might be implemented.

Procedure	New Fee	Annual Volume	Income
#1	$1,000	23	$23,000
#2	$1,450	14	$20,300
#3	$925	32	$29,600
#4	$300	95	$28,500
#5	$600	57	$34,200
			$135,600

In this example, the physician would achieve a theoretic increase in annual income of 3.4 percent ($135,600 / 131,150 = 1.034, or plus 3.4 percent).

There are other factors you should take into consideration before making adjustments to your fee schedule. First, do you frequently discover that many payers say that your charges exceed their UCRs or allowables? That is, are many of your charges above the payers' allowables? For example, suppose you bill $400 for a services and the payer allows $270 (67.5 percent of your charge) rather than $320 (the typical 80 percent of your charge). If so, your fees may be higher than those of your colleagues in your area. This may or may not be a problem depending upon the demographics of your patients and their ability or willingness to pay higher out-of-pocket amounts for your services. In any case, it alerts you to the fact that your fees are probably high compared to those being charged by your colleagues.

Second, do you frequently discover the opposite of that described above — payers routinely allow your charges? If so, your fees may be below payers' UCRs. For example, suppose you bill $200 for a procedure and the payer allows $160 (80 percent of your fee). In such a case you may want to try increasing your fee to $220 (or some other amount) to see if payers will allow 80 percent of the higher fee. Some consultants assist physicians with this process by selectively raising fees and then reviewing the payers' EOBs to determine if each raised fee has reached the maximum allowed by the payer.

Uses of Commercial Fee Data

Unless you are new to the medical field and practice management, you are probably aware of several firms that sell fee data designed to help you manage your practice's charges. Typically offered in the form of a printed custom fee report or fees on disk, these commercial products provide a listing of fee percentiles for CPT codes. A sample page from Context's *Custom Fee Report* is shown in Figure 5.2. Although report contents vary by publisher, this report provides you with the following information:

A. *Header Information:* At the top of the report you will find the practice name, medical specialty, and applicable ZIP Code. The medical specialty is used to determine which codes to list in the custom report. The ZIP Code is used to determine which payment area (for both UCR and Medicare) should be applied when calculating the listed fees.

B. *Relative Values*: Next to each code and its associated brief description is a relative value for the service. In this case, the relative values are of the fee-based type discussed earlier in this chapter. As with most other relative value scales (RBRVS excepted), the scale is unique to each section of the CPT book.

C. *Fees by Percentile*: If you find percentiles confusing, you are not alone. To help you understand what they mean, imagine that in an area, a particular code has been submitted by physicians to various insurance companies exactly 100 times. Further imagine that you have somehow been able to obtain a list of each fee submitted for the code on each claim, and that you have arranged them from the highest fee submitted to the lowest. You now have a list of 100 fees. If you were to select the fee fifth from the top, it would be the amount below which 95 percent of the submitted charges fell. That is, 95 percent of the charges submitted were for that amount or less. Similarly, if you selected the fee 20 below the highest fee in the list you know that 80 percent of the submitted charges were for that amount or less. Thus, the 80th percentile fee of $3417 for code 35286 shown in Figure 5.2 informs you that an estimated 80 percent of the charges for the code made by physician in the area were for $3417 or less. Although the actual methodology used to compute percentiles is not so straightforward as that discussed, the above examples conceptually illustrate what percentiles are intended to represent.

D. *Medicare Fees:* The Medicare fee listed is Medicare's participating allowable for the code. Note that the firm producing this report maps the ZIP Code shown at the top of the report to the specific Medicare payment area before calculating the allowable charge amount.

Several of the firms which offer custom fee reports to physicians (including Context), also sell the same data (in different formats and usually for the entire United States) to third party payers. Just as you can use the fee data in these reports to help manage your fees, payers utilize them to set ceilings on submitted charges. The mechanics of this process will be discussed later in this chapter.

Figure 5.2: Custom Fee Report

PHYSICIAN FEES - 1997

GENERAL SURGERY

ZipCode: 60521

PAGE # 22

CPT Code	Description	RVU	30th	50th	65th	80th	95th	Medicare
					Fee Percentiles			
35189	REPAIR ACQUIRED BLOOD VESSEL LESION	47.86	2759	3577	4195	4956	6523	1259.69
35190	REPAIR ACQUIRED BLOOD VESSEL LESION	33.04	1904	2469	2896	3422	4503	1010.45
35201	REPAIR BLOOD VESSEL, NECK	31.66	1825	2366	2775	3279	4315	879.56
35206	REPAIR BLOOD VESSEL, UPPER EXTREM	29.67	1710	2217	2600	3073	4044	871.90
35207	REPAIR BLOOD VESSEL, HAND/FINGER	32.32	1863	2415	2833	3347	4405	917.82
35211	REPAIR BLOOD VESSEL, CHEST W/BYPASS	50.75	2925	3793	4448	5255	6917	1484.12
35216	REPAIR BLOOD VESSEL, CHEST	39.93	2301	2984	3500	4135	5442	1224.42
35221	REPAIR BLOOD VESSEL, BELLY	42.80	2467	3199	3751	4432	5833	1172.45
35226	REPAIR BLOOD VESSEL, LOWER EXTREM	29.85	1720	2231	2616	3091	4068	861.82
35231	REPAIR/GRAFT BLOOD VESSEL, NECK	41.80	2409	3124	3664	4329	5697	1162.05
35236	REPAIR/GRAFT BLOOD VESSEL, UPP EXTR	39.69	2288	2966	3479	4110	5410	1014.82
35241	REPAIR/GRAFT BLOOD VESSEL, CHEST	58.42	3367	4366	5120	6050	7962	1527.34
35246	REPAIR/GRAFT BLOOD VESSEL, CHEST	46.17	2661	3450	4047	4781	6293	1547.03
35251	REPAIR/GRAFT BLOOD VESSEL, BELLY	47.61	2744	3558	4173	4930	6489	1128.30
35256	REPAIR/GRAFT BLOOD VESSEL, LOW EXTR	37.09	2138	2772	3251	3841	5055	1052.13
35261	REPAIR/GRAFT BLOOD VESSEL, NECK	34.10	1965	2548	2989	3531	4648	1108.43
35266	REPAIR/GRAFT BLOOD VESSEL, UPP EXTR	35.00	2017	2616	3068	3624	4770	975.97
35271	REPAIR/GRAFT BLOOD VESSEL, CHEST	53.26	3070	3980	4668	5515	7259	1444.64
35276	REPAIR/GRAFT BLOOD VESSEL, CHEST	40.20	2317	3004	3523	4163	5479	1240.58
35281	REPAIR/GRAFT BLOOD VESSEL, BELLY	41.68	2402	3115	3653	4316	5681	1505.12
35286	REPAIR/GRAFT BLOOD VESSEL, LOW EXTR	33.00	1902	2466	2892	3417	4498	1042.60
35301	RECHANNEL ARTERY,CAROTID/VERT/SUBCL	39.87	2327	2979	3471	4077	5323	1453.65
35311	RECHANNEL ARTERY, SUBCLAV/INNOMINAT	51.21	2952	3827	4488	5303	6980	2061.66
35321	RECHANNEL ARTERY, AXILLARY-BRACHIAL	35.17	2027	2628	3083	3642	4793	1127.00
35331	RECHANNEL ARTERY, ABDOMINAL AORTA	45.86	2643	3427	4019	4749	6250	1561.30
35341	RECHANNEL ARTERY,MESEN/CELIAC/RENAL	48.25	2781	3606	4229	4997	6576	1840.51
35351	RECHANNEL ARTERY, ILIAC	40.67	2344	3039	3565	4212	5543	1534.62
35355	RECHANNEL ARTERY, ILIOFEMORAL	42.33	2440	3163	3710	4384	5769	1403.80
35361	RECHANNEL ARTERY, AORTOILIAC	50.69	2922	3788	4443	5249	6909	1889.17
35363	RECHANNEL ARTERY, AORTOFEMORAL	55.72	3212	4164	4884	5770	7594	2104.28
35371	RECHANNEL ARTERY, COMMON FEMORAL	32.02	1846	2393	2806	3316	4364	1075.52
35372	RECHANNEL ARTERY, DEEP FEMORAL	31.18	1797	2330	2733	3229	4250	1074.13
35381	RECHANNEL ARTERY, FEM/POPLIT/TIBIO	36.20	2086	2705	3173	3749	4934	1289.09
35390	REOPERATION, CAROTID	8.95	516	669	784	927	1220	213.94
35450	REPAIR ARTERY BLOCKAGE, OPEN	25.06	1352	1722	1997	2348	3064	845.70
35452	REPAIR ARTERY BLOCKAGE, OPEN	17.13	924	1177	1365	1605	2094	485.07
35454	REPAIR ARTERY BLOCKAGE, OPEN	21.90	1181	1505	1745	2052	2678	647.16
35456	REPAIR ARTERY BLOCKAGE, OPEN	23.79	1283	1634	1896	2229	2909	779.51
35458	REPAIR ARTERY BLOCKAGE, OPEN	23.85	1286	1639	1901	2234	2916	899.34
35459	REPAIR ARTERY BLOCKAGE, OPEN	22.96	1238	1577	1830	2151	2807	871.80
35460	REPAIR VEIN BLOCKAGE, OPEN	17.47	942	1200	1392	1637	2136	405.06
35470	REPAIR ARTERY BLOCKAGE, THRU SKIN	20.51	1106	1409	1634	1921	2508	720.37
35471	REPAIR ARTERY BLOCKAGE, THRU SKIN	23.22	1252	1595	1850	2175	2839	845.70
35472	REPAIR ARTERY BLOCKAGE, THRU SKIN	15.86	855	1090	1264	1486	1939	382.85
35473	REPAIR ARTERY BLOCKAGE, THRU SKIN	18.04	973	1239	1438	1690	2206	534.74
35474	REPAIR ARTERY BLOCKAGE, THRU SKIN	20.59	1110	1415	1641	1929	2517	644.79

How Fee Databases are Constructed

Alluded to above, the construction of a high quality fee database is a complex undertaking and requires at a minimum an enormous number of claims that statistically represent the types of services being rendered and fees actually submitted by physicians throughout the United States. Development of a fee database includes the following undertakings:

A. *Aggregation and organization of claims data*: This process involves collecting and placing into a database claims from various sources. Editing techniques are used to remove data that appears erroneous or has problems that would adversely impact fee development. Various data elements are associated with claims and line items, such as the provider's specialty (when known), the provider's ZIP code, place and type of services, and like information.

B. *Analysis of claims and fee data:* Calculations are performed on the fees submitted for each CPT and meaningful payment areas are defined. Codes may be grouped into families of services for future analysis. At this point, statistical methods are employed to determine mean fees, standard deviations and other measures of central tendency used to compute percentiles. The analysis may become quite complex as the distribution of fees around a mean is usually skewed.

C. *Gap filling:* If you were to compare the fees for frequently performed services across different commercial fee databases you will find them to be very similar. The reason is simple, a few hundred codes account for 95 percent of all submitted charges, and the data is plentiful for these services, thus leading to virtually identical fees for these services across commercial firms. On the other hand, fees may be quite different for less frequently or rarely performed services. Why? If you had the entire listing of all fees submitted by all providers in the United States you would quickly find that many codes are so rarely reported that it would be impossible to establish percentiles ranges for these codes in most payment areas. In some areas, the codes may never be reported.

To address this problem, firms that develop fee databases employ gap filling techniques to estimate what reasonable fees should be. Each firm usually employs different approaches that may involve grouping codes into families, using relative value scales, polling providers, and the like. Payers who use these databases generally recognize these limitations and may utilize multiple sources when defending fee challenges for rarely performed services. Sources might include having access to several fee databases, relative value scales, and charges by other providers. Although gap filling is by its very nature imperfect, it does help provide rational means for estimating reasonable amounts for infrequently reported codes.

Using Fee Reports to Establish and Adjust Fees

Earlier in this chapter you learned how to adjust fees the hard way; via use of relative values. Commercial fee reports are simple to use: look up the fees for a code at various percentiles and compare them against your current charge. If your charge for a service is less than the 50th percentile, it is likely you are leaving money on the table and, at least for those payers to whom you submit on a fee-for-service basis, you can reasonably expect greater payment if you raise your fee for the service. By contrast, if your fee for a service is above the 80th percentile, you may be at or above many payers allowed amounts for the service.

After helping you realign your current fees, these reports may be used over the course of a year to help you locate fees for new or rarely performed service. Also, fee reports can be of assistance when negotiating with managed care entities.

Because these reports are easy to use their drawbacks are often overlooked. First, different payers may utilize different methods and fee databases for establishing payment ceilings. For example, payer X may set fee ceilings at the 70th percentile while payer Y uses a different commercial database and sets its fee ceilings at the 95th percentile. Yet another payer Z may employ a combination of commercial fee databases and relative values to establish payment limitations.

Second, payers are gradually shifting away form UCR to RBRVS-based payment systems. Differences between UCR-based and RBRVS-based fees for the same service, especially for surgical procedures, may be radically different. Therefore, it is important to keep in mind that the payment ceilings established by payers utilizing RBRVS may be less than the 50th percentile UCR for some services.

Negotiating Fee Schedules

It is likely that your practice has negotiated several fee schedules with HMOs, PPOs, and other organizations in your community. And, you will undoubtedly be negotiating many fee schedules in the future. You can use relative value systems and commercial fee reports to your advantage for the purpose of negotiating fees. Consider the following example (hypothetical) of a physician who is entering into a new contract with a PPO that is switching to the RBRVS system. The PPO wants to negotiate a conversion factor with the physician and has stated that they are willing to offer a conversion factor of $38.00, which is about $6.00 more than Medicare is currently paying. Is the conversion factor consistent with the fees the physician is currently charging for her services to the PPO? What conversion factor will the physician need to establish with the PPO to maintain her current income level? To answer these questions, the physician would perform the following steps.

A. List those procedures and services you currently perform (or anticipate performing) under the negotiated fee schedule. List as many as possible.
B. List your current fees for those services. (In this example, list the amounts currently being reimbursed by the PPO.)
C. Estimate the annual volume of each procedure either based on past experience with the payer or your belief about the frequency of services that will be performed.
D. Multiply your current fee for each procedure by its associated annual volume to determine how much income you are obtaining for each procedure.
E. Sum the income amounts to obtain an estimated gross income for the services as shown below. In this example, the gross income is $93,390.

Procedure	Current Fee	Annual Frequency	Income
#1	$250	123	$30,750
#2	$800	18	$14,400
#3	$650	25	$16,250
#4	$95	217	$20,615
#5	$175	65	$11,375
			$93,390

F. Again, list each procedure and its associated frequency.
G. Next to each CPT code list the RBRVS value for the service.
H. Multiply the frequency by the relative value for each procedure.
I. Sum the total of the relative values as shown below.

Procedure	Annual Frequency	Relative Value	Total RVs
#1	123	6.3	774.90
#2	18	14.5	261.00
#3	25	12.1	302.50
#4	217	2.4	520.80
#5	65	3.9	253.50
			2,112.70

J. Divide the gross income for the procedures by the total of the relative values. This amount is your current conversion factor for the payer ($93,390 / 2,112.70 = $44.20).

To maintain her current income with the PPO, the physician will need to negotiate a conversion factor of $44.20. The conversion factor of $38.00 being proposed by the PPO will result in a decrease in income.

It is important to note that this method of arriving at a conversion factor is very sensitive to volume of services. In the above example, if the physician were to bill more than the anticipated number of procedures two and three, and fewer of procedures one and four, even with a $44.20 conversion factor her income would be lower than planned.

Custom fee reports can similarly be used for those entities with whom you are negotiating that rely on UCR data. This is especially true if your fees for high frequency services are relatively low. This author has seen many instances of physician practices entering into fee negotiations without first having evaluated the reasonableness of their own fees, and being pressured to lower fees that are already absurdly low. In some cases, the fees negotiated were so low as to be unprofitable to the practice. Be aware, however, that many managed care entities are probably not going to accept the 80th percentile UCR as a negotiated fee. These organizations, in theory, are going to trade patient volume with your practice in exchange for lower fees; fees which may be a low as something equivalent to the 25th percentile UCR.

PROBLEM SET

Suggested solutions to the problems below can be found in Appendix A.

Mark the following statements true or false.

		True	False
1.	A conversion factor is also termed a multiplier.	_____	_____
2.	Conversion factors are the amounts that transform relative values into practice-specific values.	_____	_____
3.	Although used by many physicians and payers, the application of relative value systems to assist with the development of fee schedules could be considered "price fixing" by the Federal Trade Commission.	_____	_____
4.	The customary charge is the amount charged by most physicians in the area for a particular service or procedure.	_____	_____
5.	Most capitated payment plans do not include a fee-for-service component.	_____	_____
6.	The RBRVS takes into account rent costs when adjusting for local practice cost factors.	_____	_____
7.	For any specific CPT code (excluding those that must be submitted on an assigned basis) nonparticipating physicians can bill an amount 9.25 percent greater than the amount Medicare allows for participating physicians.	_____	_____
8.	Medicare's current (1997) implementation of the RBRVS system requires that different conversion factors be used for each section of CPT codes.	_____	_____
9.	Volume of services is an important factor when attempting to negotiate fee schedules with managed care plans.	_____	_____
10.	The first hospital insurance in the United States was offered by the Franklin Insurance Company of Hartford, Connecticut in 1858.	_____	_____
11.	Payers who utilize UCR typically pay at the lower of the amount charged or a percentile of UCR they establish.	_____	_____
12.	The RBRVS was developed in 1982 for the purpose of replacing the California Relative Value Scale.	_____	_____

173

13.   Problems with fee schedules can lead to, among other   _____   _____
      things, increased audit liability.

14.   Under the current Medicare Fee Schedule and assuming all   _____   _____
      other factors are equal, a physician who has been practicing
      for ten years will receive ten percent higher reimbursement
      when performing a surgical procedure than will a physician
      who has been practicing for three years.

15.   Assuming all other factors are equal, if a participating   _____   _____
      physician's allowable for a procedure is $300.00, a
      nonparticipating physician will receive an allowable of either
      $275.00 or $337.75 on the same procedure, depending upon
      whether or not she accepts assignment.

The following are multiple choice questions. Select the most correct answer(s).

16.   Dr. Connor's patients were receiving notices from their insurance companies that his fees
      were above UCR limits. Dr. Connor now knows that:

      a.   His fees are probably higher than those of many of his colleagues in the same area.

      b.   Raising his fees further probably won't cause him to lose patients.

      c.   He should lower all his fees by ten percent.

      d.   He should raise his surgical charges and lower his evaluation and management
            service charges.

      e.   None of the above.

The following information applies to problems 17 through 20.

Dr. Razzier decided to assess his current fees by use of a relative value system. His procedures,
historic charges, relative values and, frequencies are as follows:

Current Procedure	Charge	Annual Frequency	Relative Value
#1	$ 850.00	23	9.2
#2	$1,230.00	34	10.1
#3	$ 75.00	230	.9
#4	$2,500.00	10	18.7
#5	$ 435.00	75	4.5
#6	$ 170.00	132	1.5

17. Without taking into consideration the annualized frequency, what is Dr. Razzier's conversion factor?

   a. $103.32

   b. $106.87

   c. $117.15

   d. $153.33

   e. $ 95.85

18. To achieve consistency with the relative value system, for which procedures is Dr. Razzier likely to raise his fees?

   a. Procedure #1

   b. Procedure #2

   c. Procedure #3

   d. Procedure #4

   e. Procedure #5

   f. Procedure #6

19. To maintain consistency with the relative value system , for which procedures is Dr. Razzier likely to lower his fees?

   a. Procedure #1

   b. Procedure #2

   c. Procedure #3

   d. Procedure #4

   e. Procedure #5

   f. Procedure #6

20.   Dr. Razzier contracts with an HMO that is converting to the same relative value system used in these examples. What conversion factor does he need to maintain his income level? Assume that the only services involved are those identified.

a. $107.48

b. $114.85

c. $118.45

d. $104.78

e. $97.56

CHAPTER SIX:
ADVANCED CODING AND
REIMBURSEMENT PROBLEMS

The problems in this chapter are included to test your understanding of the key concepts presented throughout this text. Many different coding and reimbursement situations are provided.

Three types of problems are provided: multiple choice; story problems; and, claim form problems. For the multiple choice problems you should select one (or more) of the alternatives provided. The story problems require that you locate the appropriate codes or fees. Finally, the claim form problems require that you analyze the appropriateness of the claim, given the information about care provided to the patient.

Suggested solutions can be located in Appendix A.

Multiple Choice Questions

Select the most correct answer(s).

1.   Based on your knowledge of modifiers, which of the following physician assistant services <u>cannot</u> be billed to Medicare.

  a.   Assistant-at-surgery as a nonteam member.

  b.   Other than assistant-at-surgery as a nonteam member.

  c.   Other than assistant-at-surgery as a team member.

  d.   Assistant-at-surgery as a team member.

  e.   Any of the above can be billed.

The information below applies to problems 2 through 4.

Dr. Tens, a neurosurgeon, sees a patient in the hospital outpatient area at the request of the attending emergency room physician. The ER physician suspects that the patient has a neurological condition that may ultimately require surgery and is requesting confirmation of his opinion. The patient, a 57-year-old woman, has not been able to control her bladder, is confused, unsteady on her feet, and has pain in her lower back that gets worse when she walks. After reviewing what he considers to be a moderate amount of data on the patient, Dr. Tens notes the patient's chief complaints and takes an extensive history related to the illness, performs a complete system review, and takes a complete past, family, and social history. In addition, he performs a complete examination of the patient's nervous system. Neurological tests are ordered by Dr. Tens because the patient could have one of several conditions. Finally, Dr. Tens believes the likelihood of risk to the patient from the tests and anticipated treatment would be moderate. There are several multiple diagnoses and management options. The patient is new to Dr. Tens.

2.   Dr. Tens prescribes medication, writes a report for the emergency room physician documenting the findings of his examination, and tells the patient to call his office to set up an appointment to review the test findings and discuss treatment options. Dr. Tens services would be coded as:

   a.   A confirmatory consultation because the emergency room physician has already formed an opinion about the patient's condition that he was asking Dr. Tens to confirm.

   b.   Because Dr. Tens initiated treatment and asked the patient to see him in his office, this would be billed using an office/outpatient service code rather than a consultation code.

   c.   The services would be reported using a hospital observation code as the patient was not admitted to the hospital.

   d.   An initial inpatient consultation could be reported because the patient was seen in the hospital's outpatient facility.

   e.   None of the above.

3.   After examining the patient, Dr. Tens determines that the patient needs to be admitted to the hospital that day. How would the services rendered by Dr. Tens be reported?

   a.   99222

   b.   99223

   c.   99244 and 99221

   d.   99243 and 99222

   e.   99244

4. Dr. Tens prescribes medication to the patient, writes a report for the emergency room physician, and notes the findings of his examination, and tells the patient to call his office to set up an appointment to review the test findings and discuss treatment options. If the risk to the patient of mortality and morbidity was rather high, and if the number of management and diagnostic options were extensive, the service would be coded as:

    a. 99243

    b. 99244

    c. 99245

    d. 99255

    e. None of the above.

5. Which, if any, of the following statements about the International Classification of Disease coding system is <u>false</u>?

    a. ICD-10 is scheduled for implementation by Medicare (and therefore, most other payers) beginning January 1, 2005.

    b. Physician practices need not concern themselves with volume three of ICD-9-CM.

    c. ICD-9-CM is updates annually each December.

    d. ICD-9-CM is edited, compiled, and published by a consortium that represents many international organizations, including the Canadian Medical Association, the Center for Disease Control, International Physician Union, Oxford University and the Peoples Republic of China's Health Review Board (PRC-HRB).

    e. Claims submitted to Medicare which do not list diagnoses with required fourth or fifth digits can be fined.

6. Which, if any, of the following statements about modifiers is <u>true</u>?

    a. CPT modifiers can be used on HCPCS National codes.

    b. The HCPCS National modifier "-RT" is for reporting that only regional therapy services were provided during physical therapy.

    c. The mandated services modifier ("-32") is primarily used with consultation codes.

    d. Most Medicare carriers are in the process of phasing-out Local HCPCS codes.

    e. The discontinued procedure modifier (-53) can used in circumstances where the physician has found it necessary to perform a procedure for which the code has been deleted (discontinued) from CPT.

7.   Which of the following statements related to the Medicare major surgical package rules are <u>not</u> correct?

   a.   If you provide an unrelated E/M service to another physician's patient during the global surgical period, you should list the "-24" modifier with the E/M code to ensure payment.

   b.   Depending upon the specific code, each major surgical procedure includes either 10 or 90 days of follow-up care.

   c.   Surgical treatment of complications related to the surgery that require a return trip to the operating room may be billed. However, in such cases, Medicare will only allow the intraoperative component fee for the surgery.

   d.   Treatment of complications arising during the surgery may not be billed.

   e.   Digital anesthetics, if used, may be billed, but only if the procedure being performed is in an ambulatory surgical center with a classification of three or higher.

8.   On Halloween night, Mr. Rogers was struck by an object and sought treatment at a nearby free-standing emergency care facility which he had not previously visited. An evaluation and management service was provided and the 2.5 cm wound on his forehead was closed by use of adhesive strips. Mr. Rogers was lucky to be treated at the facility as he arrived at 11:12 pm and the facility normally closes at 11:30 pm Assuming that an expanded problem focused examination and history were performed and medical decision making was straightforward, the facility might bill Mr. Rogers as follows:

   a.   99202

   b.   99202
        12011

   c.   99202
        99052

   d.   99202
        12011
        99052

   e.   99281
        12011

   f.   99281
        12011
        99052

The information below applies to problems 9 through 11.

Dr. Wilson is three years out of residency and does not participate with Medicare. Dr. Roland, who practices across the hall from Dr. Wilson, has been in practice for ten years and participates with Medicare.

9. Dr. Roland performs an x-ray service for a Medicare patient and bills $75.00. Medicare allows $54.25 for the service. Assuming he does not except assignment, by law, what is the maximum amount that Dr. Wilson can charge a Medicare patient for the same service?

    a. $63.75

    b. $51.38

    c. $59.27

    d. $75.00

    e.   His normal charge to other patients for the same service. He just cannot bill other patients less for the same service he provides to Medicare patients.

10. Dr. Wilson performs a minor surgical procedure on a Medicare patient, accepts assignment on the case, and Medicare allows $235.00. If Dr. Roland performs the same service on Medicare patient, the maximum amount he can charge is?

    a. $256.74

    b. $223.25

    c. $247.37

    d. $276.47

    e.   His normal charge to other patients for the same service. He just cannot bill other patients less for the same service he provides to Medicare patients.

11. Dr. Roland performs a procedure on a Medicare patient and Medicare allows $723.50 for the service. If Dr. Wilson performs the same service on a Medicare patient and accepts assignment, his Medicare allowable will be?

    a. $761.58

    b. $614.97

    c. $790.42

    d. $687.32

    e.   The same allowable as received by Dr. Roland since he accepted assignment.

Story Problems

12. Mr. Olsen, a 74-year-old Medicare patient, visits your office for his periodic check-up for benign hypertension (due to nephritis). The nurse takes Mr. Olsen's interval history, blood pressure, weight, and temperature. She asks him about any recent changes in his diet, lifestyle, and medication usage. The physician reviews the nurse's notes with Mr. Olsen, performs an examination of the patient's heart and lungs, and also notes 25 skin tags on Mr. Olsen's neck, which he removes. A serum potassium test is ordered. The nurse draws blood form the patient and prepares the blood samples for pickup from an outside lab. The physician also performs an in-office urinalysis with microscopy and an EKG with supervision and interpretation. Mr. Olsen's medication is adjusted and an injection of Vitamin B-12 is given to Mr. Olsen for his general well-being.

Which codes, if any, could be reported for:

a. The office visit? (An approximation is acceptable.)

b. The examination of the heart and lungs?

c. The potassium test?

d. The EKG?

e. The urinalysis?

f. The injection of Vitamin B-12?

g. The blood draw?

h. The patient's diagnoses?

i. The excision of the skin tags?

j. The specimen handling?

13. Mr. Tucker is being examined by his urologist, Dr. Peterson, for kidney stones. Dr. Peterson recommends that Mr. Tucker have the stones treated by extracorporeal shock wave lithotripsy. Since Dr. Peterson rarely performs this procedure, Mr. Tucker is referred to another urologist, Dr. Nelson, who routinely performs lithotripsy. Dr. Peterson managed both the pre- and postop care for Mr. Tucker, while Dr. Nelson performed the lithotripsy procedure only.

How would you code for:

a. Dr. Peterson?

b. Dr. Nelson?

c. Mr. Tucker's diagnosis?

14. Bonzo the Clown crash lands after being shot from a cannon during a circus show. The physician who treats Bonzo repairs two 7.5 cm simple wounds on Bonzo's scalp and one 5.0 cm simple wound on Bonzo's hand. He also performs a 3.0 cm layer closure on Bonzo's nose. All the wounds are repaired during the same operative session. Code the service's and Bonzo's diagnoses.

15. Mrs. Taylor underwent breast reconstructions. Her surgeon, Dr. Werner, used a microsurgical technique. The reconstructions were a follow-up to the radical mastectomies that had been performed on her six months ago. Breast prostheses were placed immediately following the reconstructions (same operative session). The hospital, not the physician, provided the prostheses. Code for the surgeries.

16. Tamara had been hospitalized for an acute episode of diverticulitis of the colon by her physician, Dr. Cohen. On May 1, Dr. Cohen admitted Tamara to the hospital and performed a comprehensive examination, took a comprehensive history, ordered a radiograph, prescribed medication, and ordered that an IV be started. Medical decision making was of low complexity. The next day, May 2, Dr. Cohen visited Tamara. She reviewed her chart and radiographs, performed a problem focused exam and history, and adjusted therapy. Tamara's progress was satisfactory. Dr. Cohen's employee, Mr. Jones (a certified physician assistant) saw Tamara on May 3 and 4. During those visits, Mr. Jones performed problem-focused examinations and histories and discussed his findings with the nursing staff and Dr. Cohen. On May 5, Dr. Cohen spent 40 minutes reviewing Tamara's chart, examining her, pronouncing her fit to go home, and discussing diet and medication. Tamara is a Medicare patient. Code the services provided to Tamara. Code also Tamara's diagnosis.

17. Dr. Marcon, a radiologist, performed a transluminal balloon angioplasty via the renal artery (which is a peripheral artery). He helped position the patient, inserted the catheter, injected the dye, and gave a local anesthetic. Following the procedure he reviewed the resulting radiographs and dictated a report of the procedure and his findings. Code for Dr. Marcon.

18. Mr. Edwards is hospitalized for treatment of a gunshot wound. During the postoperative period, Dr. Price, a family practitioner who has been following Mr. Edwards in conjunction with the surgeon who removed the bullet, notes that Mr. Edwards is exhibiting symptoms of hepatitis. A famous internist who specializes in hepatic diseases, Dr. Allison, is asked to make a diagnosis and recommend treatment.

On Monday, Dr. Allison performs an in-depth evaluation of Mr. Edwards' problem. He performs a comprehensive history and examination. Medical decision making is of moderate complexity. Extensive diagnostic workups are ordered, and Dr. Allison talks with Dr. Price and the hospital nurses about Mr. Edwards' condition. On Wednesday, with the lab results in and his evaluation complete, Dr. Allison gives his diagnosis and recommendations for treatment both verbally and via a written report to Dr. Price. It is agreed, after talking with Mr. Edwards, that Dr. Allison will begin treating and following the hepatitis problem. Both Dr. Price and Dr. Allison provide Level I services to Mr. Edwards on Thursday. During the week, the surgeon who treated the gunshot wound has continued to follow Mr. Edwards and keep up-to-date with the hepatitis illness. Other than the gunshot wound and hepatitis, Mr. Edwards has not other physical problems.

Code the following:

a.   Dr. Allison's services on Monday.

b.   Dr. Allison's services on Wednesday.

c.   Dr. Allison's services on Thursday.

d.   Dr. Price's services on Thursday.

Claim Form Type Problems

These problems consist of claim information that contains errors which led to a payment delay, denial, or underpayment. Do not focus your attention on the peripheral claim details, such as ID numbers, place of service, signatures, etc. Pay close attention to the patient's gender, age, CPT codes, HCPCS codes, ICD-9-CM codes, units, and dates of service. Identify the problem(s) associated with each claim, and explain your reasoning.

19.   See claim form on the facing page. Sarah Smith was being seen by her physician, Dr. Baylor, for an upper GI endoscopy of the esophagus, stomach, and duodenum as a follow-up to her complaints about excessive indigestion and nausea, and a family history of ESRD. Immediately prior to the endoscopic procedure, Dr. Baylor performed a Level II examination. What is wrong with this claim?

Figure 6.1: Claim Form for Problem #19.

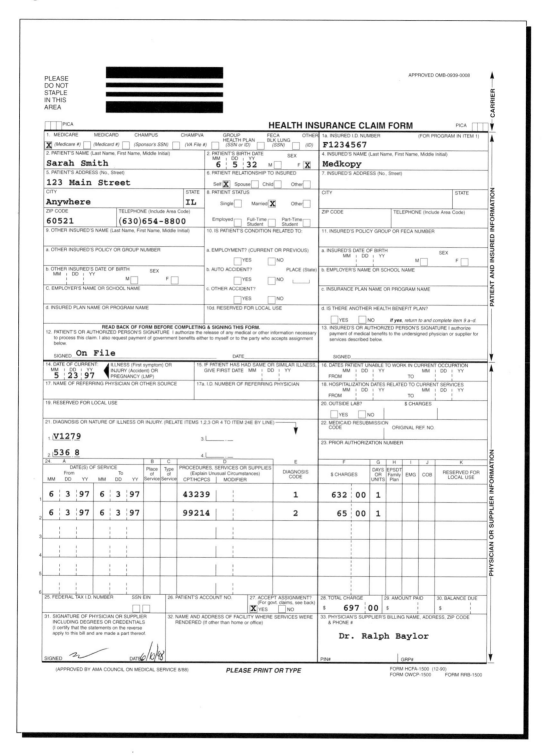

20.   See claim form on the facing page. Jimmy Jones was being seen by his physician, Dr. Cortez, for two services. First, an evaluation for an auditory processing disorder and, second, for treatment of the disorder. The services were performed in the office. Blue Cross denied all services on the claim. Why?

Figure 6.2: Claim Form for Problem #20.

APPROVED OMB-0939-0008

HEALTH INSURANCE CLAIM FORM

PICA | PICA

| 1. MEDICARE | MEDICAID | CHAMPUS | CHAMPVA | GROUP HEALTH PLAN | FECA BLK LUNG | OTHER | 1a. INSURED'S I.D. NUMBER | (FOR PROGRAM IN ITEM 1) |
| (Medicare #) | (Medicaid #) | (Sponsor's SSN) | (VA File #) | [X] (SSN or ID) | (SSN) | (ID) | M123456 | |

2. PATIENT'S NAME (Last Name, First Name, Middle Initial)
Jimmy Jones

2. PATIENT'S BIRTH DATE
MM | DD | YY
12 | 11 | 68   M [X]   F

4. INSURED'S NAME (Last Name, First Name, Middle Initial)

5. PATIENT'S ADDRESS (No., Street)
321 Main Street

6. PATIENT RELATIONSHIP TO INSURED
Self [X]   Spouse   Child   Other

7. INSURED'S ADDRESS (No., Street)

CITY
Big Thunder   STATE **MN**

8. PATIENT STATUS
Single [X]   Married   Other

CITY   STATE

ZIP CODE **44111**   TELEPHONE (Include Area Code) **(630)654-8800**

Employed   Full-Time Student   Part-Time Student

ZIP CODE   TELEPHONE (Include Area Code)

9. OTHER INSURED'S NAME (Last Name, First Name, Middle Initial)

10. IS PATIENT'S CONDITION RELATED TO:

11. INSURED'S POLICY GROUP OR FECA NUMBER

a. OTHER INSURED'S POLICY OR GROUP NUMBER

a. EMPLOYMENT? (CURRENT OR PREVIOUS)
YES   NO

a. INSURED'S DATE OF BIRTH
MM | DD | YY   SEX
M   F

b. OTHER INSURED'S DATE OF BIRTH
MM | DD | YY   SEX   M   F

b. AUTO ACCIDENT?   PLACE (State)
YES   NO

b. EMPLOYER'S NAME OR SCHOOL NAME

C. EMPLOYER'S NAME OR SCHOOL NAME

c. OTHER ACCIDENT?
YES   NO

c. INSURANCE PLAN NAME OR PROGRAM NAME

d. INSURED PLAN NAME OR PROGRAM NAME

10d. RESERVED FOR LOCAL USE

d. IS THERE ANOTHER HEALTH BENEFIT PLAN?
YES   NO   *If yes, return to and complete item 9 a-d.*

READ BACK OF FORM BEFORE COMPLETING & SIGNING THIS FORM.
12. PATIENT'S OR AUTHORIZED PERSON'S SIGNATURE I authorize the release of any medical or other information necessary to process this claim. I also request payment of government benefits either to myself or to the party who accepts assignment below.

SIGNED **On File**   DATE

13. INSURED'S OR AUTHORIZED PERSON'S SIGNATURE I authorize payment of medical benefits to the undersigned physician or supplier for services described below.

SIGNED

14. DATE OF CURRENT:
MM | DD | YY
5 | 10 | 97
ILLNESS (First symptom) OR INJURY (Accident) OR PREGNANCY (LMP)

15. IF PATIENT HAS HAD SAME OR SIMILAR ILLNESS. GIVE FIRST DATE MM | DD | YY

16. DATES PATIENT UNABLE TO WORK IN CURRENT OCCUPATION
MM | DD | YY   MM | DD | YY
FROM   TO

17. NAME OF REFERRING PHYSICIAN OR OTHER SOURCE
Dr. Bennet

17a. I.D. NUMBER OF REFERRING PHYSICIAN
21-437777

18. HOSPITALIZATION DATES RELATED TO CURRENT SERVICES
MM | DD | YY   MM | DD | YY
FROM   TO

19. RESERVED FOR LOCAL USE

20. OUTSIDE LAB? $ CHARGES
YES   NO

21. DIAGNOSIS OR NATURE OF ILLNESS OR INJURY. (RELATE ITEMS 1,2,3 OR 4 TO ITEM 24E BY LINE)

1. **125 7**   3.

2.   4.

22. MEDICAID RESUBMISSION CODE   ORIGINAL REF. NO.

23. PRIOR AUTHORIZATION NUMBER

24. DATE(S) OF SERVICE From MM DD YY	To MM DD YY	B Place of Service	C Type of Service	D PROCEDURES, SERVICES OR SUPPLIES (Explain Unusual Circumstances) CPT/HCPCS MODIFIER	E DIAGNOSIS CODE	F $ CHARGES	G DAYS OR UNITS	H EPSDT Family Plan	I EMG	J COB	K RESERVED FOR LOCAL USE
6 3 98	6 3 97			92506	1	60 00	1				
6 3 98	6 3 97			92507	1	45 00	1				

25. FEDERAL TAX I.D. NUMBER   SSN EIN

26. PATIENT'S ACCOUNT NO.

27. ACCEPT ASSIGNMENT? (For govt. claims, see back)   YES   NO

28. TOTAL CHARGE $

29. AMOUNT PAID $

30. BALANCE DUE $

31. SIGNATURE OF PHYSICIAN OR SUPPLIER INCLUDING DEGREES OR CREDENTIALS (I certify that the statements on the reverse apply to this bill and are made a part thereof.)

SIGNED   DATE 6/3/98

32. NAME AND ADDRESS OF FACILITY WHERE SERVICES WERE RENDERED (If other than home or office)

33. PHYSICIAN'S SUPPLIER'S BILLING NAME, ADDRESS, ZIP CODE & PHONE #
Dr. J. Cortez

PIN#   GRP#

(APPROVED BY AMA COUNCIL ON MEDICAL SERVICE 8/88)   **PLEASE PRINT OR TYPE**

FORM HCFA-1500 (12-90)
FORM OWCP-1500   FORM RRB-1500

PLEASE DO NOT STAPLE IN THIS AREA

CARRIER

PATIENT AND INSURED INFORMATION

PHYSICIAN OR SUPPLIER INFORMATION

21. See claim form on the facing page. Mr. Charles is being billed for lab work related to his essential hypertension by his physician, Dr. Lauer. Mr. Charles' insurance company has a problem with the billing. Why?

Figure 6.3: Claim Form for Problem #21.

										APPROVED OMB-0939-0008

PLEASE
DO NOT
STAPLE
IN THIS
AREA

HEALTH INSURANCE CLAIM FORM

PICA | PICA

1. MEDICARE	MEDICARD	CHAMPUS	CHAMPVA	GROUP HEALTH PLAN	FECA BLK LUNG	OTHER	1a. INSURED'S I.D. NUMBER	(FOR PROGRAM IN ITEM 1)
(Medicare #)	(Medicard #)	(Sponsor's SSN)	(VA File #)	[X] (SSN or ID)	(SSN)	(ID)		

2. PATIENT'S NAME (Last Name, First Name, Middle Initial)	2. PATIENT'S BIRTH DATE MM DD YY	SEX	4. INSURED'S NAME (Last Name, First Name, Middle Initial)
Charles, Cameron F.	5 17 49	M [X] F	

5. PATIENT'S ADDRESS (No., Street)	6. PATIENT RELATIONSHIP TO INSURED	7. INSURED'S ADDRESS (No., Street)
Box 5 RR 7	Self [X] Spouse Child Other	

CITY	STATE	8. PATIENT STATUS	CITY	STATE
Outback	**MT**	Single Married [X] Other		

ZIP CODE	TELEPHONE (Include Area Code)		ZIP CODE	TELEPHONE (Include Area Code)
88888	**(630) 654-8800**	Employed [X] Full-Time Student Part-Time Student		

9. OTHER INSURED'S NAME (Last Name, First Name, Middle Initial)	10. IS PATIENT'S CONDITION RELATED TO:	11. INSURED'S POLICY GROUP OR FECA NUMBER

a. OTHER INSURED'S POLICY OR GROUP NUMBER	a. EMPLOYMENT? (CURRENT OR PREVIOUS)	a. INSURED'S DATE OF BIRTH MM DD YY	SEX
	YES NO		M F

b. OTHER INSURED'S DATE OF BIRTH MM DD YY	SEX	b. AUTO ACCIDENT?	PLACE (State)	b. EMPLOYER'S NAME OR SCHOOL NAME
	M F	YES NO		

C. EMPLOYER'S NAME OR SCHOOL NAME	c. OTHER ACCIDENT?	c. INSURANCE PLAN NAME OR PROGRAM NAME
	YES NO	

d. INSURED PLAN NAME OR PROGRAM NAME	10d. RESERVED FOR LOCAL USE	d. IS THERE ANOTHER HEALTH BENEFIT PLAN?
		YES NO If yes, return to and complete item 9 a–d.

READ BACK OF FORM BEFORE COMPLETING & SIGNING THIS FORM.
12. PATIENT'S OR AUTHORIZED PERSON'S SIGNATURE I authorize the release of any medical or other information necessary to process this claim. I also request payment of government benefits either to myself or to the party who accepts assignment below.

SIGNED **On File**   DATE

13. INSURED'S OR AUTHORIZED PERSON'S SIGNATURE I authorize payment of medical benefits to the undersigned physician or supplier for services described below.

SIGNED

14. DATE OF CURRENT: ILLNESS (First symptom) OR INJURY (Accident) OR PREGNANCY (LMP) MM DD YY	15. IF PATIENT HAS HAD SAME OR SIMILAR ILLNESS, GIVE FIRST DATE MM DD YY	16. DATES PATIENT UNABLE TO WORK IN CURRENT OCCUPATION MM DD YY TO MM DD YY
		FROM TO

17. NAME OF REFERRING PHYSICIAN OR OTHER SOURCE	17a. I.D. NUMBER OF REFERRING PHYSICIAN	18. HOSPITALIZATION DATES RELATED TO CURRENT SERVICES MM DD YY TO MM DD YY
		FROM TO

19. RESERVED FOR LOCAL USE	20. OUTSIDE LAB? $ CHARGES
	YES NO

21. DIAGNOSIS OR NATURE OF ILLNESS OR INJURY. (RELATE ITEMS 1,2,3 OR 4 TO ITEM 24E BY LINE)

1. **401.9**   3. _____ . ___

2. _____   4. _____ . ___

22. MEDICAID RESUBMISSION CODE	ORIGINAL REF. NO.

23. PRIOR AUTHORIZATION NUMBER

24. A DATE(S) OF SERVICE From MM DD YY	To MM DD YY	B Place of Service	C Type of Service	D PROCEDURES, SERVICES OR SUPPLIES (Explain Unusual Circumstances) CPT/HCPCS MODIFIER	E DIAGNOSIS CODE	F $ CHARGES	G DAYS OR UNITS	H EPSDT Family Plan	I EMG	J COB	K RESERVED FOR LOCAL USE
6 3 97	6 3 97			84460	1	22 00	1				
6 3 97	6 3 97			84075	1	19 00	1				
6 3 97	6 3 97			82565	1	18 00	1				
6 3 97	6 3 97			82310	1	16 00	1				
6 3 97	6 3 97			82040	1	16 00	1				
6 3 97	6 3 97			84100	1	16 00	1				

25. FEDERAL TAX I.D. NUMBER SSN EIN	26. PATIENT'S ACCOUNT NO.	27. ACCEPT ASSIGNMENT? (For govt. claims, see back) YES NO	28. TOTAL CHARGE $ **107 00**	29. AMOUNT PAID $	30. BALANCE DUE $

31. SIGNATURE OF PHYSICIAN OR SUPPLIER INCLUDING DEGREES OR CREDENTIALS (I certify that the statements on the reverse apply to this bill and are made a part thereof.) SIGNED _[signature]_ DATE 6 3 98	32. NAME AND ADDRESS OF FACILITY WHERE SERVICES WERE RENDERED (If other than home or office)	33. PHYSICIAN'S SUPPLIER'S BILLING NAME, ADDRESS, ZIP CODE & PHONE # **Dr. Ben Lauer** PIN# GRP#

(APPROVED BY AMA COUNCIL ON MEDICAL SERVICE 8/88)   **PLEASE PRINT OR TYPE**

FORM HCFA-1500 (12-90)
FORM OWCP-1500   FORM RRB-1500

22.   See claim form on the facing page. Mr. Kaplan was initially seen by Dr. Wise as a referral from Dr. Storch. Dr. Wise performed a Level III consultation on the patient on January 9 in his office and sent a formal consult report to Dr. Storch. It was decided that Mr. Kaplan should undergo surgery to determine the nature and extent of his GI problems. On January 13, Dr. Wise admitted Mr. Kaplan to the hospital and the next day performed an exploratory laparotomy, resected the area of the intestines which contained tumors, biopsied Mr. Kaplan's liver, and performed both a choledochotomy and a biliary endoscopy. When Mr. Kaplan received payment from Acme, his insurance company, he was outraged. Why?

Figure 6.4: Claim Form for Problem #22.

PLEASE DO NOT STAPLE IN THIS AREA

APPROVED OMB-0939-0008

HEALTH INSURANCE CLAIM FORM

PICA | PICA

| 1. MEDICARE | MEDICAID | CHAMPUS | CHAMPVA | GROUP HEALTH PLAN | FECA BLK LUNG | OTHER | 1a. INSURED'S I.D. NUMBER (FOR PROGRAM IN ITEM 1) |
| (Medicare #) | (Medicaid #) | (Sponsor's SSN) | (VA File #) [X] | (SSN or ID) | (SSN) | (ID) | 432-09-8989 |

2. PATIENT'S NAME (Last Name, First Name, Middle Initial)
I.B. Kaplan

2. PATIENT'S BIRTH DATE MM 11 DD 19 YY 52 SEX M [X] F

4. INSURED'S NAME (Last Name, First Name, Middle Initial)

5. PATIENT'S ADDRESS (No., Street)
P.O. Box 9268

6. PATIENT RELATIONSHIP TO INSURED
Self Spouse Child Other

7. INSURED'S ADDRESS (No., Street)

CITY **Fort Collick** STATE **AZ**

8. PATIENT STATUS
Single Married [X] Other

CITY STATE

ZIP CODE **87654** TELEPHONE (Include Area Code) **(630) 654-8800**

Employed Full-Time Student Part-Time Student

ZIP CODE TELEPHONE (Include Area Code)

9. OTHER INSURED'S NAME (Last Name, First Name, Middle Initial)

10. IS PATIENT'S CONDITION RELATED TO:

11. INSURED'S POLICY GROUP OR FECA NUMBER

a. OTHER INSURED'S POLICY OR GROUP NUMBER

a. EMPLOYMENT? (CURRENT OR PREVIOUS) YES NO

a. INSURED'S DATE OF BIRTH MM DD YY SEX M F

b. OTHER INSURED'S DATE OF BIRTH MM DD YY SEX M F

b. AUTO ACCIDENT? PLACE (State) YES NO

b. EMPLOYER'S NAME OR SCHOOL NAME

C. EMPLOYER'S NAME OR SCHOOL NAME

c. OTHER ACCIDENT? YES NO

c. INSURANCE PLAN NAME OR PROGRAM NAME

d. INSURED PLAN NAME OR PROGRAM NAME

10d. RESERVED FOR LOCAL USE

d. IS THERE ANOTHER HEALTH BENEFIT PLAN? YES NO *If yes*, return to and complete item 9 a–d.

READ BACK OF FORM BEFORE COMPLETING & SIGNING THIS FORM.
12. PATIENT'S OR AUTHORIZED PERSON'S SIGNATURE I authorize the release of any medical or other information necessary to process this claim. I also request payment of government benefits either to myself or to the party who accepts assignment below.

SIGNED **On File** DATE

13. INSURED'S OR AUTHORIZED PERSON'S SIGNATURE I authorize payment of medical benefits to the undersigned physician or supplier for services described below.

SIGNED

14. DATE OF CURRENT: ILLNESS (First symptom) OR INJURY (Accident) OR PREGNANCY (LMP) MM 1 DD 9 YY 97

15. IF PATIENT HAS HAD SAME OR SIMILAR ILLNESS. GIVE FIRST DATE MM DD YY

16. DATES PATIENT UNABLE TO WORK IN CURRENT OCCUPATION FROM MM DD YY TO MM DD YY

17. NAME OF REFERRING PHYSICIAN OR OTHER SOURCE
Dr. Storch

17a. I.D. NUMBER OF REFERRING PHYSICIAN
1234567

18. HOSPITALIZATION DATES RELATED TO CURRENT SERVICES FROM MM DD YY TO MM DD YY

19. RESERVED FOR LOCAL USE

20. OUTSIDE LAB? YES NO $ CHARGES

21. DIAGNOSIS OR NATURE OF ILLNESS OR INJURY. (RELATE ITEMS 1,2,3 OR 4 TO ITEM 24E BY LINE)
1. **159 0** 3.
2. 4.

22. MEDICAID RESUBMISSION CODE ORIGINAL REF. NO.

23. PRIOR AUTHORIZATION NUMBER

24. A. DATE(S) OF SERVICE From MM DD YY	To MM DD YY	B. Place of Service	C. Type of Service	D. PROCEDURES, SERVICES OR SUPPLIES (Explain Unusual Circumstances) CPT/HCPCS	MODIFIER	E. DIAGNOSIS CODE	F. $ CHARGES	G. DAYS OR UNITS	H. EPSDT Family Plan	I. EMG	J. COB	K. RESERVED FOR LOCAL USE
1 13 97	1 13 97	21		99233		1	200 00	1				
1 14 97	1 14 97	21		49000		1	1500 00	1				
1 14 97	1 14 97	21		44120		1	2000 00	1				
1 14 97	1 14 97	21		47100		1	1100 00	1				
1 14 97	1 14 97	21		47420		1	2500 00	1				
1 14 97	1 14 97	21		47550		1	550 00	1				

25. FEDERAL TAX I.D. NUMBER SSN EIN

26. PATIENT'S ACCOUNT NO.

27. ACCEPT ASSIGNMENT? (For govt. claims, see back) YES NO

28. TOTAL CHARGE $ 7850 00

29. AMOUNT PAID $

30. BALANCE DUE $

31. SIGNATURE OF PHYSICIAN OR SUPPLIER INCLUDING DEGREES OR CREDENTIALS (I certify that the statements on the reverse apply to this bill and are made a part thereof.)
SIGNED *R. Wise* DATE *1/8*

32. NAME AND ADDRESS OF FACILITY WHERE SERVICES WERE RENDERED (If other than home or office)

33. PHYSICIAN'S SUPPLIER'S BILLING NAME, ADDRESS, ZIP CODE & PHONE #
Randy Wise, M.D.
PIN# **454332** GRP#

(APPROVED BY AMA COUNCIL ON MEDICAL SERVICE 8/88) **PLEASE PRINT OR TYPE**

FORM HCFA-1500 (12-90)
FORM OWCP-1500 FORM RRB-1500

CARRIER — PATIENT AND INSURED INFORMATION — PHYSICIAN OR SUPPLIER INFORMATION

23.   See claim form on the facing page. Mr. Nicholson, a Medicare beneficiary, hurt himself falling out of bed while taking an afternoon nap. His daughter drove him to a free-standing emergency clinic down the block from his house. Dr. Hall examined Mr. Nicholson, closed the nasty gash on his forehead after applying a topical anesthetic, gave him an injection of Bicillin, a prescription, and recommended that Mr. Nicholson be more closely evaluated by his primary care doctor. When payment for Mr. Nicholson's visit was received by the clinic's manager, Mrs. Brown, she called her coding staff into her office to review the claim. Medicare denied payment on all but the closure. What should Mrs. Brown tell her staff about coding similar situations in the future?

Figure 6.5: Claim Form for Problem #23.

APPROVED OMB-0939-0008

HEALTH INSURANCE CLAIM FORM

PICA | PICA

1. MEDICARE	MEDICARD	CHAMPUS	CHAMPVA	GROUP HEALTH PLAN	FECA BLK LUNG	OTHER	1a. INSURED I.D. NUMBER	(FOR PROGRAM IN ITEM 1)
[X] (Medicare #)	[ ] (Medicard #)	[ ] (Sponsor's SSN)	[ ] (VA File #)	[ ] (SSN or ID)	[ ] (SSN)	[ ] (ID)	123-45-6789B	

2. PATIENT'S NAME (Last Name, First Name, Middle Initial)
Nicholson, Chester

2. PATIENT'S BIRTH DATE MM | DD | YY **5 | 12 | 19** SEX M [X] F [ ]

4. INSURED'S NAME (Last Name, First Name, Middle Initial)

5. PATIENT'S ADDRESS (No., Street)
21 N. South Street

6. PATIENT RELATIONSHIP TO INSURED Self [X] Spouse [ ] Child [ ] Other [ ]

7. INSURED'S ADDRESS (No., Street)

CITY **Chicago** STATE **IL**

8. PATIENT STATUS Single [ ] Married [ ] Other [X]

CITY STATE

ZIP CODE **60666** TELEPHONE (Include Area Code) **(630) 654-8800**

Employed [ ] Full-Time Student [ ] Part-Time Student [ ]

ZIP CODE TELEPHONE (Include Area Code)

9. OTHER INSURED'S NAME (Last Name, First Name, Middle Initial)

10. IS PATIENT'S CONDITION RELATED TO:

11. INSURED'S POLICY GROUP OR FECA NUMBER

a. OTHER INSURED'S POLICY OR GROUP NUMBER

a. EMPLOYMENT? (CURRENT OR PREVIOUS) [ ] YES [ ] NO

a. INSURED'S DATE OF BIRTH MM | DD | YY SEX M [ ] F [ ]

b. OTHER INSURED'S DATE OF BIRTH MM | DD | YY SEX M [ ] F [ ]

b. AUTO ACCIDENT? [ ] YES [ ] NO PLACE (State)

b. EMPLOYER'S NAME OR SCHOOL NAME

C. EMPLOYER'S NAME OR SCHOOL NAME

c. OTHER ACCIDENT? [ ] YES [ ] NO

c. INSURANCE PLAN NAME OR PROGRAM NAME

d. INSURED PLAN NAME OR PROGRAM NAME

10d. RESERVED FOR LOCAL USE

d. IS THERE ANOTHER HEALTH BENEFIT PLAN? [ ] YES [ ] NO *If yes, return to and complete item 9 a-d.*

READ BACK OF FORM BEFORE COMPLETING & SIGNING THIS FORM.
12. PATIENT'S OR AUTHORIZED PERSON'S SIGNATURE I authorize the release of any medical or other information necessary to process this claim. I also request payment of government benefits either to myself or to the party who accepts assignment below.

SIGNED **On File** DATE_____

13. INSURED'S OR AUTHORIZED PERSON'S SIGNATURE I authorize payment of medical benefits to the undersigned physician or supplier for services described below.

SIGNED_____

14. DATE OF CURRENT: ILLNESS (First symptom) OR INJURY (Accident) OR PREGNANCY (LMP) MM | DD | YY

15. IF PATIENT HAS HAD SAME OR SIMILAR ILLNESS, GIVE FIRST DATE MM | DD | YY

16. DATES PATIENT UNABLE TO WORK IN CURRENT OCCUPATION FROM MM | DD | YY TO MM | DD | YY

17. NAME OF REFERRING PHYSICIAN OR OTHER SOURCE

17a. I.D. NUMBER OF REFERRING PHYSICIAN

18. HOSPITALIZATION DATES RELATED TO CURRENT SERVICES FROM MM | DD | YY TO MM | DD | YY

19. RESERVED FOR LOCAL USE

20. OUTSIDE LAB? [ ] YES [ ] NO $ CHARGES

21. DIAGNOSIS OR NATURE OF ILLNESS OR INJURY. (RELATE ITEMS 1,2,3 OR 4 TO ITEM 24E BY LINE)
1. **873 42**
2. ____
3. ____
4. ____

22. MEDICAID RESUBMISSION CODE ORIGINAL REF. NO.

23. PRIOR AUTHORIZATION NUMBER

24. A. DATE(S) OF SERVICE						B. Place of Service	C. Type of Service	D. PROCEDURES, SERVICES OR SUPPLIES (Explain Unusual Circumstances) CPT/HCPCS	MODIFIER	E. DIAGNOSIS CODE	F. $ CHARGES		G. DAYS OR UNITS	H. EPSDT Family Plan	I. EMG	J. COB	K. RESERVED FOR LOCAL USE
From MM	DD	YY	To MM	DD	YY												
1	14	97	1	14	97			12035		1	400	00	1				
1	14	97	1	14	97			99070		1	50	00	1				
1	14	97	1	14	97			00100		1	55	00	1				
1	14	97	1	14	97			90788		1	25	00	1				

25. FEDERAL TAX I.D. NUMBER SSN [ ] EIN [ ]

26. PATIENT'S ACCOUNT NO.

27. ACCEPT ASSIGNMENT? (For govt. claims, see back) [X] YES [ ] NO

28. TOTAL CHARGE $ **530 | 00**

29. AMOUNT PAID $

30. BALANCE DUE $

31. SIGNATURE OF PHYSICIAN OR SUPPLIER INCLUDING DEGREES OR CREDENTIALS (I certify that the statements on the reverse apply to this bill and are made a part thereof.)
SIGNED _William Hall_ DATE _1/14/97_

32. NAME AND ADDRESS OF FACILITY WHERE SERVICES WERE RENDERED (If other than home or office)

33. PHYSICIAN'S SUPPLIER'S BILLING NAME, ADDRESS, ZIP CODE & PHONE #
William Hall, M.D.
PIN# GRP#

(APPROVED BY AMA COUNCIL ON MEDICAL SERVICE 8/88) **PLEASE PRINT OR TYPE**

FORM HCFA-1500 (12-90)
FORM OWCP-1500 FORM RRB-1500

PLEASE DO NOT STAPLE IN THIS AREA

CARRIER

PATIENT AND INSURED INFORMATION

PHYSICIAN OR SUPPLIER INFORMATION

APPENDIX A: SUGGESTED SOLUTIONS TO PROBLEM SETS

This appendix contains suggested solutions to the problems in Chapters 1 through 6. Note that these solutions are suggested. There are more than 1500 health insurance payers in the United States, and each may have different reporting requirements, coding system interpretations, and coverage limitations. It is your responsibility to become aware of the reporting idiosyncrasies of payers with which you deal.

CHAPTER 1

1. False.   About half of all payers use this advanced editing technology.

2. True.   When a payer develops a claim, they gather the information they need to adjudicate it.

3. True.   Many benefit accrue from having a positive relationship with payers, including information that helps reduce delays and denials.

4. True.   Sadly, most claim errors originate in the physician's practice.

5. True.   Without this information the payer may establish an allowed payment which is less than reasonable.

6. False.   The typical electronic claims clearinghouse subjects your claims to payer-specific technical edits, allowing some errors to be corrected before they are submitted for payment.

7. True.   With the rare exception of a few payers, all third party payers accept the HCFA-1500 claim form.

8. False.   EFT is the abbreviation for Electronic Funds Transfer.

9. True.   Billing services may also provide other additional services that help practice's achieve greater cost efficiencies.

10. False.   A dirty claim is one which contains inaccurate, inappropriate or out-of-date information that can result in a delay or denial.

11. e.   Each of these points represents an advantage of submitting claims electronically.

12.   e.   These are all examples of problems that can cause a claim to be termed "dirty."

CHAPTER 2

1.   False.   You would use CPT codes.

2.   False.   CPT is published each year, usually in late November, by the American Medical Association.

3.   True.   The sections are: Evaluation and Management; Anesthesia; Surgery; Radiology; Pathology and Laboratory; and, Medicine.

4.   False.   These codes are found in the radiology section of CPT.

5.   False.   An eponym refers to the naming of a procedure/service after the person(s) who developed it. TURP is an abbreviation for transurethral resection of the prostate.

6.   True.   Without indentations, the CPT book would be nearly twice its current size.

7.   False.   It's pronounced "hick picks."

8.   False.   International Classification of <u>Diseases</u> - Ninth Revision - Clinical <u>Modification.</u>

9.   True.   The braces connect a series of terms to a common stem.

10.   True.   Using "rule out," "suspected," "possible," and other terms are not acceptable ICD-9-CM coding conventions. Most payers will simply assume the patient has the condition being ruled out as the basis for meeting medical necessity guidelines. If the patient is found not to have the condition, the provider may be viewed as submitting false bills for his services.

11.   False.   The Health Care Financing Administration currently has no plans to replace CPT with HCPCS National or any other coding system.

12.   False.   Medicare will not accept HCPCS codes for services it does not cover (such as dental), even when medical necessity has been established.

13.   False.   HCPCS National codes always consist of a letter (A through V) followed by four numbers.

14.   False.   Depending upon medical specialty, a physician may make frequent use of HCPCS National modifiers when submitting claims to Medicare.

15.   True.   HCPCS National codes begin with the letters A through V.

16.   True.   Failure to provide medical necessity can lead to a denial.

17.   True.   Always report the underlying condition instead of the manifestation as the primary diagnoses. You can, however, report the manifestation as a secondary diagnosis.

18.   True.

19.   False.   Like CPT and HCPCS, it is updated annually.

20.   True.   They are published in the carrier Medicare bulletins sent to physicians.

21.   e.   Using the provider's diagnostic statement, you first locate references to codes in the Index and then review the code in the Tabular list.

22.   e.   The services would be reported using codes from the HCPCS National range (G0071-G0094).

23.   b and c.

24.   d.   Option a. is incorrect as Medicare will not accept CPT's all purpose supply code 99070. Answer b. is not correct as many other payers now accept HCPCS National and/or Local codes. There is no Local code Z1094 in Utah (refer to Figure 2.3), so option c. is not correct.

25.   d.   The first lesion is coded with 17000, the second and third lesions with code 17001, and the final two lesions with code 17002.

26.   a.   The method of destruction is irrelevant to code selection.

27.   c.   The lesion was malignant and, therefore, the series of code shown is not the correct series. Answer e. would be acceptable if you did not have a CPT book to confirm c. as the correct answer.

28.   d.   The pneumonia is a manifestation and cannot be listed as the primary disease. Also, the cytomegalovirus infection (code 771.1) is for congenital conditions. The problem stated that this disease was not congenital.

29.   b. and c.   It is not required that E codes be used. Note that the Old Bucket Handle diagnosis is inappropriate.

30.   This condition is also termed Spina bifida with hydrocephalus and is coded as 741.03. Look in the ICD-9-CM index under Arnold-Chiari syndrome, type II.

31.   Code 270.0.   To find this code you would look under Blue in the ICD-9-CM index and then locate the reference to blue diaper syndrome.

32.   Code 330.1.   You would look under the condition "idiocy" in the ICD-9-CM index to locate reference to the proper code.

33.   The correct code (either V09.80 or V09.81) can be found by looking under the term "Resistance" in the Index to ICD-9-CM.

34.   Rat-bite fever can be located by looking in the in the Index under either "Rat-bite" or "Fever." The correct code is either 026.0, 026.1 or 026.9 depending upon the type of bacteria involved.

35.   You will find the code (from the range 102.0-102.9 or 373.4) using the Index under the term 'Yaws." Note that the manifestation code, 373.4, is not to be used as a primary diagnosis.

CHAPTER 3

1.   False.   Time is used only when counseling and/or coordination of care dominate the E/M service, and only for those E/M codes which define time.

2.   True.

3.   False.   They must be requested by another physician.

4.   False.   Only one initial consultation service is allowed per admission.

5.   True.   Refer to the notes associated with code 99288.

6.   True.   Documenting the examination of an affected body area or organ system is part of the E/M examination component.

7.   True.

8.   False.   The emergency department codes may only be used for services provided in a hospital emergency department.

9.   True.   Review the notes associated with hospital observation services.

10.   True.   For example, if counseling comprised the entire service, you would select the code based on time spent face-to-face with the patient.

11.   False.   These are the prolonged service codes that are to be used when the "-21" modifier is not applicable.

12.   True.

13.   False.   Where appropriate, CPT modifiers may be reported with HCPCS National or Local codes.

14.   False.   Each surgeon in the two surgeon or surgical team setting would report the "-62" or "-66" modifier.

15. False. The modifier is to be used to report the services of an assistant surgeon in a teaching hospital in situations where the qualified resident that would normally perform the assist was not available.

16. True.

17. True.

18. False. The Rhythm ECG (code 93042) is defined as being for supervision and interpretation only, making the modifier unnecessary.

19. True for 1997.

20. True.

21. False. Although the fee may be reduced, the purpose of the modifier is to report that something less than the procedure, as described, was performed.

22. True. In addition to the standard two digit modifiers, CPT provides five-digit modifiers: they consist of the two digit modifier preceded by "099."

23. False. The "-QI" modifier is no longer used by Medicare.

24. False. Modifier "-79" is for an unrelated procedure by the SAME physician.

25. False. This HCPCS National modifier is used for a procedure performed on the patient's toe. Specifically, the fourth digit on the left foot.

26. False. The immunization procedure can be billed but only if it is the only service rendered during the patient visit.

27. True. As an example, refer to the cardiac catheterization procedure codes (93501 series).

28. False. Medicare does not allow billing for an injection service provided in conjunction with an E/M visit.

29. False. Per day ESRD services may be billed if provided for less than one month.

30. True. Refer to the notes proceeding the ophthalmoscopy codes.

31. False. Code 96545 is provided for this purpose.

32. False. Osteopathic manipulative treatment is reported by codes from the range 98925-98929.

33. True. Refer to the note in CPT immediately above code 93539.

34. True. Refer to notes at the start of psychiatry codes in the CPT Medicine section.

35. False. The specimen must be transferred to an outside laboratory.

36. False. You would look under the appropriate anatomic site within the body system to find the unlisted procedure code which applies.

37. True. Provision of local, topical, and digital anesthetics are bundled with the surgery charge.

38. False. Follow-up days may vary from procedure to procedure, depending upon payer guidelines.

39. True. Refer to the surgical package guidelines listed in the beginning of the Surgery section of CPT.

40. True. Refer to the discussion on follow-up care for diagnostic procedures in the CPT Surgery section guidelines.

41. False. The opposite is true. A "separate procedure" is one that is usually included in a global surgical service and is, therefore, not billed separately unless performed by itself, not in conjunction with the global service.

42. False. They are only found in the Surgery Section of CPT.

43. True. Medicare regulations require that treatment of complications arising postsurgically (except those requiring a trip to the operating room) be included with the original surgery charge.

44. False. The closure billing rules apply to excision of both benign and malignant lesions.

45. False. You sum together only those wounds in the same classification (indented group).

46. False. The charge for the graft can be listed in addition to the charge for the mastectomy.

47. True. Refer to the removal of cast codes in CPT.

48. True. See the "add-on" codes discussion in the CPT Surgery section guidelines.

49. False. This service would be reported by use of codes in the range 59610-59614.

50. True.

51. True.

52. False. There are four subsections. Cyclotronic imaging is fictitious.

53. False. It includes only the supervision and interpretation.

54.　True.　CPT Surgery codes are used to report the injection services associated with many radiological procedures.

55.　True.

56.　False.　Most payers will only allow payment for one reading.

57.　True.

58.　False.　Code 76140, for consultation on x-ray examination made elsewhere, including the written report, would be listed.

59.　False.　Medicare mandates assignment, but other payers, including managed care plans, are free to establish their own guidelines.

60.　True.

61.　False.

62.　False.　The panel would be billed and each test not listed in the panel would be itemized.

63.　False.　Refer to the notes associated with the surgical pathology codes which state that "…services designated in codes 88311 through 88365…" are not included in codes 88300 through 88309. The Morphometric analysis code is 88358.

64.　c.　Physicians are not accountable to their staff for accuracy of their documentation; it is the other way around.

65.　e.　Based on the information provided, Dr. Daniels performed a comprehensive examination, comprehensive history, and decision making was moderate. Since the patient is established and being seen in the office, and as such only two of the three key components need be met, code 99215 should be reported.

66.　a.　The patient is new to Dr. Daniels. If she had been seen by the other Dr. in the practice within the past three years, then she would be established. Note that you must have all three components meeting the minimum levels listed for the new patient codes. Therefore, 99204 is the appropriate answer.

67.　d.　How Dr. Daniels sent his required report to the internist is irrelevant to the problem, that he sent the consult report is relevant. Note that this is a level four office consultation (rather than a level five), as all three of the key component requirements must be met.

68.　d.　Refer to the notes in CPT associated with the initial observation care codes.

69.　b.　Review the time duration table for prolonged service codes in CPT.

70.   e.   This problem would be coded using:

99291 with 1 unit (first hour)
99292 with 3 units (each additional 30 minutes)
12002 (wound closure)

The arterial puncture to collect blood, interpretation of a bilateral chest x-ray, and ventilator management are by definition included as part of the critical care services. The wound closure may be itemized. Refer to the notes associated with critical services in CPT.

71.   d.   Since referrals may originate with managed care entities and other sources, this is the correct answer.

72.   d.   Note that you may bill both a hospital discharge (code 99239 since we know he spent more than 30 minutes related to discharge activities) and the skilled nursing E/M service.

73.   A review of the notes associated with the nursing facility service codes in CPT shows that if other services related to the admission are performed outside the nursing facility, then only the comprehensive nursing facility assessment should be billed. Based on the information provided, the most likely answer is a.

74.   b.   The modifier "-E3" is a HCPCS National modifier for identifying the upper right eyelid.

75.   d.   Refer to the discussion of the "-GC" and "-GE" modifiers.

76.   e.   The "-YY" and "-ZZ" modifiers were deleted. In this case a code from the range 99271-99275 would be used with modifier "-SF."

77.   e.   Answer a. is not correct because code 99216 does not exist. Answer b. is not correct because the "-21" modifier must be used on the highest level of service in a group of codes. Answer c. is not correct because in order to use modifier "-24" the patient must be established and the code is for a new patient. Answer d. is not correct because the unusual services modifier is not appropriate for E/M codes.

78.   b. and d.   Answer a. is not correct, a laryngoscopy cannot be performed bilaterally. Answer b. is potentially correct, the procedure can be performed bilaterally. Answer c. is not correct, the procedure cannot be performed bilaterally—there is only one appendix. Answer d. is potentially correct as the procedure can be done on each eye. Answer e. is not correct.

79.   e.   Answer a. is not correct as the diagnostic laryngoscopy (31505) is included in the laryngoscopy with removal of lesion (31512) and cannot be billed separately. Answer b. is not correct as 97261 is an "add-on" code (note wording of "each additional" in the code's definition) and as such does not require modifier "-51." Answer c. is not correct, code 59525 is an "add-on"

code (refer to the note immediately following the code which states "list in addition to 59510…"). Answer d. is not correct as the second procedure (40801) is the higher valued service.

80.   Answers a., b., c. and d. are each potentially correct.

81.   Answers a. and d. could be correct. Answer b. is not correct if the visit led to a decision for surgery, it would be more appropriate to report an office/outpatient visit service than the preventive medicine service. Answer c. is not correct because modifier "-QI" is no longer valid. Answer d. could be correct.

82.   Answer a. is not appropriate as modifiers "-78" and "-79" would not be reported on the same code. Answer b. could be correct. Answer c. is not correct as modifier "-77" is usually reserved for repeating a surgical procedure, not a lab service. Answer d. is not correct as code 80053 does not exist.

83.   e.   The wound repair procedures listed are minor and would not warrant the services of an assistant surgeon.

84.   d.   The patient is considered new and the level of service is comprehensive. The prescription of the spectacles is included in the examination and is billed separately.

85.   e.   Code 93312 would be used to report the service. Note that use of the professional component modifier, "-26," would be inappropriate as the description of the service in both the problem and CPT includes the interpretation and report.

86.   d.   The hospital services were significant and distinct from the psychotherapy.

87.   With the exception of answer a., each of the services listed is included as part of the cardiac catheterization procedure. Refer to the notes preceding code 93501 in CPT.

88.   f.   The physician may elect to add-on charges for the services rendered at night, for services rendered on a Sunday, or for both. However, the vast majority of third party payers will deny coverage of these add-on services.

89.   e.   The code to be used for reporting the diet counseling services—99078 for physician educational services rendered to patient in a group setting—can be found in the special services and reports area of the Medicine section of CPT.

90.   e.   Each of the factors should be considered.

91.   b., c., e.   Answer a. is not correct as treatment of complications arising during the surgery are included. Answer c. is correct as the follow-up period for major surgical procedures is 90 days, which also means that answer d. is incorrect. Nonincisional endoscopies are consider by Medicare to be minor surgeries and, therefore, the major surgery rules do not apply. Thus answer e. is also

correct.

92.   a., b.   Although all the choices were for biopsy-related services, answers a. and b. are correct as they are starred procedures.

93.   c.   Of the codes listed, the only service which is included in the OBG care code 59510 is the routine urinalysis (81000).

94.   All but c.   In c., the surgeon performs another major procedure through the incision site and the exploration then becomes a component of the major procedure. Note that exploration procedure is a "separate procedure."

95.   All but b. and e.

Answer a. is not appropriate as code 17001 is an "add-on" code and the "-51" modifier does not apply. Answer b. could be an example of appropriate billing. Answer c. is inappropriate as you would sum together the lengths of repairs in the same indented group of codes. Answer d. is inappropriate as the surgical arthroscopy (29820) includes the diagnostic arthroscopy (29815). Thus, all the answers except b. and e. are correct.

96.   d.   The layer closures are in different indented code groups and would, therefore, be reported separately. The simple wounds are in the same indented group, thus their lengths would be added together and one code (12004) listed.

97.   a.   Medicare automatically converts total time into units and then adds the time units to the units associated with the reported CPT anesthesia code. This total number of units is multiplied by a conversion factor (dollar amount allowed by unit) to determine the Medicare allowable.

CHAPTER 4

1.   False.   Each physician is legally responsible for his/her coding and regulatory compliance. Despite the practice's staff's training and capabilities, the physician still needs to be involved in these activities on a regular basis.

2.   True.   For example, a procedure code substantially changes in definition and the physician continues to bill on the basis of the old, not the new definition. Since the physician is not billing for those services that were actually rendered, he/she might be accused of fraudulent billing practices.

3.   True.

4.   True.   However, in cases where both surgical and other services are performed on the patient on the same day, it is always a good idea to keep surgical procedures together on the claim, allowing for the application of modifiers and readability on the part of the payer.

5.   True.

6. False.   Payment turnaround on electronic claims is typically faster than for paper claims. Plus, electronic claims tend to receive higher reimbursement as the electronic claims submission process forces practices to submit cleaner claims.

7. True.

8. True.

9. False.   An equivalency code refers to a CPT code that describes a service similar in content and difficulty to one that is being reported by use of an unlisted service code. The purpose of the equivalency code is to help the payer's medical review staff better understand the nature of the unlisted service and hopefully, make a payment decision in favor of the physician.

10. False.   Unbundling is either the reporting of the components of a global service instead of the global service itself or, the reporting of one or more component code(s) in addition to the global service.

11. True.

12. True.   The patient is the insurance company's customer, the physician is the supplier.

13. False.   Although some of the larger third party payers may provide limited training, most do not, and there are no laws which require such training.

14. True.

15. e.

16. Answer c. is most correct, though answers a. and b. are possible. Generally, the physician will list the most definitive diagnosis known at the time the service was rendered. Although the physician suspected tumors at the time of the office visit, tumors were not a certainty making rectal bleeding the diagnosis of choice. Similarly, the tumors were not confirmed until the day after the hospital admission, thus the hospital admission would be coded in association with the rectal bleeding diagnosis. Billing in this manner is most appropriate when done on a daily basis. If the physician waited until all services had been rendered before submitting a claim, then the tumor diagnosis would be acceptable on all services.

17. c.   There is no such thing as a provider SSD number.

CHAPTER 5

1. True.   This is dollar amount multiplied times a relative value to establish a fee.

2. False.   See answer #1 above.

3. False.   However, this was true 15 years ago.

4.   True.

5.   False.   Specific services, such as complex surgical procedures, may be paid on a fee-for-service basis under capitation plans.

6.   True.   However, such adjustments are global (state or geographic area specific) and not individual office specific.

7.   True.

8.   False.   Medicare currently uses three conversion factors, but could use one for the entire system. Unlike other relative value systems, the relative values in RBRVS allow for one conversion factor for all codes.

9.   True.

10.   False.   Hospital insurance was first offered in the twentieth century.

11.   True.

12.   False.   It was developed at Harvard University in the mid-1980's for the purpose of replacing Medicare's fee-for-service payment system.

13.   True.

14.   False.   Years in practice are not a factor in determining Medicare's allowed payments.

15.   False.   The amounts would be $285.00 (five percent less than the participating doctor's $300.00 allowable) when the physician accepts assigned and $327.75 (that is 109.25 percent of the $300.00 allowable) when the physician does not accept assignment.

16.   a.   Unless he specializes in the carriage trade (wealthy patients who have the means to pay out-of-pocket) his high fees could drive patients away. Lowering all fees by 10 percent would likely have the effect of reducing some fees which are already too low and not reducing others which are far too high.

17.   b. and c.   Two methods of determining conversion factors were provided in the text. The first method (sum current fees and sum relative values, then divide the sum of the fees by the sum of the relative values) gave a conversion factor of $117.15 ($5260 / 44.9 = $117.15). The second method (divide each fee by its associated relative value and then sum the resulting amount and divide it by the number of procedures) yielded a conversion factor of $106.87 ($641.19 / 6 = $106.87).

18.   The clearly correct answers are a., c. and e. However, depending upon the method you used to derive the conversion factor, answer f. may also be correct. Using the conversion

factor of $106.87 derived in problem 17. (or $117.15, if you prefer) you can compare the current charge for each procedure divided by its relative value to the conversion factor. Negative differences identify opportunities where the practice may want to consider increasing fees.

Procedure	Current Fee	Relative Value	Fee/Value	Conversion Factor	Difference
#1	$ 850.00	9.2	$ 92.39	$106.87	- **$14.48**
#2	$1,230.00	10.1	$121.78	$106.87	+ $14.91
#3	$ 75.00	.9	$ 83.33	$106.87	- **$23.54**
#4	$2,500.00	18.7	$133.69	$106.87	+ $26.82
#5	$ 435.00	4.5	$ 96.67	$106.87	- **$10.20**
#6	$ 170.00	1.5	$113.33	$106.87	+ $ 6.46

19. Based on the calculations made for problem 18 above, the answers would be b., d., and possibly f.

20. d. To compute the amount, first array the procedures with associated fees and frequencies, and then multiply by the fee as shown below.

Procedure	Current Fee	Annual Volume	Annual Income
#1	$ 850.00	23	$ 19,550.00
#2	$1,230.00	34	$ 41,820.00
#3	$ 75.00	230	$ 17,250.00
#4	$2,500.00	10	$ 25,000.00
#5	$ 435.00	75	$ 32,625.00
#6	$ 170.00	132	$ 22,440.00
		TOTAL	$ 158,685.00

The second step is to multiply the relative values times the annual volume as follows:

Procedure	Annual Volume	Relative Value	Total RVs
#1	23	9.2	211.6
#2	34	10.1	343.4
#3	230	.9	237.0
#4	10	18.7	187.0
#5	75	4.5	337.5
#6	132	1.5	198.0
		TOTAL	1,514.5

To determine the income maintenance conversion factor, divide gross revenue for the procedures ($158,685) by the sum of the total RVs (1,514.5) which gives a result of $104.78 ($158,685 / 1514.5 = $104.78).

CHAPTER SIX

1.   d.   Review the definitions of HCPCS National modifiers "-AN," "-AS" and "-AU."

2.   e.   An office/outpatient consultation code would be listed.

3.   a.   You would not bill for both a consultation and initial hospital care on the patient on the same day.

4.   c.   This is the correct answer for a Level 5 office/outpatient consultation. The examination and history as described were comprehensive, and the medical decision making was of high complexity.

5.   Answers a., c., and d. are not true and thus correct. Medicare has announced no formal plans for implementing ICD-10. ICD-9-CM is updated annually in September. Finally, the consortium members listed are a product of the author's imagination.

6.   Answers a., c., and d. are true and thus correct.

7.   Answer a. is false, and thus correct, the "-24" modifier applies only to the physician who performed the surgery. Answer b. is false, and thus correct. Medicare defines major surgeries as those with 90 days of follow-up. Answer e. is not true, and thus correct. Digital blocks are always included in the charge for the surgery.

8.   a.   The facility is defined as an office, not an emergency department of a hospital. The wound repair is not billed, as adhesive strips were applied, not sutures. In such cases, the wound repair is included in the office visit.

9.   c.   The limiting charge is set at 1.0925 times the participating physician allowable. Thus, 1.0925 x $54.25 = $59.27.

10.   e.   Since Dr. Roland participates in the Medicare program, he is not subject to limiting charge regulations.

11.   d.   When accepting assignment, the nonparticipating physician's allowable from Medicare is five percent less than that given to participating physicians. Thus, $723.50 x .95 = $687.32.

12. Suggested solutions are as follows:

    a.   Code 99212, 99213, or 99214 might be appropriate, depending upon the full extent of the examination, history, and medical decision making involved. Because the physician also excised the skin tags during the visits, which is considered minor surgery, it may be necessary to add the "-25" modifier, for unrelated E/M services on the same day as surgery, to ensure payment. The office visit diagnoses and skin tag diagnoses need to be appropriately associated with the services.

    b.   The examination of the heart and lungs are part of the E/M service.

    c.   Federal regulations require that the lab bill Medicare for the potassium test.

    d.   Medicare may allow payment for the technical component of the EKG (code 93005), but will bundle in the supervision and interpretation with the E/M service.

    e.   Code 81000 would be used to report the urinalysis.

    f.   Code J3420 would be listed. However, without a supporting diagnosis (such as pernicious anemia), Medicare will deny the service as not being medically necessary.

    g.   Medicare may allow payment for the blood draw as long as the specimen is sent to an outside lab and the purpose of the visit was not for specimen collection. The code for reporting this service to Medicare is HCPCS National code G0001.

    h.   Diagnoses would be as follows:

        Hypertension - 405.19
        Skin Tag - 701.9

i.   Removal of the skin tags would require two codes:

            11200 for the first 15 tags
            11201 for each additional tag

            Recall that you would not place the "-51" multiple procedure modifier on
            code 11201 as it is an add-on code.

j.   Medicare considers the specimen handling to be part of the E/M service and
            it may not be billed to the patient.

13.   The suggested solutions are as noted below:

a.   Dr. Peterson could charge for the pre- and postoperative care in either of two
            ways. First, he could list the lithotripsy surgery code and add modifiers for
            pre- and postoperative management only as follows:

            50590-99 56/55

            Alternatively, he could list office and hospital visits as appropriate, possibly
            adding the pre- and postoperative modifiers, "-56" and "-55," respectively.

b.   Dr. Nelson would only charge for the lithotripsy itself. To do so, the "-54"
            surgery only modifier to the code as shown below:

            50590-54

c.   The diagnosis code for kidney stones is 592.0.

14.   In coding this problem, pay particular attention to the notes associated with wound repairs
        (codes 12001-13300). The lengths of the three simple repairs would be added together and
        reported as one repair as they fall within the same indented group, codes 12001 through
        12007. Summing together the lengths of these repairs results in a 20 cm closure (7.5 +
        7.5 + 5.0 = 20.0) which would be reported by use of code 12005.

        The layer closure is an intermediate repair and the 3.0 cm closure on the nose would be
        reported by use of code 12052.

        Diagnosis codes for the injuries would be as follows:

        Scalp wounds - 873.0
        Hand wound - 882.0
        Nose wound - 873.2

        Collective, the services would be reported as follows:

        Procedures Diagnoses

        12052   873.2
        12005-51 873.0, 882.0

15.   This problem was designed to illustrate the use of modifiers. The reconstructions could be coded by use of 19366. Two reconstructions were performed, one on each breast. Since the procedures are bilateral, the "-50" modifier would be added to one of the codes. A microsurgical technique was utilized, so the "-20" modifier needs to be added to both procedures.

The insertion of the prostheses would be coded using 19340. Again, the bilateral modifier, "-50," would be applicable, as well as the multiple procedure modifier, "-51." For both the reconstructions and insertions, the RT and LT modifiers for right and left would also be appropriate.

Codes and modifiers could be reported as follows:

19366-99/20/LT
19366-99/20/50/RT
19340-99/51/LT
19340-99/50/RT

16.   Dr. Cohen would report the following services on his claim(s):

May 1   99222

The problem described a comprehensive history, comprehensive examination, and medical decision making of low complexity—the criteria for a Level II hospital admission charge.

May 2   99231

The problem provided enough information to determine that a Level I follow-up hospital service was rendered.

May 3   99231-AN

May 4   99231-AN

Medicare allows the physician to bill for the services of a certified physician assistant in such settings, provided that the assistant is employed by the physician. The "-AN" modifier is added to communicate to Medicare that the services of a physician assistant are being reported.

May 5   99239

This is the code for hospital discharge day management services, more than 30 minutes.

Tamara's diagnosis is 562.11.

17.   Dr. Marcon would have two charges for his services. One for the injection, code 35471 (the renal artery), and one for the supervision and interpretation of the procedure, code 75962.

18.   The services provided to Mr. Edwards by Dr. Allison on Monday and Wednesday are part of the same consultation, and as such, Dr. Allison would bill on Wednesday for a Level IV initial inpatient consultation via code 99254. (Note that the criteria for this service was provided in the problem.) Dr. Allison's Thursday charge would be for a Level I follow-up hospital visit (code 99231). Dr. Price would bill using the same code (99231), but it is unclear why his services are needed since Dr. Allison has taken over management of the hepatitis problem and the surgeon is handling follow-up for the gunshot wound. It is likely that Dr. Price's claim will be denied as being medically unnecessary.

19.   There are two problems with this claim. First, Medicare will deny payment for an office visit provided on the same day as surgery unless significant, separately identifiable E/M services were provided. The modifier "-25," if appropriate, would be listed with code 99214 to communicate this issue. Second, the upper GI endoscopy with biopsy service (code 43239) is one of the procedures for which Medicare allows a surgical tray charge when the procedure is performed in the office. Thus, a billing opportunity (A4550) was overlooked.

20.   Two problems are demonstrated. The first is that the diagnosis of Dracontiasis is not logically related to the speech and hearing evaluation and therapy services. The claim could be denied on this basis. Second, the two listed services (92506 and 92507) are mutually exclusive of each other and should not be reported together on the same day.

21.   Five of the lab service codes listed are components of an automated multichannel test and should not be billed separately. Code 80005 should be used instead of codes 84460, 84075, 82310, 82040, and 84100. This is an example of unbundling.

22.   This relatively complex claim contains several errors. First, the exploratory laparotomy (49000), the bile duct exploration (47420), and the bile duct endoscopy (47550) are components of a cholecystectomy, with cholangiogram (code 47605) and should not be billed separately. The insurance company would deny the unbundling of the component procedures and allow for the cholecystectomy. Second, the initial hospital care (99223) may be perceived as being included in the charge for the surgery and would be denied without a "-57" modifier noting decision for surgery. Third, multiple procedure modifiers are absent, reflecting Dr. Wise's failure to rank surgical procedures performed on the same date from highest to lowest charge. As a result, the insurance company denied nearly $4,000 of the charges submitted.

23.   There are three key problems with this claim. First, the charge for a surgical tray is included in the repair service. If it had been billable to Medicare, code A4550 would be used instead of CPT's all purpose supply code, 99070. Second, the topical anesthetic is also included in the charge for the procedure. Code 00100 for anesthesia services is therefore inappropriate. Finally, the injection itself for the Bicillin (90788) would not be billed separately in addition to the surgical procedure. However, the supply of the Bicillin could be reported by use of a HCPCS "J" code, such as J0550.

APPENDIX B:
DOCUMENTATION GUIDELINES
FOR EVALUATION &
MANAGEMENT SERVICES

I. WHAT IS DOCUMENTATION AND WHY IS IT IMPORTANT?

Medical record documentation is required to record pertinent facts, findings, and observations about an individual's health history including past and present illnesses, examinations, tests, treatments, and outcomes. The medical record chronologically documents the care of the patient and is an important element contributing to high quality care. The medical record facilitates:

* the ability of the physician and other health care professionals to evaluate and plan the patient's immediate treatment, and to monitor his/her health care over time;

* communication and continuity of care among physicians and other health care professionals involved in the patient's care;

* accurate and timely claims review and payment;

* appropriate utilization review and quality of care evaluations; and

* collection of data that may be useful for research and education.

An appropriately documented medical record can reduce many of the "hassles" associated with claims processing and may serve as a legal document to verify the care provided, if necessary.

What Do Payers Want and Why?

Because payers have a contractual obligation to enrollees, they may require reasonable documentation that services are consistent with the insurance coverage provided. They may request information to validate:

* the site of service;

* the medical necessity and appropriateness of the diagnostic and/or therapeutic services provided; and/or

* the services provided have been accurately reported.

II. GENERAL PRINCIPLES OF MEDICAL RECORD DOCUMENTATION

The principles of documentation listed below are applicable to all types of medical and surgical services in all settings. For Evaluation and Management (E/M) services, the nature and amount of physician work and documentation varies by type of service, place of service and the patient's status. The general principles listed below may be modified to account for these variable circumstances in providing E/M services.

1.   The medical record should be complete and legible.

2.   The documentation of each patient encounter should include:

  *   reason for the encounter and relevant history, physical examination findings and prior diagnostic test results;

  *   assessment, clinical impression or diagnosis;

  *   plan for care; and

  *   date and legible identity of the observer.

3.   If not documented, the rationale for ordering diagnostic and other ancillary services should be easily inferred.

4.   Past and present diagnoses should be accessible to the treating and/or consulting physician.

5.   Appropriate health risk factors should be identified.

6.   The patient's progress, response to and changes in treatment, and revision of diagnosis should be documented.

7.   The CPT and ICD–9–CM codes reported on the health insurance claim form or billing statement should be supported by the documentation in the medical record.

III. DOCUMENTATION OF E/M SERVICES

This publication provides definitions and documentation guidelines for the three *key* components of E/M services and for visits which consist predominately of counseling or coordination of care. The three key components—history, examination, and medical decision making—appear in the descriptors for office and other outpatient services, hospital observation services, hospital inpatient services, consultations, emergency department services, nursing facility services, domiciliary care services, and home services. While some of the text of CPT has been repeated in this publication, the reader should refer to CPT for the complete discriptors for E/M services and instructions for selecting a level of service. **Documentation guidelines are identified by the symbol DG.**

The descriptors for the levels of E/M service recognize seven components which are used in defining the levels of E/M services. These components are:

* history;

* examination;

* medical decision making;

* counseling;

* coordination of care;

* nature of presenting problems; and

* time

The first three of these components (i.e., history, examination and medical decision making) are the *key* components in selecting the level of E/M services. An exception to this rule is the case of visits which consist predominantly of counseling or coordination of care; for these services time is the key or controlling factor to quality for a particular level of E/M service.

For certain groups of patients, the recorded information may vary slightly from that described here. Specifically, the medical records of infants, children, adolescents and pregnant women may have additional or modified information recorded in each history and examination area.

As an example, newborn records may include under history of the present illness (HPI) the details of the mother's pregnancy and the infant's status at birth; social history will focus on family structure; family history will focus on congenital anomalies and hereditary disorders in the family. In addition, information on growth and development and/or nutrition will be recorded. Although not specifically defined in these documentation guidelines, these patient group variations on history and examination are appropriate.

A. Documentation of History

The levels of E/M services are based on four types of history (Problem Focused, Expanded Problem Focused, Detailed, and Comprehensive). Each type of history includes some or all of the following elements:

* Chief Complaint (CC);

* History of present illness (HIP);

* Review of systems (ROS); and

* Past, family and/or social history (PFSH).

The extent of history of present illness, review of systems and past, family and/or social history obtained and documented depends on clinical judgment and the nature of the presenting problem(s).

The chart below shows the progression of the elements required for each type of history. To qualify for a given type of history, **all three elements in the table must be met.** (A chief complaint is indicated at all levels.)

History of Present Illness (HPI)	Review of Systems (ROS)	Past, Family and/or Social History (PFSH)	Type of History
Brief	N/A	N/A	*Problem Focused*
Brief	Problem Pertinent	N/A	*Expanded Problem Focused*
Extended	Extended	Pertinent	*Detailed*
Extended	Complete	Complete	*Comprehensive*

DG: *The CC, ROS and PFSH may be listed as separate elements of history, or they may be included in the description of the history of the present illness.*

DG: *A ROS and/or a PFSH obtained during an earlier encounter does not need to be re-recorded if there is evidence that the physician reviewed and updated the previous information. This may occur when a physician updates his or her own record or in an institutional setting or group practice where many physicians use a common record. The review and update may be documented by:*

*   describing any new ROS and/or PFSH information or noting there has been no change in the information; and

*   noting the date and location of the earlier ROS and/or PFSH.

DG: *The ROS and/or PFSH may be recorded by ancillary staff or on a form completed by the patient. To document that the physician reviewed the information, there must be a notation supplementing or confirming the information recorded by others.*

DG: *If the physician is unable to obtain a history from the patient or other source, the record should describe the patient's condition or other circumstances which precludes obtaining a history.*

Definitions and specific documentation guidelines for each of the history elements are listed below.

CHIEF COMPLAINT (CC)

The CC is a concise statement describing the symptom, problem, condition, diagnosis, physician recommended return, or other factor that is the reason for the encounter.

> *DG: The medical record should clearly reflect the chief complaint.*

HISTORY OF PRESENT ILLNESS (HPI)

The HPI is a chronological description of the development of the patient's present illness from the first sign and/or symptom or from the previous encounter to the present. It includes the following elements:

*   location,

*   quality,

*   severity,

*   duration,

*   timing,

*   context,

*   modifying factors, and

*   associated signs and symptoms.

Brief and **extended** HPIs are distinguished by the amount of detail needed to accurately characterize the clinical problem(s).

A **brief** HPI consist of one to three elements of the HPI.

> *DG: The medical record should describe one to three elements of the present illness (HPI).*

An **extended** HPI consists of four or more elements of the HPI.

> *DG: The medical record should describe four or more elements of the present illness (HPI) or associated comorbidities.*

REVIEW OF SYSTEMS (ROS)

A ROS is an inventory of body systems obtained through a series of questions seeking to identify signs and/or symptoms which the patient may be experiencing or has experienced.

For purposes of ROS, the following systems are recognized:

*   Constitutional symptoms (e.g., fever, weight loss)

*   Eyes

*   Ears, Nose, Mouth, Throat

*   Cardiovascular

*   Respiratory

*   Gastrointestinal

*   Genitourinary

*   Musculoskeletal

*   Integumentary (skin and/or breast)

*   Neurological

*   Psychiatric

*   Endocrine

*   Hematologic/Lymphatic

*   Allergic/Immunologic

A **problem pertinent** ROS inquires about the system directly related to the problem(s) identified in the HPI.

> *DG:*   *The patient's positive responses and pertinent negatives for the system related to the problem should be documented.*

An *extended* ROS inquires about the system directly related to the problem(s) identified in the HPI and a limited number of additional systems.

> *DG:*   *The patient's positive responses and pertinent negatives for two to nine systems should be documented.*

A *complete* ROS inquires about the system(s) directly related to the problem(s) identified in the HPI <u>plus</u> all additional body systems.

> *DG:*   *At least ten organ systems must be reviewed. Those systems with positive or pertinent negative responses must be individually documented. For the remaining systems, a notation indicating all other systems are negative is permissible. In*

the absence of such a notation, at least ten systems must be individually documented.

PAST, FAMILY AND/OR SOCIAL HISTORY (PFSH)

The PFSH consists of a review of three areas:

* past history (the patient's past experiences with illnesses, operations, injuries and treatments);

* family history (a review of medical events in the patient's family, including diseases which may be hereditary or place the patient at risk); and

* social history (an age appropriate review of past and current activities).

For those categories of subsequent hospital care, follow–up inpatient consultations and subsequent nursing facility care, CPT requires only an "interval" history. It is not necessary to record information about the PFSH.

A **pertinent** PFSH is a review of the history area(s) directly related to the problem(s) identified in the HPI.

> *DG:*   *At least one specific item from <u>any</u> of the three history areas must be documented for a pertinent PFSH.*

A ***complete*** PFSH is a review of two or all three of the PFSH history areas, depending on the category of the E/M service. A review of all three history areas is required for services that by their nature include a comprehensive assessment or reassessment of the patient. A review of two of the three history areas is sufficient for other services.

> *DG:*   *At least one specific item from <u>two</u> of the three history areas must be documented for a complete PFSH for the following categories of E/M services: office or other outpatient services, established patient; emergency department; subsequent nursing facility care; domiciliary care, established patient; and home care, established patient.*

> *DG:*   *At least one specific item from <u>each</u> of the three history areas must be documented for a complete PFSH for the following categories of E/M services: office or other outpatient services, new patient; hospital observation services; hospital inpatient services, initial care; consultations; comprehensive nursing facility assessments; domiciliary care, new patient; and home care, new patient.*

B. Documentation of Examination

The levels of E/M services are based on four types of examination that are defined as follows:

* **Problem Focused** — a limited examination of the affected body area or organ system.

* **Expanded Problem Focused** — a limited examination of the affected body area or organ system and other symptomatic or related organ system(s).

* **Detailed** — an extended examination of the affected body area(s) and other symptomatic or related organ system(s).

* **Comprehensive** — a general multi–system examination or complete examination of a single organ system.

For purposes of examination, the following *body areas* are recognized:

* Head, including the face

* Neck

* Chest, including breasts and axillae

* Abdomen

* Genitalia, groin, buttocks

* Back, including spine

* Each extremity

For purposes of examination, the following *organ systems* are recognized:

* Constitutional (e.g., vital signs, general appearance)

* Eyes

* Ears, nose, mouth and throat

* Cardiovascular

* Respiratory

* Gastrointestinal

* Genitourinary

* Musculoskeletal

* Skin

* Neurologic

* Psychiatric

* Hematologic/lymphatic/immunologic

The extent of examinations performed and documented is dependent upon clinical judgment and the nature of the presenting problem(s). They range from limited examinations of single body areas to general multi–system or complete single organ system examinations.

DG: *Specific abnormal and relevant negative findings of the examination of the affected or symptomatic body area(s) or organ system(s) should be documented. A notation of "abnormal" without elaboration is insufficient.*

DG: *Abnormal or unexpected findings of the examination of the unaffected or asymptomatic body area(s) or organ system(s) should be described.*

DG: *A brief statement or notation indicating "negative" or "normal" is sufficient to document normal findings related to unaffected area(s) or asymptomatic organ system(s).*

DG: *The medical record for a general multi–system examination should included findings about 8 or more of the 12 organ systems.*

C. Documentation of the Complexity of Medical Decision Making

The levels of E/M services recognizes four types of medical decision making (straight–forward, low complexity, moderate complexity and high complexity). Medical decision making refers to the complexity of establishing a diagnosis and/or selecting a management option as measured by:

*   the number of possible diagnoses and/or the number of management options that must be considered;

*   the amount and/or complexity of medical records, diagnostic tests, and/or other information that must be obtained, reviewed and analyzed; and

*   the risk of significant complications, morbidity and/or mortality, as well as comorbidities, associated with the patient's presenting problem(s), the diagnostic procedure(s) and/or the possible management options.

The list below shows the progression of the elements required for each level of medical decision making. To qualify for a given type of decision making, two of the three elements in the list must be either met or exceeded.

• Number of diagnoses or management options
(Minimal, Limited, Multiple, Extensive)

• Amount and/or complexity of data to be reviewed
(Minimal or none, Limited, Moderate, Extensive)

• Risk of complications and/or morbidity or mortality
(Minimal, Low, Moderate, High)

• Type of decision making
(Straightforward, Low Complexity, Moderate Complexity, High Complexity)

Each of the elements of medical decision making is described below.

NUMBER OF DIAGNOSES OR MANAGEMENT OPTIONS

The number of possible diagnoses and/or the number of management options that must be considered is based on the number and types of problems addressed during the encounter, the complexity of establishing a diagnosis and the management decisions that are made by the physician.

Generally, decision making with respect to a diagnosed problem is easier than that for an identified but undiagnosed problem. The number and type of diagnostic tests employed may be an indicator of the number of possible diagnoses. Problems which are improving or resolving are less complex than those which are worsening or failing to change as expected. The need to seek advice from others is another indicator of complexity of diagnostic or management problems.

DG: *For each encounter, an assessment, clinical impression, or diagnosis should be documented. It may be explicitly stated or implied in documented decisions regarding management plans and/or further evaluation.*

* *For a presenting problem with an established diagnosis the record should reflect whether the problem is: a) improved, well controlled, resolving or resolved; or, b) inadequately controlled, worsening, or failing to change as expected.*

* *For a presenting problem without an established diagnosis, the assessment or clinical impression my be stated in the form of a differential diagnoses or as "possible," "probable," or "rule out" (R/) diagnoses.*

DG: *The initiation of, or changes in, treatment should be documented. Treatment includes a wide range of management options including patient instructions, nursing instructions, therapies, and medications.*

DG: *If referrals are made, consultations requested or advice sought, the record should indicate to whom or where the referral or consultation is made or from whom the advice is requested.*

AMOUNT AND/OR COMPLEXITY OF DATA TO BE REVIEWED

The amount and complexity of data to be reviewed is based on the types of diagnostic testing ordered or reviewed. A decision to obtain and review old medical records and/or obtain history from sources other than the patient increases the amount and complexity of data to be reviewed.

Discussion of contradictory or unexpected test results with the physician who performed or interpreted the test is an indication of the complexity of data being reviewed. On occasion the physician who ordered a test may personally review the image, tracing or specimens to supplement information from the physician who prepared the test report or interpretation; this is another indication of the complexity of data being reviewed.

DG: If a diagnostic service (test or procedure) is ordered, planned, scheduled, or performed at the time of the E/M encounter, the type of service, e.g., lab or x–ray, should be documented.

DG: The review of lab, radiology and/or other diagnostic tests should be documented. An entry in a progress note such as "WBC elevated" or "chest x–ray unremarkable" is acceptable. Alternatively, the review may be documented by initialing and dating the report containing the test results.

DG: A decision to obtain old records or decision to obtain additional history from the family, caretaker or other source to supplement that obtained from the patient should be documented.

DG: Relevant findings from the review of old records and/or the receipt of additional history from the family, caretaker or other source should be documented. IF there is no relevant information beyond that already obtained, that fact should be documented. A notation of "Old records reviewed" or "Additional history obtained from family" without elaboration is insufficient.

DG: The results of discussion of laboratory, radiology or other diagnostic tests with the physician who performed or interpreted the study should be documented.

DG: The direct visualization and independent interpretation of an image, tracing or specimens previously or subsequently interpreted by another physician should be documented.

RISK OF SIGNIFICANT COMPLICATIONS, MORBIDITY, AND/OR MORTALITY

The risk of significant complications, morbidity, and/or mortality is based on the risks associated with the presenting problem(s), the diagnostic procedure(s), and the possible management options.

DG: Comorbidities/underlying diseases or other factors that increase the complexity of medical decision making by increasing the risk of complications, morbidity, and/or mortality should be documented.

DG: If a surgical or invasive diagnostic procedure is ordered, planned or scheduled at the time of the E/M encounter, the type of procedure, e.g., laparoscopy, should be documented.

DG: If a surgical or invasive diagnostic procedure is performed at the time of the E/M encounter, the specific procedure should be documented.

DG: The referral for or decision to perform a surgical or invasive diagnostic procedure on an urgent basis should be documented or implied.

The following table may be used to help determine whether the risk of significant complications, morbidity, and/or mortality is **minimal, low, moderate,** or **high**. Because the determination of risk is complex and not readily quantifiable, the table includes common clinical examples rather than absolute measures of risk. The assessment of risk of the presenting problem(s) is based on the risk

Table 1: Risk Assessment

TABLE OF RISK

Level of Risk	Presenting Problem(s)	Diagnostic Procedure(s) Ordered	Management Options Selected
Minimal	• One self-limited or minor problem, eg cold, insect bite, tinea corporis	• Laboratory tests requiring venipuncture • Chest x-rays • EKG/EEG • Urinalysis • Ultrasound, eg. echocardiography • KOH prep	• Rest • Gargles • Elastic Bandages • Superficial dressings
Low	• Two or more self-limited or minor problems • One stable chronic illness, eg well controlled hypertensive or non-insulin dependent diabetes, cataract, BPH • Acute uncomplicated illness or injury, eg, cystitis, allergic rhinitis, simple sprain	• Physiologic tests not under stress, eg, pulmonary function tests • Non-cardiovascular imaging studies with contrast, eg, barium enema • Superficial needle biopsies • Clinical laboratory tests requiring arterial puncture • Skin biopsies	• Over-the-counter drugs • Minor surgery with no identified risk factors • Physical therapy • Occupational therapy • IV fluids without additives
Moderate	• One or more chronic illnesses with mild exacerbation, progression, or side effects of treatment • Two or more stable chronic illnesses • Undiagnosed new problem with uncertain prognosis, eg, lump in breast • Acute illness with systemic symptoms, eg, pyelonephritis, pneumonitis, colitis • Acute complicated injury, eg head injury with brief loss of consciousness	• Physiologic tests under stress, eg, cardiac stress test, fetal contraction stress test • Diagnostic endoscopies with no identified risk factors • Deep needle or incisional biopsy • Cardiovascular imaging studies with contrast and no identified risk factors, eg arteriogram, cardiac catheterization • Obtain fluid from body cavity, eg lumbar puncture, thoracentesis, culdocentesis	• Minor surgery with identified risk factors • Elective major surgery (open, percutaneous or endoscopic) with no identified risk factors • Prescription drug management • Therapeutic nuclear medicine • IV fluids with additives • Closed treatment of fracture or dislocation without manipulation
High	• One or more chronic illnesses with severe exacerbation, progression, or side effects of treatment • Acute or chronic illnesses or injuries that may pose a threat to life or bodily function, eg multiple trauma, acute MI, pulmonary embolus, severe respiratory distress, progressive severe rheumatoid arthritis, psychiatric illness with potential threat to self or others, peritonitis, acute renal failure • An abrupt change in neurologic status, eg seizure, TIA, weakness, or sensory loss	• Cardiovascular imaging studies with contrast with identified risk factors • Cardiac electrophysiological tests • Diagnostic Endoscopies with identified risk factors • Discography	• Elective major surgery (open, percutaneous or endoscopic) with identified risk factors • Emergency major surgery (open, percutaneous or endoscopic) • Parenteral controlled substances • Drug therapy requiring intensive monitoring for toxicity • Decision not to resuscitate or to de-escalate care because of poor prognosis

related to the disease process anticipated between the present encounter and the next one. The assessment of risk of selecting diagnostic procedures and management options is based on the risk during and immediately following any procedures or treatment. The highest level of risk in any one category (presenting problem(s), diagnostic procedure(s), or management options) determines the overall risk.

D. Documentation of an Encounter Dominated by Counseling or Coordination of Care

In the case where counseling and/or coordination of care dominates (more than 50%) of the physician/patient and/or family encounter (face–to–face time in the office or other outpatient setting or floor/unit time in the hospital or nursing facility), time is considered the key or controlling factor to qualify for a particular level of E/M services.

> *DG:*   *If the physician elects to report the level of service based on counseling and/or coordination of care, the total length of time of the encounter (face–to–face or floor time, as appropriate) should be documented and the record should describe the counseling and/or activities to coordinate care.*

INDEX